SECRETS OF THE BIBLE PEOPLE

Kamal Salibi

INTERLINK BOOKS
An Imprint of Interlink Publishing Group, Inc.
NEW YORK

Library of Congress Cataloging-in-Publication Data

Salibi, Kamal S. (Kamal Suleiman), 1929-
Secrets of the Bible People / Kamal Salibi.
p. cm.
Includes index.
1. Bible. O.T.—Geography. 2. Arabian Peninsula in the Bible.
3. Hebrew language—Etymology—Names. 4. Bible. O.T.—Criticism, interpretation, etc. I. Title.
BS630.S24 1988 87-21920
22.9′1—dc19 CIP

ISBN 0-940793-16-4

First American edition published 1988 by
Interlink Books
An imprint of Interlink Publishing Group, Inc.
99 Seventh Avenue
Brooklyn, New York 11215

Published simultaneously in Great Britain by Saqi Books

Typeset by Theatretexts, London

Printed in Great Britain by
Billing & Sons Ltd
Worcester

Cover illustration: detail from *Moses brings forth water out of the rock* by F. Lippi. Courtesy of the National Gallery.

Contents

Maps

Key to Hebrew and Arabic Transliteration

Hebrew	*Arabic*	*Technical Transliteration*	*Alternative Transliteration*
א	ء	’ (glottal stop)	’ (omitted at beginning of words)
ב	ب	b	b
ג	ج	g (Arabic ğ)	j (in Arabic)
ד	د	d	d
ה	ه	h	h
ו	و	w	w
ז	ز	z	z
ח	ح	ḥ (voiceless pharyngeal fricative)	ḥ
ט	ط	ṭ (t as in ‘toy’)	ṭ
י	ي	y	y
כ	ك	k	k
ל	ل	l	l
מ	م	m	m
נ	ن	n	n
ס	س	ś (as in ‘see’)	s
ע	ع	‘ (voiced pharyngeal fricative)	‘
פ	ف	p (Arabic ṕ)	ṕ or f (Hebrew) f (Arabic)
צ	ص	ṣ (as in ‘saw’)	s
ק	ق	q (voiceless uvular stop)	q
ר	ر	r	r
שׁ	ش	š (sh as in ‘sheep’)	sh
שׂ	س	s (as in ‘see’)	s
ת	ت	t (as in ‘tea’)	t
	ث	ṯ (th as in ‘thaw’)	th
	خ	ḫ (voiceless uvular fricative)	kh
	ذ	ḏ (th as in ‘them’)	dh
	ظ	ẓ (voiced alveolar fricative)	ẓ, dh
	ض	ḍ (voiced alveolar stop)	ḍ, dh
	غ	ġ (voiced uvular fricative)	gh

Common Consonantal Transformations

Hebrew	*Arabic*
' (glottal stop)	w; y
g	ġ; q
d	ḏ; z
h (as feminine suffix)	t (normally silent)
w	' (glottal stop); y
z	ḏ; ṣ; ẓ; ḍ
ḥ	ḫ
ṭ	t
y	' (glottal stop); w
k	q
m	n
n	m
ś	s; ṣ; sometimes z
' (voiced pharyngeal fricative)	ġ
ṣ	ḍ; z; ẓ; sometimes s
q	ǧ; ġ; k
š	s; ṯ
s	š; sometimes ṣ
t	ṯ; š; ṭ

Note: In reproducing Arabic names consonantally, I have normally omitted the transliteration of the feminine suffix, and also the semi-vowels *w* and *y* where they feature only as vowels. In some cases, however, these Arabic characters have been transliterated for closer comparison between the Arabic and Biblical forms of the same name. In *The Bible Came from Arabia*, I transliterated the Hebrew ס as ś, and the ש as s, the common practice being the reverse. I have kept my own unorthodox transliteration of the two characters in the present book for consistency.

Preface

As such a vital part of the heritage of the modern world, the Hebrew Bible deserves to be properly understood. This is why, during the last two centuries, it has been the subject of extensive critical study by Christian and Jewish scholars, many of them practising believers of deep religious conviction, eager to understand the origins of their faith. At the hands of these scholars, the Hebrew text of the Bible has been subjected to thorough investigation, and various theories concerning the composition of its different parts have been advanced. Attempts were also made to study the Bible texts in the light of history in order to gain a better understanding of their narrative, devotional and doctrinal contents. Where the stories of the Bible are concerned it is today generally conceded that some involve chronicled or telescoped history, while others are only tangentially historical, preserving a rich fund of ancient myth and legend — the body of immemorial lore which forms the pagan background of Judaism and ultimately of Christianity.

To this extent the present book, which examines some of the better known Bible stories, is in the tradition of modern Biblical criticism, but with one important difference. While Biblical scholars today generally adhere to the traditional belief that the land of the Hebrew Bible was Palestine, the present book proceeds on the assumption that this land was actually in peninsular Arabia. This concept of Biblical geography is not entirely new. A number of references to Arabia in the Bible texts are so obvious that they can hardly pass unnoticed. It has always been known, for example, that the Biblical land of Sheba is present-day Yemen, and that the valley of Hadramut, which lies there, still carries the name of Biblical Hazermaveth in an Arabicized form. It has long been speculated that the Yemen could have been the original Arabian setting of the Biblical story of Job. In the nineteenth century many scholars were convinced that Arabia was much more closely connected with the Bible than was commonly thought. These scholars had read early Arabic literature where a number of intriguing references to the Israelites as an ancient West Arabian people are to be found. In 1864 the great orientalist Reinhart Dozy published a book called *The Israelites of Mecca in David's Time*, in which he suggested that the lost Israelite tribe of Simeon was already firmly established in the West Arabian land of the Hijaz by King David's time. Even before the time of Dozy, there was widespread conviction among scholars that the Biblical Israelites were originally Arabian desert tribes who later came to settle in Palestine.

Today Biblical scholars scoff at the idea that the Hebrew Bible could have had much connection with Arabia beyond the undeniable fact that the ancient Israelites had a certain familiarity with the peninsula. When I first came forward with the proposition that the West Arabian highlands, rather than Palestine, were the original land of the Bible and the setting of its entire history (*The Bible Came from Arabia*, London, Jonathan Cape, 1985; Pan Books, 1987), my work was condemned, in the words of Professor George Mendenhall, formerly of the University of Michigan, as 'a quixotic absurdity that cannot be taken seriously', and 'an extreme example of the misuse of specialized learning, based on nineteenth-century ideas that have long ago been proved false'. Yet were these ideas ever really proved false? And if so, how? Moreover, what if some major archaeological discovery, in Arabia or in Palestine, should one day prove these ideas — and my own, more extreme thesis — to be correct?

In the field of learning, as I see it, there is no orthodoxy and heresy, but only the search, involving reasoned conjecture tested against evidence. Until such time as proper evidence is brought to prove beyond doubt that Biblical history ran its course in Palestine, I shall continue to search for it in Arabia, not because I want it to be there, but because I remain fully convinced by reason and evidence that its dramas were played out there. Hence I venture to write a new book on the subject. Time may ultimately prove my thesis correct in its essence and perhaps even in most of its details, or it may prove to be entirely wrong. If it turns out to be correct, then many an accepted concept of the ancient history of the Near East will have to undergo a radical change. If the thesis turns out to be incorrect, it will still have served a useful purpose: that of stirring modern scholarship in the field to rethink its basic position — an exercise which is always in order. The plain fact is that in our own century Biblical scholars and historians of the ancient Near East have come to form a closed circle which resents unsolicited intrusions into the field. They have built an edifice based on foundations which are, in most cases, assumptions which they attempt to pass for facts, while refusing any radical re-examination of the subject matter. To any attempt at such re-examination, they react in anger, defending the edifice they have constructed and turned into a citadel and hurling condemnations at their critics from its ramparts. This does not imply that all their theories and hypotheses are necessarily incorrect. In the final analysis they may turn out to be right on many counts. However, their insecurity in the citadel, where they have chosen to lock themselves, is paramount, as they refuse to accept in good grace external challenges which may be right or wrong.

For readers who have not read my previous book, *The Bible Came from Arabia*, it would be useful to summarize its thesis here. While undertaking an etymological study of Arabian place names, I was struck by what seemed to be a high concentration of Biblical place names in the West Arabian territory of Asir bordering the Red Sea, between the city of Taif and northern Yemen. Upon closer scrutiny, I discovered that the coordinates of the towns and villages in the area bearing Biblical names conform to a stunning degree to the coordinates given to the places mentioned by the same names in the Bible — a far more telling fact than the actual existence of the names. When I went back to the massive body of scholarly literature on Biblical geography to check my findings against it, I found this literature more confusing than illuminating. First, after more than a century of research, scholars have only found a handful of Biblical place names which actually survive in a recognizable form in Palestine. Second, many of the Palestinian places which have come to be known by Biblical names have been given these names, either anciently or recently, by itinerant pilgrims, or by scholars or archaeologists who took them, on no conclusive evidence, to be

Biblical sites. Third, in nearly all cases, the coordinates of the places which actually carry Biblical names in Palestine do not conform to the coordinates given to the places by the same names in the Bible, although they do in Arabia. Fourth, Biblical scholars have doubted the historicity of many events related by the Bible because they cannot easily be fitted into the geography of Palestine. Fifth, no one has yet found the slightest trace of an ancient Hebrew or Israelite presence in Egypt, and scholars remain in disagreement as to when, and by what route, the Israelites made their exodus out of Egypt, ultimately to reach Palestine. There also exists a host of other problems of Biblical geography about which scholars continue to argue, pitting one awkward hypothesis against another, but refusing to accept any suggestions from outside their closed circle. The one factor that appears to have united these scholars, since 1985, has been my own suggestion that the Bible need not have come from Palestine at all, and that one might seriously entertain the possibility that its origin is West Arabian. So far most scholars who have publicly expressed opinions about this suggestion have haughtily dismissed it as 'worthless rubbish and nonsense from beginning to end', often without further comment.

Among those who cared to explain why they thought my suggestion about the relocation of Biblical geography to be absurd, a number of arguments were presented. First, some said that place names alone are not sufficient evidence to establish where Biblical history ran its course. I was not just guided by place names, but also by comparative coordinates, and furthermore, I took matters of topography, natural resources, flora and fauna, along with other matters into consideration, yet all this was invariably slurred over. Some scholars remarked that, going by place names alone, one might relocate the Bible land almost anywhere in the Near East, because of the strong similarity between the different Semitic languages from which place names in that part of the world are derived. Because this criticism was made by Biblical scholars of recognized eminence, there were many who accepted it. Before he could have read a word of my book, Professor James Sauer of the University of Pennsylvania, president of the American Schools of Oriental Research, permitted himself to announce to the world through the pages of *Newsweek* that, going by my method, one could demonstrate that Israelite history had its geographical setting in Kenya, and that the Biblical

Jerusalem was actually Nairobi. This statement was made in September 1984, more than a year before my book was first published. What Professor Sauer and others who argued against the validity of my method were unaware of was the fact that I had done my homework carefully on this point. Before daring to consider my thesis about the West Arabian origin of the Bible, let alone advance it, I had examined the map of every part of the Near East in detail to determine whether or not I could find any concentrations of Biblical place names, no matter how small, in areas other than West Arabia, until I was completely satisfied that there were none. Outside West Arabia the only territory in which I could find an appreciable, though small, concentration of Biblical place names, but with coordinates that do not fit Biblical accounts, was Palestine. If Professor Sauer seriously believes that going by place names, he can make a case for relocating the Biblical Jerusalem in Nairobi, there is nothing to prevent him from trying.

Second, there were many critics who pointed out that the parallels I draw between the place names mentioned in the Bible and those that survive in West Arabia are frequently not valid. John Day, editor of the *Oxford Bible Atlas*, apart from generally condemning them as 'total nonsense', declared them to be 'inadmissible on philological grounds'. There were those who maintained, for example, that I make too much of metathesis — the change in the order of consonants in a given word, whereby a name such as Hermon (*ḥrmn*) could become Hemron (*ḥmrn*). My critics here, granting that they are experts in the Semitic languages, were simply dishonest, because they must know better; their aim was to confuse non-specialists on a technicality with which only a specialist would be familiar. I will cite here the simplest example of metathesis between Biblical Hebrew and modern Arabic. In Biblical Hebrew the word for 'with' is *'m* (vocalized as *'am*). In Arabic, it is *m'* (vocalized as *ma'*). All one has to do is go through an etymological dictionary of Biblical Hebrew to discover the countless cases in which metathesis is involved in the consonantal structure of words having the same meanings, or related meanings, between the different Semitic languages. Moreover, it is because metathesis is a generally acknowledged phenomenon of comparative and diachronic linguistics that the technical term for it exists. Centuries before modern western scholars called it 'metathesis', the Arabic dictionaries had labelled it *istibdāl*.

Also taking advantage of the unfamiliarity of non-specialist readers with Semitic linguistics, a number of my critics cast doubts on the comparisons I made between Biblical and modern Arabian place names in which changes of consonants are involved. These have been done according to a pattern of consonantal changes between the different Semitic languages, and between different dialects of the same language (see table preceding Preface). The validity of such changes has always been accepted by scholars in the field. Again, the standard etymological dictionaries of Biblical Hebrew are replete with examples of such consonantal changes between one Semitic language and another in the same word. Here also, my critics were plainly dishonest. For example, they accept, without batting an eyelid, the identification of the Biblical Bethel (*byt 'l*) with the modern Palestinian village of Beitin (*bytn*), and of the Biblical Gibeon (*gb'n*) with the modern Palestinian village of al-Jib (*ğb*), although the change of the Hebrew *l* into the Arabic *n* to turn Bethel into Beitin is not a commonly attested consonantal change between Hebrew and Arabic, and the name of al-Jib actually lacks two consonants that are found in the name Gibeon. In my own studies, I identify Bethel as the West Arabian Batīlah (*btl*) or Buṭaylah (*bṭyl*), and Gibeon as the West Arabian Jib'an (*ğb'n*), whose names, in their Biblical and modern Arabic forms, are absolutely identical in consonantal structure. On the other hand, where I do recognize consonantal changes, as in the case of the Biblical Cush (*kwš*) being the modern West Arabian Kuthah (*kwṯ*), I follow the rules of consonantal changes between Hebrew and Arabic which my most ardent critics are bound to recognize as eminently valid. Why they make a point of not recognizing these generally accepted rules in the case of my work is a matter which I leave for them to explain, if they can. In the small minority of cases where I do make comparisons between Biblical and Arabian place names which do not strictly follow the accepted rules regarding consonantal change, I am careful to point out that such comparisons are no more than guesses subject to reconsideration. My predecessors in the field, who identified Bethel with the Palestinian Beitin, and Gibeon with the Palestinian al-Jib, presented their identifications, which are linguistically untenable on more than one count, as definitive and beyond doubt.

One of the first critics to attack my book in the press, shortly after its publication, was Tudor Parfitt, lecturer in Hebrew at the

School of Oriental and African Studies of the University of London. In an article politically entitled 'The hijacking of Israel', which he wrote for the *Sunday Times*, Parfitt dismissed my work as utterly worthless on a number of grounds — among others that I treated Biblical Hebrew as a dead language whose texts have to be deciphered afresh, whereas Hebrew, he claims, has been in continuous existence as a living language from Biblical times to the present day. This criticism was echoed from Cambridge University by no less eminent a scholar than Regius Professor John Emerton in the pages of the *Guardian*. The implication of this criticism was that I had no reason to doubt the validity of the traditional, or Masoretic, vocalization of the Bible texts, arguing that the Jewish scholars called the Masoretes, who undertook the vocalization of the consonantal Hebrew of the Bible in Palestine and Iraq between the sixth and tenth centuries AD, were people to whom Hebrew was a language of religious scholarship and not one of common daily speech. As it happens, I am far from being the person who actually discovered that Biblical Hebrew ceased to be a language of day to day speech long before the time of the Masoretes. Any article on the history of the Hebrew language in any standard encyclopaedia will say as much. The normal estimate is that Hebrew ceased to be a living language in about the third century BC. I would say that the death of Hebrew as a spoken language occurred a century or two earlier, but I would not split hairs on this point.

As for the doubts about the Masoretic vocalization of the Bible texts, they have existed since the earliest days of Biblical criticism, when it was suggested, for example, that the 'ravens' that brought bread and meat every morning and evening to the prophet Elijah, while he was hiding in the wilderness, could not really have been 'ravens' (*‘rbym*, vocalized by the Masoretes to read *‘ōrbīm*) but Arabs (*‘rbym*, revocalized to read *‘arbīm*) from the nearby desert. It has been standard practice since then for scholars engaged in the textual criticism of the Bible to doubt the Masoretic vocalization of problematical Biblical words and phrases now and then. What I do is go all the way and read the Hebrew Bible in its unvocalized text, paying no regard to the Masoretic vocalization, in order to discover what sense I can make out of it by myself, before turning to find out what sense the Masoretes had made of it. I simply carry to its logical conclusion what scholars have been doing for nearly two centuries. In most cases my own reading of the Bible turns out to be no different from that of the Masoretes. In a number of cases, however, it does turn out to be radically different, and I explain in detail the reasons. If Emerton, Parfitt and others disagree with me, where I disagree with the Masoretes, they would also have to go into detailed explanation, in which case they might convince me of my errors of Biblical interpretation. If they choose to make sweeping condemnations of my Biblical readings, without bothering to explain their reasons, I shall take it that they have none.

Then there is the question of archaeology. My critics have generally maintained that the case for Palestine being the true land of the Bible has been fully proven on this basis. Professor James Sauer was emphatic on this point: 'Archaeologists have come up with incontrovertible evidence in the ground that Hebron and Jerusalem are where the Bible says [*sic*] that they are.' As I pointed out in *The Bible Came from Arabia*, there are a number of serious archaeologists and other scholars who disagree, and who have expressed unequivocal opinions on this matter. The fact that jar handles have been found in some Palestinian sites bearing Canaanite inscriptions that say *lmlk ḥbrn* (read to mean 'to the King of Hebron'), and such like, prove nothing — certainly nothing conclusive. One might for instance ask who was the Biblical King of Hebron in question. Moreover, one might read *lmlk ḥbrn*, for example, to mean 'for the ownership of Hebron' (an attested personal name) rather than 'to the King of Hebron', especially as jars of ordinary earthenware are hardly worthy of dedication to a king. Granted, archaeological excavations in West Arabia are needed to provide more conclusive proof or disproof of my thesis that the land of the Hebrew Bible was in fact there. Archaeologically, however, the case for Palestine, after decades of intense excavation, remains completely unproven, and, moreover, the comparative toponymical evidence is far more against than for it. Biblical archaeologists are hardly ready to admit this, but there are scientific archaeologists who do so. In doubting the validity of Biblical archaeology to date, I am satisfied that I am in good company.

Let me set the record straight: I do not pretend in any way that my own findings in the field of Biblical geography and general Biblical study are, beyond doubt, the truth, the whole truth and nothing but the truth. On the other hand, I do maintain that they are findings whose possible validity must be seriously considered rather than hastily accepted, or even more hastily dismissed. I arrived at these findings by following a method which I described in detail in the second chapter of *The Bible Came from Arabia*. My critics, in anger rather than in reason, have dismissed my method as a non-method. Yet by pursuing this method, I have arrived at conclusions which have a distinct advantage over the standing propositions of modern 'Bible Science': they provide an explanation of Biblical geography which facilitates rather than complicates the understanding of the Hebrew Bible as history. Some of my ardent critics, in their more reflective moments, have admitted this. Therefore, I shall venture to present interested readers with this second book of Bible studies, which I hope they will find more readable than the first, where the more tedious technicalities of geography and linguistics had to be covered.

In ending this preface I must acknowledge the assistance of four people who helped me in my work: John Munro of the American University of Beirut, who edited the first draft of the completed text; Leila Salibi and Margo Matta, who made the first typescripts of it; and Josephine Zananiri, who edited the book in its final form before it was sent to press.

Kamal Salibi
Amman, 24 April 1987

SECRETS OF THE BIBLE PEOPLE

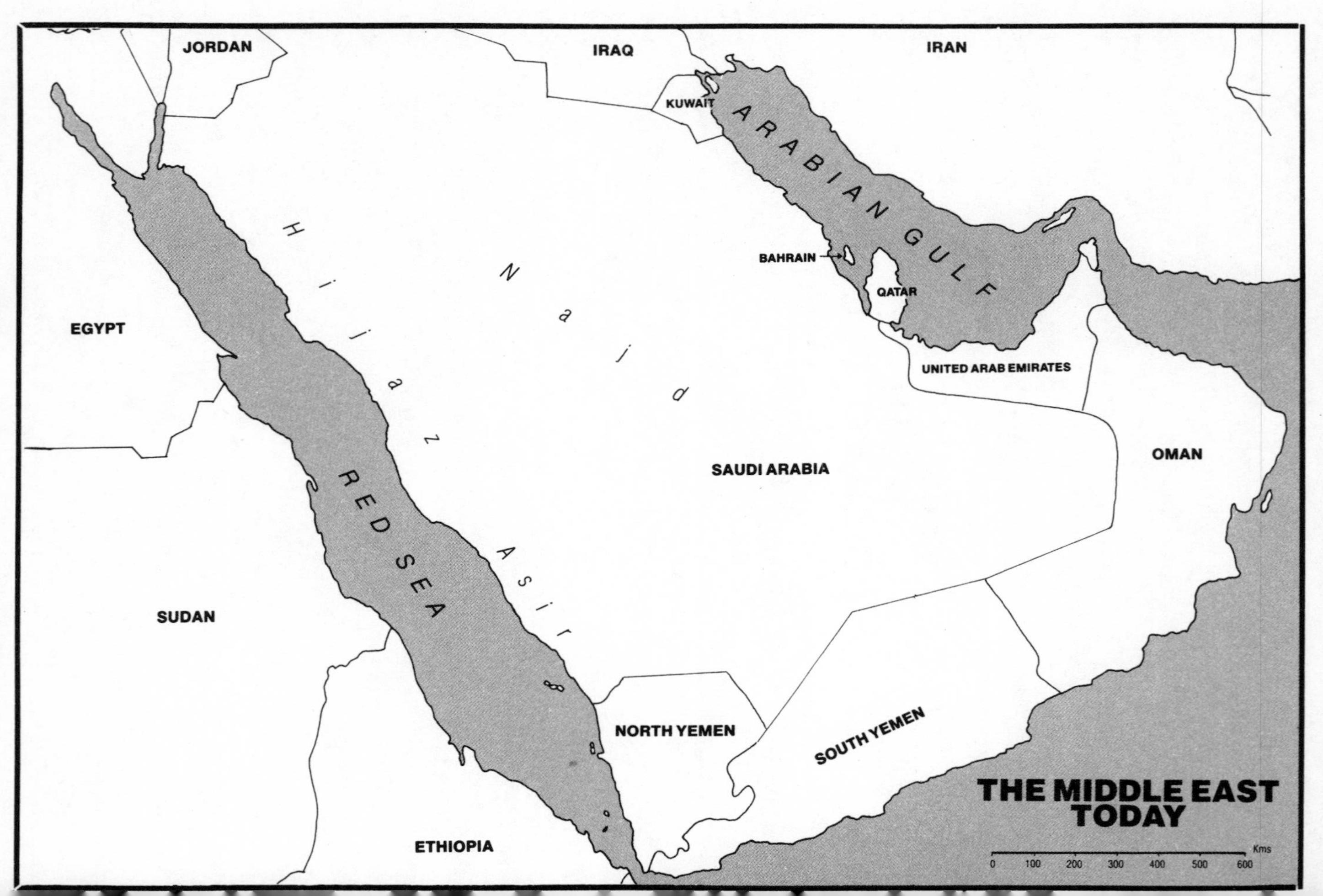
JORDAN
IRAQ
IRAN
KUWAIT
ARABIAN GULF
BAHRAIN
QATAR
EGYPT
Hijaz
Najd
UNITED ARAB EMIRATES
OMAN
SAUDI ARABIA
RED SEA
Asir
SUDAN
NORTH YEMEN
SOUTH YEMEN
THE MIDDLE EAST
TODAY
Kms
0 100 200 300 400 500 600
ETHIOPIA

Introduction
Defining the Objective

In my earlier book, *The Bible Came from Arabia*, I argued largely, but not entirely, on the basis of place names that the true land of the Hebrew Bible (to Christians the Old Testament) was not Palestine, but the southern Hijaz and Asir in West Arabia. Hostile critics have pronounced my argument of the case as worthless rubbish on the grounds that the archaeology and palaeography of Palestine have already proved beyond doubt that the history of the Biblical Israelites was enacted there. A number of specialists express strong reservations about the truth of this claim. Where my own theory of the West Arabian geography of the Bible is concerned, I admit that it still needs to be substantiated by archaeological excavation. On the other hand the fact that hundreds of Biblical place names survive in West Arabia, whereas barely a handful are to be found in Palestine cannot be lightly dismissed. Another matter that commands even more serious attention is the fact that the geographical coordinates, which the Hebrew Bible gives to places whose names happen to survive in both areas, invariably apply to West Arabia and not to Palestine.

In the present book I shall examine some well-known Bible stories with two aims in view: first, to put my new theory of Biblical geography to further test, and to introduce certain corrections; second, to reappraise the content of these Bible stories when examined in the light of what I contend is their true Arabian setting. If you have a Bible near you while you read this book, it will help; all the better if you can read the Bible in Hebrew, although this is not vital. Where I think the English Bible mistranslates the original, I will point out the error, and give what I believe to be a more accurate reading of the original Hebrew. If you do not mind reading seventeenth-century English, I would recommend the Authorized Version (AV) rather than the Revised Standard Version (RSV), or other modern translations. The old translators took fewer liberties in translation, particularly in the rendering of place names.

In *The Bible Came from Arabia*, I pointed out that the Hebrew Bible, as we know it, may be considered an accurate version of the Jewish scriptures as they were put together in about 500 BC; certainly before 300 BC. What is not always accurate, however, is the vocalization of the Hebrew Bible text, which was carried out about a thousand years later by the Palestinian and Mesopotamian Masoretes (sixth to tenth centuries AD) — Jewish scholars whose spoken language was Aramaic, or more likely Arabic, rather than Hebrew. By the most conservative estimate, Hebrew, by that time, had not existed as a language of ordinary speech since the third century BC. Any standard encyclopaedia article on the subject will support this view. In Hebrew, as in Arabic, there are no real vowels in the alphabet, and vocalization can only be indicated by vowel signs. With different vocalizations, words spelled in the same way can yield widely different meanings. When I read my Arabic newspaper every morning, I have to vocalize the unvowelled words in the columns in my mind, as I read them, according to the context. When I read the Hebrew Bible, I discount the Masoretic vocalization and do the same thing; then I turn to find out what sense the Masoretes had made of the same text. In most cases I find they were correct. In many cases, however, they were not as correct, and sometimes they were plainly wrong.

In no way can I claim that it was I who first discovered that the Masoretic vocalization of the Hebrew Bible can often be misleading. This fact has been known since the earliest days of modern Biblical criticism. One well-known example, already alluded to in the Preface, comes from the story of the 'ravens' that 'brought... bread and flesh in the morning, and bread and flesh in the evening' to the prophet Elijah while he was hiding himself near the brook of Cherith (1 Kings 17:6). In vocalizing the original Hebrew of this story, the Masoretes rendered the word *'rbym* as *'ōrbīm*, which produced the meaning 'ravens'. Had they rendered it as *'arbīm*, as some Biblical scholars have suggested, it would have meant 'Arabs', which makes better sense. Another example comes from one of the best-known Psalms (23:4). Here the Masoretes vocalized the word *ṣlmwt* to read *ṣal-māweth*, which means 'the shadow of death'. To some Biblical scholars a more plausible vocalization of the same word would have been *ṣalamōth*, meaning 'darknesses'. Hence the 'valley of the shadow of death' of which this psalm speaks could have simply been the 'valley of darknesses'. The literature of modern Biblical criticism is replete with other examples of passages of Biblical text, where the Masoretic vocalization of the original Hebrew has been seriously doubted. I simply go a step further than my predecessors in the field, discounting the Masoretic vocalization of any Biblical text I examine as a matter of principle, assuming that it could be wrong until I can establish the degree to which it is correct.

In the present book, therefore, I shall proceed on two assumptions: first, that Biblical geography belongs in West Arabia, not Palestine; second, that the Bible ought to be read afresh in the original Hebrew without regard to the Masoretic vocalization which was introduced to its text much later. In this light I shall examine the more familiar stories told in the Torah or Pentateuch — the first five books of the canonical Hebrew Bible (Genesis, Exodus, Leviticus, Numbers and Deuteronomy). I shall also examine the story of Jonah which is told in the book of Jonah. First, however, there are some technicalities to explain to those readers who are not specialists.

The texts I shall examine have been thoroughly studied and restudied before, and much of what I have to say about them is not new. In the field called 'Bible Science', one must distinguish between the remarkable work carried out since the last century by scholars who have concentrated on the textual analysis of the Hebrew Bible; the often ingenious work of others who have tried to evaluate the Bible as history, even in the context of what I contend is the wrong geography; and the work of Biblical archaeologists, who continually announce discoveries of what they claim are Biblical sites and Biblically relevant inscriptions and records in Palestine and other parts of the Near East. Some Biblical scholars have taken the work of these archaeologists seriously; others less so. My own conviction is that the case of Biblical archaeology, as it stands today, remains completely unproven, despite all claims to the contrary.

Let us consider, however, the highly important insights which the textual criticism of the Bible has yielded, relating to the books whose narrative contents we shall subsequently examine. Regarding the book of Jonah, it is believed that the text comes from a time after the fall of Jerusalem in 586 BC. Estimates of the period when it could have been written vary between 500 and 350, even 250 BC. On the five books of the Torah, textual criticism has much more to say, and learned opinion varies. There is general agreement, however, that certainly three of these five books — Genesis, Exodus and Numbers — are redactions from older texts or sources, commonly called 'traditions'. These traditions can be distinguished from one another, in the standing text of the Torah, by differences in vocabulary, style and content. The main ones are considered to be the following:

1. The Yahwist tradition, called J (from the German spelling of Yahweh, which is comparable to the English Jehovah). This tradition is readily recognizable in the Torah texts from its reference to the God of the Bible by name as Yahweh (Hebrew *yhwh*, usually rendered in English translation as 'the Lord'). The Yahwist in the Torah is a master story-teller with a compact and forceful style all his own. Scholars have distinguished between different Yahwist or J traditions from some variations in style.

2. The Elohist or E tradition, which refers to God as Elōhīm (Hebrew *'lhym*, meaning 'God'). Again, the Elohist tradition (or perhaps traditions) is a narrative one, though somewhat more reflective. While the Yahweh of J is anthropomorphic and behaves like a human being, the Elōhīm or 'God' of E is more transcendental. To describe passages where the Elohist tradition is not clearly distinguishable from the Yahwist, the term JE is used. In the Torah, the J and E traditions are discernible in Genesis, Exodus and Numbers, but not in Leviticus or Deuteronomy.

3. The Priestly or P tradition is marked by its concern with detailed genealogies and ritual instruction, which do not feature in the mainly narrative J and E traditions. It is generally considered that the P author or authors were the ones who put together the J and E materials in Genesis, Exodus and Numbers for the first time, probably in the seventh century BC, along with the P additions to these texts. Subsequent redactions of the unified text are attributed to a Redactor or Redactors called R. Like E, P generally refers to God

as Elōhīm. The book of Leviticus, which has no narrative content, is considered to be a P text.

4. Standing in a class by itself in the Torah is the book of Deuteronomy, whose authorship is attributed to the so-called Deuteronomist or D tradition — like P a priestly tradition, but of a later school. The style of D is marked by injunction, and its content emphasizes the status of Israel as Yahweh's chosen people. Apart from the book of Deuteronomy, which forms part of the Torah, the books of Joshua, Judges, Samuel and Kings are also attributed to the D tradition or school and considered 'Deuteronomic history'.

There are other theories regarding the composition of the text of the Torah which challenge the documentary theory summarized above. Some of these theories dwell on literary forms; others on the assumption that oral traditions preceded the written traditions; yet others on the findings of Biblical archaeology and palaeography. On the whole, however, the theory described above makes good sense, and most scholars accept at least its basis as a useful working principle, although they might split hairs with some of the finer details. Personally, I maintain that there is enough truth in the theory to make it impossible to ignore it. The same, to my mind, is true of form criticism, which distinguishes between the different literary forms in the Torah texts — tribal legends, religious myths, cultic laws and rites, and so on. I make these distinctions in my present study, though mostly in my own way. I am also convinced that there is much oral tradition of immemorial antiquity behind the text of the Torah, which the master story-tellers of Genesis, Exodus and Numbers picked up and wove into their yarns. As for archaeological criticism, I consider it invalid. My opinion in this instance can hardly be otherwise, since I am convinced that Biblical archaeology has searched and continues to search for Biblical history in the wrong places.

In the chapters that follow, I shall go into some analysis of the following Torah stories: from Genesis, the stories of Adam and Eve, Noah, the Tower of Babel, the Patriarchs (Abraham, Isaac, Jacob), and Joseph; from Exodus and Numbers, the story of Moses, and from the latter book, the story of Balaam. Rather than confuse the reader with abstruse references to J, E, P, R and D sources and traditions, I shall simply take the stories as they appear in the Bible texts and make some preliminary analysis of their content in the light of what I assume to be the Arabian geography of the Bible. My analysis will not be exhaustive; in some cases, as in the studies of the stories of Jacob and Moses, it will barely scratch the surface. It is not my intent to demolish one 'Bible truth', only to put another in its place. Where one cannot arrive at certainty, however, one can always guess: advance a hypothesis, experiment with it, and ultimately find out to what extent it stands up to evidence and reason. This, after all, is exactly what the scientific method is all about.

What I shall attempt, in short, is an investigation of some well-known Bible stories, no more no less. I shall examine the original Hebrew text of each story to determine exactly what it indicates. Where I detect more than one narrative strand in the same story, I shall disentangle them and study them separately, each against what I shall estimate to be its proper geographic setting in Arabia. Where it will be necessary for me to have recourse to linguistics, I shall try to do so with economy: enough to demonstrate to the specialist what I mean; not so much as to clutter the text of the book at every point with transliterated Hebrew and Arabic. Wherever possible I shall have the linguistic explanations in parentheses, so that non-specialist readers can skip them if they wish. In relating the story of the historical Moses and the exodus, I have relegated the more detailed geographical reconstruction of the wanderings of the Israelites in Arabia to an appendix, where the interested reader may find it.

One thing is certain: the Bible stories which I shall examine in this book have been examined many times before on the accepted but unproven assumption that their setting was in Palestine and the northern lands of the Near East. There they yielded none of their secrets, perhaps because the land is alien. Would they be coaxed to yield their secrets in Arabia, if Arabia is their true land? Do they make better sense there? Readers may judge for themselves.

1
Did Adam Exist?

Legend is not history, yet its fabric is woven from the same yarn. While history is factual, often to the point of being dull, legend is fanciful and engaging. In its imagery, peoples, nations, tribes, countries and towns are, more often than not, transformed into men and women, gods and goddesses. Political alliances become personal friendships; tribal and regional confederations mould into marriages; migrations become voyages of adventure; colonies, sons and daughters; political and economic conflicts and wars seethe into quarrels over points of personal and family honour. Nevertheless, legend, in its own way, serves the same purpose as history: it attempts to explain how particular social realities came about; and this is what distinguishes legend from pure fiction. In fiction the names of the characters are usually invented; the story is intended to entertain and, in some cases, to edify, and no pretence is made to the contrary. In legend, however, the names of characters are real, although the characters themselves may be territories or communities — and in some instances civilizations, cults or institutions — rather than persons. While in fiction the geography of the story as well as the characters may be pure invention, in legend, as in history, geography has to be real; otherwise the legend cannot serve its purpose.

In myths, as in legends, geography is factual as well. While legends, however, are fanciful history, myths are fanciful speculation of a philosophical rather than historical nature, which seek to explain basic questions such as the origin of the world; of mankind and human behaviour; of society and the social order. In the Hebrew

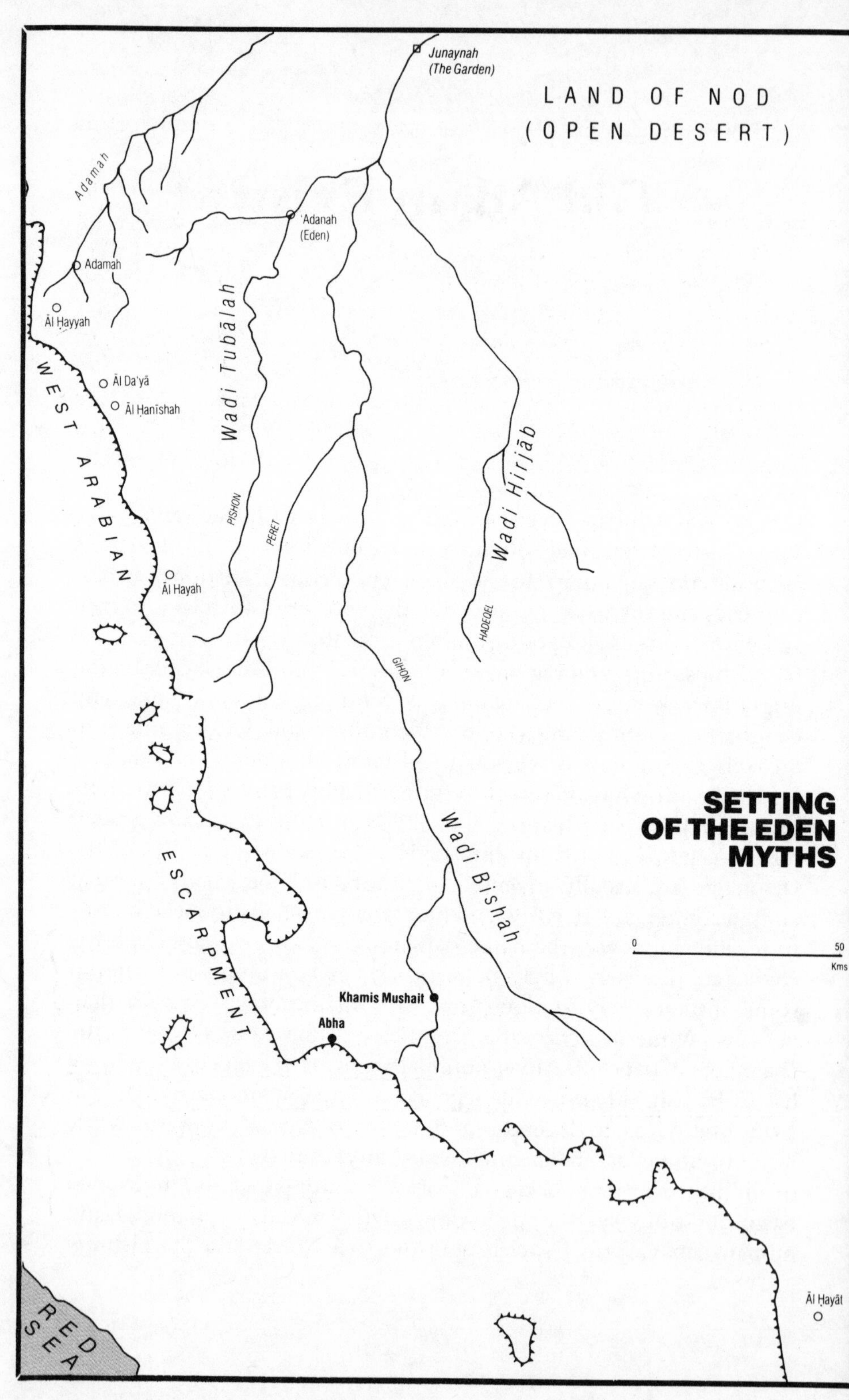
Junaynah
(The Garden)
LAND OF NOD
(OPEN DESERT)
Adamah
'Adanah
(Eden)
Adamah
Āl Ḥayyah
Wadi Tubālah
WEST ARABIAN
Āl Da'yā
Āl Ḥanīshah
PISHON
PERET
Wadi Hirjāb
Āl Hayah
HADEQEL
GIHON
Wadi Bishah
ESCARPMENT
SETTING
OF THE EDEN
MYTHS
0
50
Kms
Khamis Mushait
Abha
RED
SEA
Āl Ḥayāt

Bible many of the stories told are strictly historical, and some are legends or myths, but I have still not found a single one which is fiction.

In the book of Genesis we have a particularly varied collection of myths and legends whose antiquity antedates their written form by many centuries. During this long interval many generations of story-tellers must have embellished this lore with additional touches of fancy, fusing different myths and legends together and sometimes merging different characters. Biblical scholars hold different views on how the book of Genesis was actually compiled and at what time. On one point, however, they agree: Genesis is an anthology of stories from different sources or traditions, and the existing text of this anthology was clearly rewritten in the final stage by an editor — the Redactor, as Biblical scholars call him.

I shall leave aside the question of the literary composition of Genesis as my concern in this chapter lies elsewhere: the story of Adam and his family, which is the first story the book relates. Regardless of how this story was originally collated, then redacted, one thing is certain; it is composed of at least three different strains:

First, the story of 'the man' (Hebrew *h-'dm*, vocalized *hā-ādām*, with the definite article) personifying mankind, who was created by the Biblical God Yahweh and placed in the garden of Eden, then expelled from it for his disobedience (Genesis 2:7-3:24).

Second, the passing mention of 'the man' (*h-'dm*, again with the definite article) who features in the story of the primeval brothers Cain and Abel as their unnamed father (4:1).

Third, the reference to the man actually called Adam (*'dm*, vocalized *ādām*, without the definite article) who was the father of Seth (4:25) and the ancestor of Seth's descendants (5:1).

The Genesis text nowhere specifically says that 'the man' of the Eden story and 'the man' who was the father of Cain and Abel were the same person: nor does it identify 'the man' in either case as the person who was actually called Adam, and who was the father of Seth. The way the three stories are narrated in succession, with some deft interpolation here and there, simply leaves us with the impression that 'the man' of the first two stories and the Adam of the third story were one and the same person, whose wife was called Eve (actually mentioned by name only twice, 3:20, 4:1, in both cases as the wife of 'the man', not of Adam). Thus, we are left to conclude that what is involved is one story about the first human family whose head was called Adam, the ancestor of all mankind. The fact that the Hebrew word *ādām*, meaning 'man', is identical with Adam as the name of the father of Seth plays a fundamental role in fusing the three stories into one.

Upon closer scrutiny we discover that the composite Genesis story of Adam and his family is a fusion of not only three, but of at least four different stories, each of them originally independent of the others. First, the myth about the creation of man and his fall, presented as the story of the first 'man' (*h-'dm* or *h-'yš*) and the first 'woman' (*h-'šh*) (2:7-3:24). This is followed by another myth illustrating the origin of human conflict, presented as the story of the brothers Cain and Abel (4:2-16). Then there is a legend about the origins of a people called the Cain (4:17-24), followed by another legend about the origins of a people called the Seth (4:25-5:32). While the story of the first 'man' and the first 'woman' is set in the garden of Eden, the other three stories (if indeed there are only three) are set elsewhere. Assuming that there are only four stories in question, we might turn to examine them one by one.

The Eden myth

In *The Bible Came from Arabia*, I devoted a chapter to the question of the garden of Eden (*gn 'dn*), which I identified in terms of the geography of Arabia as the oasis of Junaynah (Arabic for 'garden'), in Wadi Bishah in inland Asir, downstream from the village of 'Adanah (*'dn*, identical with the Biblical form of the name for Eden). All four 'rivers' of Eden, and much else besides, are found there (see map p. 28). The characters in the Genesis myth of the first 'man' and the first 'woman', whose narrative is made to unfold in this setting, are the following, in order of appearance:

1. Yahweh (*yhwh*), the God of the Hebrew Bible
2. The 'man' (*h-'dm*)
3. The 'tree of life' (*h-ḥyym*)
4. The 'tree of knowledge' (*h-d'h*) of good and evil
5. The 'woman' (*h-'šh*)
6. The 'serpent' (*h-nḥš*)
7. The 'cherubim' (*h-krbym*)
8. The 'flaming sword' (*lhṭ h-ḥrb*, literally the 'flame of the sword')

The sequence of events in the story deserves careful consideration. Yahweh first creates the man (2:7); next he plants a garden 'in Eden in the east' (*b-'dn m-qdm*, 2:8, literally 'in Eden from the east'). In this garden he plants 'every tree that is pleasant to the sight and good for food'. Whether or not it was Yahweh who planted the 'tree of life' as well as the 'tree of knowledge' is left ambiguous. What is said about these two trees is exactly this: 'And the tree of life is in the midst of the garden, and the tree of the knowledge of good and evil' (*w-'ṣ h-ḥyym b-twk h-gn w-'ṣ h-d't twb w-r'*, 2:9). The ambiguity in the story regarding the origin of these trees may have been deliberate. Next Yahweh takes the man and puts him in the garden (2:15). He commands him to eat freely of every tree there, but forbids him to eat from the tree of knowledge (2:17a). At this point Yahweh says nothing to the man about the tree of life, the possible implication being that the man was not yet aware of its existence. All he does tell him is that if he eats from the tree of knowledge (with no mention of the tree of life) he will immediately die (2:17b). This, however, proves to be untrue, as when the man disobeys Yahweh and eats from the fruit of that tree, he does not die.

Now the woman enters the scene. Yahweh, having put the man to sleep, takes one of his ribs, forms the woman out of it, and brings her to the man (2:21-22). Next, the serpent appears. 'More subtle than any other wild creature that God Yahweh had made', the serpent explains to the woman the real reason why God had forbidden her and her husband to eat from the tree of knowledge: it was not because they would die, but because they would become like gods (*k-'lhym*), knowing good and evil (3:4-5). The serpent thus prevails on the woman to defy the command of Yahweh and eat from the forbidden tree. Then the woman gives some of its fruit to her husband to eat (3:6). Surmising what had happened, Yahweh summons the man (by implication, alone) and admonishes him for what he has done, and the man lays the blame on the woman. When Yahweh proceeds to question the woman, she lays the blame on the serpent. Thereupon, Yahweh tells each of the three what will become of them (3:9-19). At this point the story is interrupted by the announcement that the man named his wife Eve (*ḥwh*), because she was the mother of 'everything living' (*kl ḥy*, 3:20). The woman, it must be noted, had not borne any offspring yet to deserve this name.

The woman called Eve and the serpent now vanish from the scene as Yahweh turns to deal with the man. Having eaten from the tree of knowledge, he had become like Yahweh and the other gods — in the words of Yahweh, 'like one of us' (*k-'ḥd m-m-nw*, 3:22) — knowing good from evil. Yahweh therefore expels him from the garden, lest he should eat from the tree of life and so live for ever (3:22). As an added precaution, Yahweh places the 'cherubim' and the 'flame of the sword' outside the garden to guard the way to the tree of life (3:24).

The initial point worthy of note in this story is that Yahweh first created the man; then he planted the garden in Eden *in the east*; then he took the man and placed him in the garden — which, as already noted, was the oasis of Junaynah, a short distance downstream from the confluence of Wadi Bishah in inland Asir; the implication is that Yahweh created the man somewhere *west* of Wadi Bishah. Here the name of Yahweh (*yhwh*, verbal noun from *hwh* or *hyh*) survives to this day as Āl Hayah (*'l hyh*, or 'the god *hyh*') — the name of a village in the Asir highlands, which overlook Wadi Bishah from the west, near the town of Nimas. As the Genesis myth has it, Yahweh used *'pr mn h-'dmh* (usually taken to mean 'dust from the ground') to form the man. Here, however, the Hebrew could mean 'dust' (*'pr*) from a place called *h-'dmh* — today a tributary of Wadi Bishah called Wadi Adamah (exactly *'dmh*), whose course starts from the Asir highlands north of Āl Hayah and Nimas. Eden (present 'Adanah) and its 'garden' (Junaynah) are located almost directly east of this Wadi Adamah, which argues well for the geographical accuracy of the myth.

From the content of the myth as already observed, it is clear that Yahweh, who created the man in Adamah and not in Eden or its garden, is not considered the only god in existence, but one of a number: a class of beings who enjoyed eternal life, and who originally had a monopoly of ethical knowledge, until the man created by Yahweh disobeyed him and began to use this knowledge himself. The myth apparently assumes that the tree of life and the tree of knowledge, whose fruits were the preserves of Yahweh and his fellow gods, were already in the garden of Eden before Yahweh planted other trees around them. In *The Bible Came from Arabia*, I pointed out that these two sacred trees must have represented a god of life and a god of knowledge, whose names survive as those of the present villages of Āl Ḥayāt (*ḥyt*, Arabic form of *ḥyym*, 'life') and Āl Da'yā (*d'y'*, Aramaic form of *d'h*, 'knowledge'). The *Āl* in both names is the common Semitic *'l*, or *Ēl*, denoting a 'god'. While the village of Āl Ḥayāt is located near the headwaters of Wadi Bishah, Āl Da'yā is located in the Asir highlands north of Nimas, close to the headwaters of Wadi Adamah.

In Genesis 6:1-4, it is made quite clear that Yahweh was one god among many. So far, translators of this passage of Genesis have been thrown off course by the Hebrew *ydwn* (6:3a), which is only attested in Biblical Hebrew in this context. The word must be translated 'approach, come near' (Arabic *yadnū*, the verbal root being *dny*, unattested in Hebrew form). Instead, as in the Revised Standard Version translation (RSV), it has been taken to mean 'abide, dwell', which in Hebrew would be *ylwn*, not *ydwn*. Some translators were also confused by the expression *b-šgm* (6:3b), which simply means 'in weakness', in the sense of 'weak' (said of mankind; cf. Arabic *sqm*, vocalized *suqm*, 'weakness'). The word *šgm*, instead, was taken to be essentially *šg*, as the infinitive of *šgg*, 'go astray', with the suffixed *m* as the third person plural pronoun in the genitive case; hence *šgm* as a construct, allegedly meaning 'the going astray of them', i.e. 'their going astray'. I would translate the passage in question as follows, leaving it to the reader to compare it with the existing translations:

> Mankind began to multiply on the face of the earth, and daughters were born to them. The sons of the gods (*bny h-'lhym*) saw that the daughters of man were fair, and they took wives for themselves from all the ones they chose. Yahweh said: 'My spirit shall never approach man (*l' ydwn rwḥy b-'dm l-'lm*); he is weak (*b-šgm hw'*), flesh (*bsr*), and his days are a hundred and twenty years (*w-hyw ymyw m'h w-'srym šnh*)'. The Nephilim (*h-nplym*) were on the earth in those days. Again after that, the sons of the gods came in to the daughters of man, and they bore them children; those are the Gebor folk (*h-gbrym*) who have always been the people of Hashem (*'šr m-'wlm 'nšy hšm*).

noble tribe even today

Here it must be noted that the 'Nephilim' (*h-nplym*, plural of *npl*, cf. Arabic *nwp̄l*, vocalized *nawfal*, 'handsome young man') must have been the ancient inhabitants of the present twin villages of Nawāfil and Nawāfilah (both *nwp̄l* in the plural form), near the border of

North Yemen. The 'Gebor folk' (*h-gbrym*, plural of *gbr*, usually translated 'mighty men') are an ancient tribe of North Yemen called the Jabr (*ǧbr*), still found there to this day. 'Hashem' (*hšm*, hitherto misread as *h-šm*, 'the name', and taken to mean 'renown') is today the oasis of Āl Hāshim (*hšm*) in nearby Wadi Najran. Here again actual geography validates the new translation of the Biblical Hebrew.

Aside from the geography of this added piece of Biblical mythology, what it also indicates is a picture of Yahweh as a god who chose to be different from others — the *bny h-'lhym*, perhaps meaning the 'tribe of the gods' rather than the 'sons of the gods', as the word *bny* or 'sons', in constructs, normally denotes a 'tribe, people', in ancient Hebrew as well as in modern Arabic. While the other members of this 'tribe of the gods' had intimate relations with people, consorted with their daughters, and begot progeny from them, Yahweh, eminently conscious that he was essentially 'spirit' (*rwḥ*), abstained from such behaviour, maintaining his aloofness from mankind.

This special character of Yahweh is brought out in the myth of the garden of Eden. In this myth the main characters are really Yahweh and the man he had created. The woman and the serpent in it vanish from the scene after they persuade the man to eat from the tree of knowledge, and the man alone is subsequently expelled from the garden. It is only at this point in the story that the woman is identified by name as being Eve. Could it be that the 'serpent' (*h-nḥš*, cf. Arabic *ḥnš*, 'serpent, snake') and Eve (*ḥwh*) were actually gods?

When the woman in the myth is first called Eve it is explained that the name was given to her by the man because she was the 'mother' not of all mankind, but of 'everything living' (*kl ḥy*, 3:20). It is interesting that the man gives her this name before he actually makes her his wife, and before she has borne him any children; add to this the fact that nowhere is it said that she was expelled from the garden along with the man. She was apparently a mother goddess who belonged there, along with the serpent, who was perhaps a god of 'prudence, subtlety' (Hebrew *'rmh*). As a goddess of 'living' (*ḥy*), in the sense of fertility or procreation, Eve must have been subordinated to the god of 'life' (*ḥyym*), whose sacred tree was in the garden of Eden. It has already been noted that the village of Āl

Ḥayāt, at the headwaters of Wadi Bishah, still carries the name of an ancient 'god of life'. In Wadi Bishah itself, west of the village of 'Adanah (Eden) and the oasis of Junaynah (the 'garden'), the name of Eve (*ḥwh*) also exists as that of the village of the 'living goddess', Āl Ḥayyah (*'l ḥyh*). As a goddess of procreation, subordinate to the god of life, Eve is presented in the myth as a created being. The punishment she receives for her disobedience is the association of her powers of procreation, first with labour pain, second with subordination to man (3:16).

The status of the 'serpent' (*h-nḥš*) in the myth as a deity is equally obvious. He was a god of 'prudence, subtlety', and as such a subordinate of the god of knowledge — Āl Da'yā, as his name still survives as a place name in the Wadi Bishah vicinity. It is not surprising that the 'serpent' should have introduced the 'living goddess' Eve, and ultimately the man, to the forbidden fruit of the tree of knowledge — the tree sacred to its master, Āl Da'yā, the god of knowledge. Again, the name of the 'serpent' stands immortalized as that of the village of Āl Ḥanīshah (*'l ḥnš*), the 'serpent god', located in the immediate vicinity of its master, Āl Da'yā, the 'god of knowledge', in the Asir highlands overlooking the Wadi Bishah confluence.

The correct story must probably be retold as follows: Yahweh created a man out of the soil of Wadi Adamah. He then trespassed on the territory of Āl Ḥayāt, the god of life, and Āl Da'yā, the god of knowledge, in the oasis of Junaynah at the confluence of Wadi Bishah, where each of these two gods had a sacred tree in his name. Yahweh, apparently, had earlier sought to encroach on the prerogatives of Āl Da'yā by creating his own subordinate god of prudence and subtlety, Āl Ḥanīshah. According to the standing text of Genesis the 'serpent' was among the creatures which Yahweh himself had made (3:1). Now Yahweh planted his own garden in Junaynah, placed his own man there, took one of his ribs (singular *ṣl'h*), and fashioned it into a woman who was actually Āl Ḥayyah (alias Eve), Yahweh's own goddess of procreation. Having already encroached on the prerogatives of the god of knowledge, Yahweh was apparently no less determined to encroach also on those of the god of life. The 'rib' which he took from the man to fashion into Eve or Āl Ḥayyah, seems also to have been revered at one time as a divine being: a secondary deity called Ṣal'ah (*ṣl'h*), whose name survives in the Asir highlands as that of the village of Āl Sal'ī (*'l sl'y*), in Jabal Faifa not far from Āl Ḥayāt.

Things, however, did not end with the results Yahweh had planned. Though originally created by Yahweh, Āl Ḥanīshah betrayed him and made common cause with Āl Da'yā, persuading Āl Ḥayyah to do the same. This occurred when the 'serpent' met the 'woman' alone (the story, as told in 3:1-6, does not mention the presence of the 'man' at the meeting), and persuaded her to eat from the tree of knowledge. Then Āl Ḥayyah prevailed on the man to eat from the tree against Yahweh's bidding. Yahweh, who was determined to keep the 'garden' of Junaynah for himself, was furious; more than that, he was afraid that the 'man' he had created would become a god in his own right. The measures he proceeded to take were radical: he demoted Āl Ḥanīshah from the status of a secondary god to a creature that crawled on its belly and ate dust (3:14) — an ordinary snake. Āl Ḥayyah was also depotentized to become an ordinary woman, subordinate to man, whose destiny was to bear children in pain (3:16). The two former associates in divine conspiracy were also turned into mortal, mutual enemies (3:15). As for the man who was the dupe of their conspiracy, he was expelled from the garden, as Yahweh feared that should he stay he might eat of the tree of life and become a complete god. He had already gained one of the fundamental attributes of divinity by eating from the tree of knowledge.

To keep his 'garden' at Junaynah under proper control and to prevent his 'man' from ever entering it again, Yahweh entrusted its guardianship to the cherubim (*h-krbym*) — literally, the 'priests' (cf. *krb*, also *mkrb*, in ancient South Arabian, meaning 'priest, high priest'). Here the myth attempts to explain the origin of the priesthood, apparently as a class of people entrusted with preventing ordinary human creatures from trespassing on the prerogatives of the gods; in this case, on the prerogatives of Yahweh, who was resolved to turn the other gods — mainly the god of life and the god of ethical knowledge — into his subordinates. Moreover, Yahweh saw to it that the 'flame' (*lhṭ*) of a 'sword' (*ḥrb*) guarded the access to the tree of life. Here again what we have in question is a secondary divinity: the 'one of the flame', whose name survives as that of two villages at the headwaters of Wadi Bishah called today Āl Bū-Hatalah (*'l b-htl* , cf. *lhṭ*), the 'god with the flame'. Yahweh was determined that the man he had created, and who had acquired ethical knowledge by daring to consort with other gods, should at least remain mortal.

The myth of Cain and Abel

The myth concerning Yahweh's creation of man and his condemnation of him to mortality is immediately followed in Genesis (4:1-16) by another myth concerning the origin of human conflict. In this story also, a fundamental reality is explained in terms of a story whose geographical setting, at least, is real. Here the characters in order of appearance are the following:

1. The 'man' (*h-'dm*)
2. Eve (*ḥwh*)
3. Cain (*qyn*), their first son
4. Abel (*hbl*), their second son
5. Yahweh

The story begins with the 'man', who is still nameless, making Eve his wife. Considering what we have already surmised from the first myth, this marriage appears to have been consummated between an ordinary man who has ethical knowledge but is mortal, and Āl Ḥayyah, the goddess of procreation. Āl Ḥayyah, having previously been reduced by Yahweh to the status of an ordinary woman, is subordinate to his 'man', who now actualizes his sexual dominance over her. She was also condemned by Yahweh to painful child-bearing, so she conceives by the 'man' and bears two sons in succession: Cain, then Abel. The 'man' and the depotentized goddess who has become his wife now vanish from the scene, leaving their two sons to deal with Yahweh on their own.

Cain is a cultivator and he makes an offering to Yahweh of his agricultural produce. His brother Abel is a pastoralist and he makes an offering to Yahweh of his choice flocks. Yahweh accepts the offering of Abel, showing no regard to the offering of Cain. When Cain is angered by this arbitrary discrimination, Yahweh explains to him that his choice is between accepting what has happened in good grace, or resorting to sinful action.

In his anger, Cain follows the second course and kills his brother Abel. Yahweh questions Cain about Abel, eliciting an evasive answer: 'Am I my brother's keeper?' But the voice of Abel's blood calls to Yahweh from the ground, and Cain, as his murderer, is condemned to become a permanent fugitive and wanderer on the earth. Cain protests against the severity of the sentence; he is particularly afraid that the exposure could lead him to be slain by whoever finds him. Yahweh, therefore, alleviates the sentence by placing a mark on him for his protection, declaring that vengeance will be taken sevenfold on anyone who kills him. Cain then goes to live 'east of Eden', in the 'land of Nod' (*'rṣ nwd*) — literally the 'land of wandering'. Actually what lies east of 'Adanah and Junaynah in Wadi Bishah is open desert.

Here again the Genesis myth is obviously set in Wadi Bishah, where the name of the murdered Abel (*hbl*) still survives, carried by the oasis of Hubal (exactly *hbl*). In apotheosis this son of a demoted goddess and an ordinary man could well have come to be worshipped as the well-attested Arabian god Hubal (also *hbl*), whose cult survived in the peninsula until the coming of Islam. Actually a number of places carrying variant forms of the same name are to be found in different parts of Arabia, which attests to the popularity of the Hubal cult in its time. As for Cain (*qyn*), his name survived into early Islamic times as that of the Arabian tribe of the Qayn (exactly *qyn*), who were regarded by their contemporaries as the humble remnants of a vanished Arabian people. In Arabian tradition it is not only a grave offence, but also a disgrace, for a member of a respectable tribe to attack or kill a member of the humbler desert folk, who are considered protected. Such, today, are the gypsy-like Ṣulubah — the defenceless tinkers and entertainers of the Syro-Arabian desert. In Hebrew the name Cain (*qyn*, vocalized *qayīn*) means 'smith'. In Arabic the same word means 'smith' and is also used to denote a 'tinker' in a more general sense, a jack of all trades who does menial work of all kinds. Yahweh, it seems, condemned Cain to become the prototype of the modern Arabian Ṣulubah. The 'mark' of Cain must have been the sort of tattoo by which the Ṣulubah are still distinguished today from other desert people.

In the myth of Cain and Abel, we may have more than meets the eye. On one level, the story deals with the theme of human conflict. It says, effectively, that there is an intrinsic unfairness in the world, which pits the unfavoured against the favoured and leads to violence. Yet in the story there is a reason why Yahweh showed favour to Abel, but paid no regard to Cain, and thus turned brother against brother. Abel had offered Yahweh an animal sacrifice, which he accepted; Cain had offered him a vegetable sacrifice, which he refused. Is it possible that the myth, rather than dealing with the question of human conflict, or in addition to that, preserves the memory of an ancient Arabian vegetarian cult, possibly associated with the Cain or Qayn people, which was strongly disapproved of by the followers of the original and definitely non-vegetarian Yahweh cult? For the moment we shall simply pose the question and return to it in later chapters as more evidence becomes available.

The Cain legend

Until the point in the story where Cain kills Abel, what is involved is definitely myth. Beyond this point, however, legend begins, where the Cain are actually a people, personified by their eponymous ancestor. The people in question, in fact, are none other than the Kenites (*h-qyny*), as they are called elsewhere in the Bible (Genesis 15:19; Numbers 24:21; Judges 1:16; 4:11, 17; 5:24; 1 Samuel 15:6; 27:10; 30:29; as *h-qynym*, 1 Chronicles 2:55). The historical Qayn tribe of Arabia, as already noted, bore the same name and could have been the remnants of the same Biblical people.

As the myth of Cain and Abel begins to turn into the legend concerning the origin of the Cain folk, a geographical switch occurs. In the myth Yahweh condemns Cain, after he had murdered his brother, to become a 'wanderer' (Hebrew *nd*, 4:12, 14) in the land of Nod (*nwd*), meaning the land of 'wandering' — the open desert east of Wadi Bishah beyond 'Adanah (Eden) and Junaynah (the 'garden'). The Genesis text actually specifies that this land of 'wandering' lay east of Eden (4:16). In the same sentence, however, we are told that Cain went to 'dwell' or 'settle' (*y̌b*), not 'wander', in the land of Nod; and precisely at this point the myth in the story ends and the legend commences. The juncture between the two tales involves a play on the word *nwd*, which can mean 'wandering' and which is also a place name, today Nawdah (exactly *nwd*) — either of two villages having the same name in the highlands of northern Yemen. While the Cain of the myth was condemned to become an eternal 'wanderer' (*nd*) in the land of 'wandering' east of Wadi Bishah, the Cain of the legend, as the personification of a people by that name, went to 'settle' (*yšb*) in the territory of Nawdah in northern

Yemen. Considering that tribes and peoples normally take their names from their lands of origin, I would guess that the Cain folk, or Kenites (Arabic Qayn, and in all cases *qyn*) were originally established in the valley of Wadi Qāyinah (exactly *qyn*), in the southern part of the Yemen, before they migrated to the highlands further north to settle in the 'land of Nod', which was in the vicinity of one of the two North Yemen villages called Nawdah to this day.

After noting the settlement of Cain in the land of Nawdah, the legend turns to concentrate on the proliferation of the Cain people and their geographical whereabouts (4:17-24). Cain, we are told, marries and begets a 'son' called Enoch (*ḥnwk*); then he builds a city and calls it after his son's name. Enoch then begets a 'son' called Irad (*'yrd*). What is indicated here, beyond doubt, is a northward migration of the Cain folk from the territory of Nawdah in the Yemen, into the highlands of Asir: first to an Enoch which is the present village of Ḥanakah (*ḥnk*), near the town of Dhahrān al-Janūb; then further north to an Irad which is today Āl 'Irād (*'rd*), near Abha. Irad's 'son' is Mehujael (*mḥwy'l*), today Muḥāyil (*mḥyl*), a town on the maritime side of Asir north-west of Abha. This Mehujael, in turn, has a 'son', Methushael (*mtwš'l*, to be parsed *mtwš 'l*) — today probably Ḥawd al-Mushayṭ (the 'well' of *'l mšyṭ*, metathesis of *mtwš*), near Muḥāyil, rather than Āl Mushayṭ (*'l mšyṭ*), near the town of Khamis Mushait (which is again *mšyṭ*), east of Abha.

Methushael's son, whose name is Lamech (*lmk*), takes two 'wives', Adah (*'dh*) and Zillah (*ṣlh*). The nearest 'Lamech' to Muḥāyil and Ḥawd al-Mushayṭ is Āl Kāmil (*kml*, metathesis of *lmk*), in the Ballahmar region not far to the north. Here the 'Lamech' or Āl Kāmil folk must have formed tribal coalitions with two neighbours: those of 'Idwah (*'dwh*), in the adjacent Bani Shahr hill country to the north (Lamech's 'wife' Adah); and those of Ṣilah (*ṣlh*), in the Rijal Alma' hill country to the south (Lamech's 'wife' Zillah). Of the two 'wives' of Lamech, Adah becomes the mother of Jabal (*ybl*) and Jubal (*ywbl*). Zillah, on the other hand, becomes the mother of Tubal (*twbl*) and his 'sister' Naamah (*n'mh*). In terms of Arabian geography, the places indicated appear to be the following:

1. Buwālah (*bwl*, cf. *ybl*, for 'Jabal'), near Muḥāyil.
2. Buwaylah (*bwyl*, cf. *ybwl*, for 'Jubal') in the Taif region of the southern Hijaz.

3. The valley of Wadi Tūlab (*twlb*, cf. *twbl*, for 'Tubal'), in central Najd, west of the present city of Riyadh.
4. Nā'imah (exactly *n'mh*, for 'Naamah', the 'sister' of Tubal), also in central Najd.

More evidence emerges regarding the proliferations of the Cain people as the legend continues. The original Hebrew proceeds to say that 'Jabal' (that is to say, present Buwālah, near Muḥāyil) was 'the father of the inhabitants of Ōhel and Miqneh' (*'by yšb 'hl w-mqnh*, 4:20, traditionally taken to mean 'the father of those who dwell in tents and have cattle'). Ōhel (*'hl*) is today Āl Yāhil (*yhl*), in the northern Asir highlands; Miqneh (*mqnh*) is the valley of Wadi Maqniyah (*mqnyh*), north of Muḥāyil, and downhill from Āl Yāhil. As for 'Jubal' (that is to say, present Buwaylah, in the Taif region), he is described as 'the father of all Tōpēsh, Kīnōr and 'Ōgāb' (*'by kl tpš knwr w-'wgb*, 4:21, hitherto translated as 'the father of all those who play the lyre and pipe' (RSV)). Actually Shaṭfah (*šṭp*, cf. *ṭpš*), Qurayn (*qryn*, cf. *knwr*) and 'Uqūb (*'qb*, cf. *'wgb*) still exist as three villages of the Taif region where Buwaylah (Biblical 'Jubal') is also located.

There remains 'Tubal' (Wadi Tūlab), Lamech's 'son' by his wife Zillah, and the brother of Naamah. In the Hebrew of Genesis he is described as follows: 'Tubal, a smith (*twbl qyn*), the forger of all tools of copper and iron' (*lṭš kl ḥrš nḥšt w-brzl*, 4:22). So far, the Hebrew *twbl qyn*, rather than being taken to mean 'Tubal, a smith' or 'Tubal, the smith', which is its obvious meaning, has been rendered in translation as the double-barrelled name Tubal-cain. It seems to me certain that the Tubal folk — the ancient inhabitants of Wadi Tūlab in central Najd — were in their time the prototypes of the modern Ṣulubah, the tinkers (singular *qyn*) of the Arabian desert, as Genesis actually indicates.

From this geographical analysis of the Genesis story of the Cain folk, one can learn exactly why this legend was made to dovetail so closely with the myth of Cain and Abel, which must originally have been an entirely different story. According to the legend, descendants of Cain (i.e. a branch of the Cain people) inhabited Ōhel, today Āl Yāhil, in the northern Asir highlands, as already noted. This Āl Yāhil is located at the headwaters of a valley called today Wadi Kanahbalah (*knhbl*). The name makes no sense at all unless it is understood as a construct of some kind. In ancient times some Arabian story-teller must have taken it to be *kn hbl*, recognizing in it a combination of the names of Cain (*qyn*) and Abel (*hbl*). Cain was known to be the name of a people, and Abel (as Hubal, see above) the name of a god; so the legend of Cain and the myth of the god Abel were combined in one story which began as myth and ended as legend. It is of such stuff that popular lore is often made.

The legend of Seth

After the legend of Cain comes the legend of Adam, Seth and Enosh (4:25-26). When the Genesis stories were put together, some redactor, using a simple device, identified the Adam (*'dm*) of this legend, who was the 'father' of Seth by an unnamed wife, with 'the man' (*h-'dm*) of the Eden myths, who was the husband of Eve and the father of the mythological Cain and Abel. Where the original opening sentence of the Seth legend probably said, 'Adam knew (i.e. had intercourse with) his wife, and she bore a son', the redactor, interpolating only one word into the text, wrote: 'Adam knew his wife *again* (Hebrew *'wd*), and she bore a son.' At the same stage of redaction or at some later stage, the confusion between the legendary Adam and the mythological 'man' of Eden was compounded by making Adam's unnamed wife say after the birth of their son Seth: 'God has appointed for me another child instead of Abel, for Cain slew him' (4:25b). This second and more tendentious interpolation not only identifies Adam's wife as being the 'Eve' of the Eden myths, but also ties the legend of Adam and his descendants with the myth of Cain and Abel, as well as with the legend of Cain. The wife of the Adam of the Seth legend is not actually called Eve in the text of Genesis because she was not Eve at all. She was simply the unnamed 'woman' (*'šh*) who was the mother of Seth.

What the Adam legend seeks to explain is the relationship between two tribes or communities of the southern highlands of the Yemen, whose names both survived into Islamic times: the Thāt (*ṯṯ*, cf. *št*, or 'Seth') and the Anas Allāh (the *'ns* of 'God', cf. *'nwš*, for 'Enosh'). The legend also explains why the Anas folk were called Anas Allāh: 'In the days of Enosh,' it says, 'the name of Yahweh was first invoked' (4:26b); therefore, by implication, the Anas or Enosh were, in their time, God's special people. Indeed the Hebrew *'nwš*, as the Arabic *'ns*, actually means 'people'. These two tribes or communities, it seems, came originally from the mountain region of Jabal Adim (*'dm*, also the Biblical name for Adam), the Anas Allāh being a branch of the Thāt. Thus 'Seth' (i.e. the Thāt) is depicted in the Genesis legend as the 'son' of 'Adam' (i.e. Jabal Adim), while 'Enosh' (i.e. the Anas Allāh) is depicted as the 'son' of 'Seth'.

How was it that the legend of the 'sons' of Jabal Adim (or Mount Adam, if we may so call it) became confused with the myth of Yahweh's creation of 'man'? First, the name of Jabal Adim happens to be the same in its consonantal spelling as the Hebrew word for man (*'dm*). Furthermore, the myth of the creation of 'man' is set in the vicinity of an Eden which is today 'Adanah (*'dn*), in Wadi Bishah in inland Asir. The legend of 'Adam' and his progeny also belongs to a land of 'Eden' — the southern highlands of the Yemen which form the hinterland of the present city of Aden — in Arabic, 'Adan (also *'dn*). Apart from this, there is no relationship between the myth regarding the 'man' of Eden and the legend of Adam, his 'son' Seth, and his 'grandson' Enosh. The first is a beautiful and highly thoughtful story which elaborates on the fundamental human predicament: how man gained the ethical knowledge which was originally the preserve of the gods, but failed to become a god by being denied immortality. The second is no more than a piece of ancient South Arabian lore concerned with the origins of two local folk whose historicity is beyond question.

In the myth of Eden, as in the myth of Cain and Abel, there are elements for endless reflection on themes of universal import. This much has long been realized. What has not so far been adequately appreciated is the extent to which the humdrum legends about the progeny of Cain, of the Adam who was not his father, and of the Seth who was not his brother, provide precious insights into the ancient history of Arabia — a history of which so little is known.

2
The Mystery of Noah

In the book of Genesis, Noah features most prominently as the hero of the flood saga (6:11-8:22) — a myth found in many cultures, concerning a great deluge which destroys the world because of its rampant wickedness, leaving only a chosen group of the good and the faithful to survive. In some of the Polynesian flood myths, the flood is caused by a catastrophic rising of the ocean waters, which indicates a tidal wave — the type of catastrophic inundation with which the Polynesian world of the Pacific Ocean is familiar. In the Chinese myth the flood is a primordial condition which is finally brought under control by damming the waters and arranging outlets to the sea for them. Here the theme clearly relates to the taming of great rivers, like those found in China, where the inundations are caused not by heavy rainfall, but by the seasonal melting of snows at the source. In the Genesis story of the flood, the deluge is caused by torrential rains which continue for forty days. The same is true of the Mesopotamian flood story told in the Epic of Gilgamesh, and it is generally believed that the Genesis story is a borrowing from a Mesopotamian original. I believe it must have been the other way round, as floods in Mesopotamia are river inundations mainly caused by the melting of mountain snows. Had the Mesopotamian flood story been indigenous, it would have proved closer to the Chinese saga than to the Biblical one, which more eminently fits the Arabian setting. One would have expected at least to find a mention of rivers in an indigenously Mesopotamian flood myth. In Arabia, on the other hand, floods can only be caused by rains, there being no major

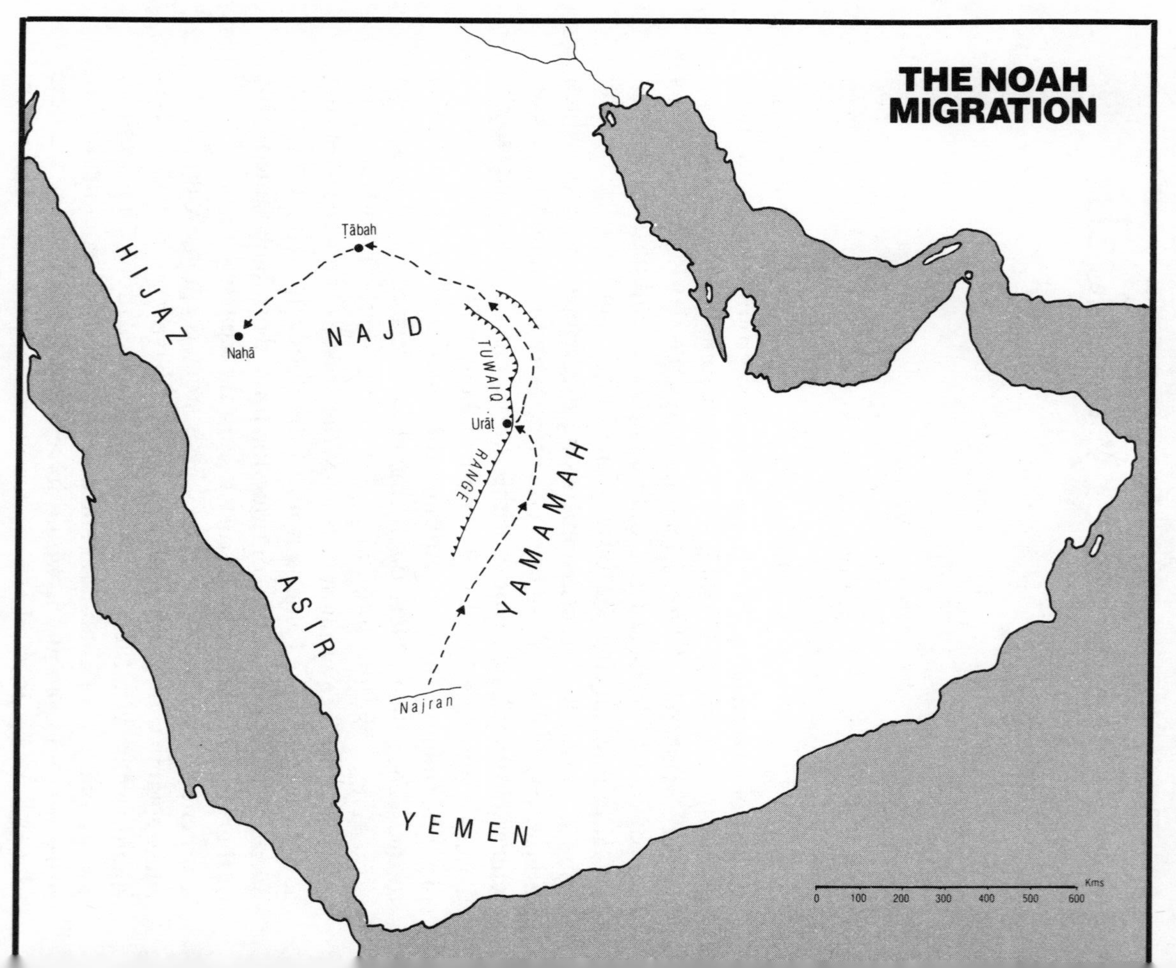
THE NOAH MIGRATION
Ṭābah
HIJAZ
NAJD
Naḥā
TUWAIQ
Urāṭ
RANGE
YAMAMAH
ASIR
Najran
YEMEN
Kms
0 100 200 300 400 500 600

rivers to inundate, and no snow-capped mountains to cause such inundation. Most likely the Genesis story of the flood has its origins in an indigenous Arabian mythology, and the ancient Mesopotamians borrowed the theme from that same mythological source.

In Genesis, however, Noah is not only the hero of the flood story; he is other things as well:

1. He is a descendant of the tenth generation of Adam, born 1056 years after the birth of Adam (5:3-19); and the span of his own life is 950 years (9:29).
2. He sires three sons, Shem, Ham and Japheth, after he is 500 years old (5:32); and his three sons become the ancestors of related groups of peoples (10:2-30).
3. The flood occurs when he is 600 years old (7:6), when his sons are already there, and also married (7:7).
4. He is a saintly figure: 'a righteous man, blameless in his generation', and 'he walked with God' (6:9).
5. After the flood subsides, God makes a covenant with Noah and his descendants after him (9:8), whose 'sign' is the rainbow (9:12-17); he also provides them with a summary code which establishes the principle of *lex talionis*, specifies that food must consist of animal flesh as well as vegetables, but forbids the eating of the flesh of an animal with its blood (9:3-6).
6. Noah is the 'man of *hā-adāmāh* (*h-'dmh*)' (usually taken to mean 'man of the soil', in the sense of 'farmer') who plants a vineyard and makes wine of its produce (9:20-21). This story tells how he became drunk with the wine he made; how his son Ham saw him lying naked in his drunkenness and did nothing about it; and how the misbehaviour of Ham on this occasion had negative consequences on the social status of some of his progeny (9:22-27).

As already noted in the previous chapter, the book of Genesis is an anthology of ancient lore compiled and redacted from different stories. The Noah story, like the other Genesis stories, is in itself a composite piece of lore. In view of the range of information it provides, one would be justified in thinking that its hero, Noah, actually personifies four different things: first, an ancient society, people or tribe from which other social communities proliferated; second, the hero of an indigenous Arabian story about a great flood;

third, an ancient mystery religion whose 'sign' was the rainbow; fourth, a legendary maker of wine who is also a wine-bibber. For a better understanding of what Noah actually was, it would be helpful to treat these four different aspects of him separately.

The Noah people

A tribe is a social community with a sense of common identity, bound together by common loyalties and traditions, normally claiming a common ancestor and inhabiting a contiguous territory. In tribal societies tribal loyalties shift with time as old tribes break up and new ones are formed from the fragments. Tribes, however, are called after their territories, or give their names to their lands, and such appellations usually survive and endure as local place names. These same names are often adopted by new tribes which have no historical connection with their older namesakes, except for the geographical location. Hence, many tribal names found in the Hebrew Bible came to survive in Arabia, not only as place names but also often as the names of historical or existing tribes.

Whatever the actual origins of its name, a tribe normally maintains that its appellation is derived from that of a legendary ancestor. Moreover, tribal lore frequently telescopes the history of a vanished tribe — or that of a tribal kingdom or principality — into a legend recounting the deeds of the eponymous ancestor. In the tribal societies in which such legends circulate, metaphorical language is readily understood. Should the legend say, for example, that its hero's life spanned the better part of a thousand years, the implication is clear: this was the estimated life span of the tribe, or of the kingdom or principality founded by this tribe, not of the eponymous hero who is made to personify its history.

The Noah (*nḥ*) who reportedly lived 950 years, who sired Shem, Ham and Japheth when he was over 500, and who also witnessed the flood at the age of 600, was beyond doubt a tribe. So were his alleged ancestors, nine in all, the first three of them being Adam, Seth and Enosh (chapter 1). The six remaining alleged ancestors in order of descent from Enosh (historically the Anas Allāh tribe of southern Yemen) are the following: Kenan (*qynn*), Mahalalel (*mhll'l*), Jared (*yrd*), Enoch (*ḥnwk*), Methuselah (*mtwslḥ*) and Lamech (*lmk*). Of these six names, those of Jared, Enoch and Lamech are historically attested as those of three tribes of the same region of the Yemen:

the Ward (*wrd*) tribe and two of its branches, the Ḥināk (*ḥnk*) and the Mālik (*mlk*). The name of Kenan is practically identical with that of the great historical tribal confederation of the Kinānah (*knn*), also of the Yemen. Methuselah (*mtw slḥ,* the 'man' of *slḥ),* as a name, seems to be that of the historical Salīḥ (*slḥ*): a tribe of the Yemen who migrated to Syria in the early centuries of the Christian era. Mahalalel (*mhll 'l,* the 'praise of God', the root of *mhll* being *hll,* 'praise') is possibly an older form of the name of the South Arabian Hilāl (*hll*) tribe of the coastlands of the Red Sea, who crossed over to Egypt in Islamic times and overran North Africa in the tenth century AD.

The Noah people, it seems, were originally a tribe from the Yemen, where they were apparently organized for a time as a kingdom or principality, as will be seen. When the central authority in the Noah state began to weaken with time, different branches of the Noah folk — the Shem, the Ham and the Japheth — broke away from the main body of the Noah and asserted their separate tribal independence in their respective localities. In the Noah legend, as reported by Genesis, Shem, Ham and Japheth were born to him after he was 500 years old, and they were already married with households of their own before he was 600. As the Noah society in the Yemen began to disintegrate, possibly to the accompaniment of tribal wars, it was only natural for some of the Noah people to migrate and settle elsewhere. It could well have been a natural catastrophe, such as a flood, which triggered off one of these migrations, which resulted in the establishment of a Noah (*nḥ*) community in the Medina region of the central Hijaz, near the oasis of Khaibar. There one finds to this day a tribe called the Naḥāyīn (Arabic for the *nḥ* folk), in the vicinity of a village called Naḥā (exactly *nḥ*). Historically, tribal migrations from the Yemen to the Hijaz, and further north into Syria, are well attested. According to an Arabian legend, as recorded by Arab historians of early Islamic times, one such migration in late pre-Islamic times followed the breaking of the great dam at Maarib and the resulting flood, which caused large areas in the inland parts of the Yemen to be devastated.

While the name of the Noah, as I have shown, survives to this day in the Hijaz, the names of the Shem (*šm*), the Ham (*ḥm*) and the Japheth (*ypt*) survive in different parts of the Yemen. The village of Shumm (*šm*), in one part, still carries the name of Shem, as did also at one time the historically attested tribe of the Sumayy (*smy*). The name of Ham, in another part, is that of the valley of the Wadi Ḥām (exactly *ḥm*); and the name of Japheth is that of the mountain called Jabal Wafīt (*wṗt*). The Shem, the Ham and the Japheth were apparently branches of the Noah people who belonged to these different localities. Considering that their names are not found in the Hijaz, one might assume that they did not join the migration of their fellow Noah folk in that direction. Unlike the Noah with whom they had originally been associated, their home territories may not have been devastated by the great flood which could have caused the Noah to migrate.

The flood

In the inland-draining valleys of South-West Arabia, floods can be terrifying, taking little more than a few hours of heavy rain to produce a substantial torrent. Should the rain last for days, these floods are bound to cause massive devastation. The flood, which reportedly occurred when the Noah tribe or tribal state was in its six hundredth year, was caused by rains which continued for 'forty days and forty nights' (7:12). A fraction of the time would have sufficed to produce a memorable inundation. Considering the frequency of floods in those parts, it is possible that the local people had learned to prepare wooden floaters covered with pitch (6:14) for the emergency — hence the legend of Noah's 'ark'.

Putting together evidence from the book of Genesis and the Koran, one can determine the exact place where the flood of Noah occurred. According to the Genesis story (6:14), Noah's 'ark' was made of 'gopher wood' (*'ṣy gpr*, literally the 'wood' or 'trees' of *gpr*). This *gpr* is not mentioned as a particular kind of wood anywhere else in the Bible. The indicated wood is most probably from the forests of Jafar (exactly *ğpr*), in north-east Yemen, at the headwaters of the flood-prone valley of Wadi Najran. In the Koran (11:40; 23:27), the flood of Noah's time is attributed to the inundation of al-Tannūr — no doubt the sandstone hillocks of Jabal al-Tannūr, flanking Wadi Najran from the south. Incidentally, many rocks of these hillocks are engraved with ancient sketches. One may safely conclude, therefore, that the Noah folk who were hit by the Biblical flood were the inhabitants of Wadi Najran before the flood forced them to move elsewhere.

In the Genesis account (8:3-4), it is said that the waters of the flood took 150 days to abate, whereupon Noah's 'ark' came to rest upon the 'mountains' — not the 'mountain' — of Ararat (*hry 'rrṭ*), so far taken to refer to Mount Ararat in Armenia, in Asia Minor. Apart from the actual location of the Biblical 'mountains of Ararat', the following must be observed here:

1. Genesis notes the exact date when the flood began: 'In the six hundredth year of Noah's life, in the second month, on the seventeenth day of the month' (7:11).

2. Genesis also notes the exact day when the ark came to rest on the 'mountains of Ararat': 'in the seventh month, on the seventeenth day of the month' (8:4), the intervening period being 'a hundred and fifty days' (8:3).

3. Genesis further notes that the waters of the flood were finally dry 'in the six hundred and first year, in the first month, on the first day of the month' (8:13); moreover, that Noah and his family left the ark 'in the second month, on the twenty-seventh day of the month' of that same year (8:14).

The calendar involved here must have been an ancient one marking a particular era in the history of South-West Arabia — what we might call the Noah era. Considering that the period of the inundation lasted exactly five months, amounting to 150 days, the month in this calendar must have been 30 days, which indicates a solar calendar of 360 days to the year, periodically adjusted somehow to fit the real solar year. Unless such an adjustment was due in the year of the flood, the total number of days which Noah and his family spent in the ark would have been 370. Had the calendar been adjusted annually to 365 days by the addition of five feast days to the twelve-month year, their stay in the ark would have been 375 days. Had the calendar been adjusted every six years, from the very beginning of the Noah era, by the addition of a thirteenth month, the year 600 would have been one in which such an adjustment was due, in which case the stay in the ark would have amounted to 400 days.

For a society to follow a regular solar calendar requiring periodical adjustments, it must have an organization that transcends the tribal level, indicating that it must be organized as a state of some type. Moreover, it is difficult to maintain a calendar without some form of writing, in order to keep a fixed record. This should lead us to suspect that the Noah people, at the time when they were established in the Yemen, were a literate society organized as a state, with its centre perhaps (but not necessarily) in Wadi Najran. In the lore of the Yemen to this day, Noah is one of the more dominant figures, and his son Shem is credited as the founder of the city of Sanaa, which was the capital of the Yemen at different periods, and remains the present capital of North Yemen. According to recorded Arab tradition, the later kings of the Himyar dynasty who ruled the country in the sixth century AD, and who were Jews, regarded themselves as the successors of Noah and the followers of a monotheism of which he was the original founder. One is left wondering here whether the Biblical Noah could have been the Noah dynasty rather than the Noah people. And is it possible that all his Biblical predecessors, to whom Genesis assigns life spans covering hundreds of years (5:3-31), were also ruling dynasties rather than tribes or peoples?

Turning from the question of the Noah calendar, there are other points to consider in the Genesis account of the flood. In Arabia floods can be highly destructive, but their waters do not last; they rapidly find their natural outlets to the desert, where they vanish into the sands. The pools and mud they leave behind do not take long to dry. Certainly, no flood waters in Arabia can last for five months, leaving the land wet and muddy for the better part of a year. The 150 days it took Noah's ark to settle on the 'mountains of Ararat', and the additional minimum of 220 days it took for Noah and his family to leave the ark, must be interpreted in terms other than the inundation and the sodden earth it left behind. To my mind it must denote the time the Noah folk took, after abandoning their devastated territory in Wadi Najran, to complete the first two stages of their northward migration.

Following the course of the Yamamah valley towards Central Arabia (see map p. 46), tribesmen with their families, travelling at the slow average pace of five kilometres a day, would have taken 150 days to cross the 750 kilometres from Wadi Najran to 'Ararat' (*'rrṭ*), today's Urāṭ (*'rṭ*) — an oasis nestling in the Tuwayq hills which form the dorsal spine of the Najd plateau — the Biblical 'mountains of Ararat'. An additional 220 days at the minimum would have provided them with enough time to rest at this oasis, then proceed further north to reach the village of Ṭābah (*ṭbh*) — one of the landmarks of the Hail region, in the northern part of Najd, at the foot of the ridge of Jabal Salmā. As it happens, the word for an 'ark' in Biblical Hebrew is *tebāh* (*tbh*, in constructs *tbt*). In Biblical myth and legend, as in Near East lore in general, there is much play on words; the simple are left to take what is said literally, but the more percipient are expected to derive more. According to the Genesis story (8:19), Noah, his family and all the living creatures that were with them finally 'went out of the ark' (*yṣ'w mn h-tbh*) when it became possible for them to do so. The same Hebrew sentence would also mean that they 'went out of Ṭābah'. From there they would have had to cross another 500 kilometres to reach the Medina region in the central Hijaz, where they appear to have finally settled, and where their name still survives as that of the village of Naḥā, and the local tribe of the Naḥāyīn.

The Noah cult and the mystery of the rainbow

As I see it, the story of Noah, as told in Genesis, is not only an account of a tribal migration in prehistoric Arabia; it is also a cultic allegory with inner meanings to be resolved. In this allegory the principal figures appear on the surface to be two: Yahweh, sometimes simply referred to as God, and Noah. Upon closer examination other figures appear. Here, to begin with, is the sequence of the action:

1. Yahweh is deeply grieved by the wickedness of man and the corrupt ways of all 'flesh' (*bsr*) on the earth, so he decides to 'make an end of all flesh' (6:11-13).
2. Yahweh secretly divulges his intentions to Noah (*nḥ*); he instructs him to build an ark (*tbh*, in constructs *tbt*, cf. Arabic *tābūt*, or *tbt*, 'ark, coffin') large enough for him, his family and male and female samples of all living 'flesh'. He is ordered to stock this ark with adequate provisions, as the devastation of the earth shall be by flood. Noah does as he is commanded (6:13-22).
3. Yahweh, convinced of Noah's righteousness before him, instructs him to enter the ark with his household and all the living creatures in their company and tells him that the flood will begin after seven days, and will last forty days and nights. Again Noah obeys (7:1-5).

4. When the flood comes exactly as predicted, producing an inundation which covers the highest mountains, the ark floats on the surface of the waters. When the waters begin to abate, the ark finally comes to 'settle' on dry land (7:12 - 8:4). The word used for 'settle' here is *tnḥ*, from *nwḥ*, the root from which the name Noah, or *nḥ*, is derived. Noah, as a name of this derivation, means 'settlement'.

5. Noah stays in the ark until Yahweh instructs him to leave with his family and all the living 'flesh' that was with him, whose species are now enjoined to breed abundantly and multiply on the earth (8:15-19).

6. Having left the ark, Noah builds an altar and makes sacrifices to Yahweh of every animal and bird that is considered ritually clean (8:20).

7. Yahweh is greatly pleased by the odour of Noah's sacrifices, and decides in his heart never 'to curse the ground' again because of the wickedness of man, which he admits to be part of human nature, being innate rather than volitional. Therefore, he announces: 'While the earth remains, seedtime and harvest, cold and heat, summer and winter, day and night, shall not cease' (8:21-22).

8. Yahweh blesses Noah and bids his sons to multiply and fill the earth. He gives them command over all living creatures, which could be food for them without restriction, provided they did not eat the 'flesh' (again *bsr*) of a creature while it retained its blood, which stood for its 'life'. He ordains a ban on people and on creatures of the same species killing one another. For the human species he establishes a firm principle on this point: 'Whoever sheds the blood of mankind, by mankind shall his blood be shed' (9:1-7).

9. Yahweh establishes a covenant with Noah and his descendants after him, and with all the creatures that 'came out of the ark' (9:10). It is a covenant between him and the 'earth' (9:13), promising that it will never again be destroyed by flood. The 'sign' of the covenant is to be the rainbow (*qšt*, essentially *qšh*) in the cloud (*'nn*): 'I set my bow (*qšty*) in the cloud (*'nn*), and it shall be a sign of the covenant between me and the earth... When the bow is in the cloud, I will look upon it and remember the everlasting covenant between God and every living creature of all flesh that is upon the earth' (9:13, 16).

This is not tribal legend, but pure religious mythology. At one time it was part of the stock in trade of a mystery religion or cult, whose hidden meanings and nuances only a select group of initiates could understand. In the light of Arabian topography, the long-hidden secrets may, perhaps, be unravelled. Here, still alive as place names, are the names of all the principal participants — not only Yahweh and Noah, but also the 'flesh', the 'ark', the 'cloud' and the 'rainbow':

1. Yahweh (*yhwh*): the name of the God of the Hebrew Bible survives as a place name in many parts of Arabia – for example Āl Hayah (*'l hyh*), in the Asir highlands (see chapter 1).

2. Noah (*nḥ*), in this instance the name of a god rather than that of a people and a probable dynasty: the name survives intact as that of the Āl Nayīḥ village (*'l nyḥ*, cf. *nwḥ*, 'god of settlement', or 'god of the settler') in the Asir highlands north of Āl Hayah.

3. The 'flesh' (*bsr*, cf. Arabic *bšr*, for 'mankind'): there is at least one South Arabian inscription which speaks of a god called Bashar (*bšr*), apparently a god of 'living flesh'. This god must have had a consort called Basharat (*bšrt*, feminine form of *bšr*), whose name was recently found in the Abha vicinity of the Asir highlands, north of Najran, on a rock drawing which depicted her as a cow (see *Atlal, The Journal of Saudi Arabian Archaeology*, V (1981), plate 41b). One might assume, on this basis, that the god Bashar was worshipped as a bull. The village of Āl Bashar (*'l bšr*), in the Asir highlands south of Abha, continues to carry the name of this god; so does Āl Bashīr (also *'l bšr*), in the southern Hijaz, where the neighbouring village of Basharah (*bšrh*, *bšrt*) carries the name of his bovine consort.

4. The 'ark' (in the form *tbt*, as in constructs and also in the attested Arabic form): there appears to have been an ancient Arabian god called Āl Thābit (*'l ṯbt*), whose name survives in this form as a place name in different parts of West Arabia. There are no less than three villages called Āl Thābit in the Asir highlands, two of them south of Āl Hayah (Yahweh) and Āl Nayīḥ (Noah). There are also three Arabian tribes today called Thābit. One of these three tribes carries the highly indicative name of Thābit al-Basharī, after the village in the Hijaz called Basharah (see above), which may indicate a connection between the ancient cult of the god Āl Thābit on the one hand, and the cult of Āl Bashar and his consort Basharat on the other. The verbal root *ṯbt*, in Arabic, means 'be fixed, constant,

stable'. Noah's 'ark' (as *tbt*), allegorically, maintained its stability in the midst of the terrifying instability of the flood by floating on the surface of the water. Āl Thābit, it seems, was an ancient Arabian god of 'stability'.

5. The 'cloud' (*'nn*): two villages of the Asir highlands, one of them between Āl Hayah and Āl Thābit, are called Āl 'Aynayn (*'l 'ynyn*, essentially *'nn*), which suggests that the 'cloud' of the Noah myth was no ordinary cloud, but a god (Semitic *'l*) in its own right. The name of this cloud god is also the name of a village of the Yamamah region of Central Arabia called 'Inān (exactly *'nn*), not far from the oasis of Urāṭ — the Biblical Ararat (see above).

6. The 'rainbow' (*qšh*, Arabic *qaws*, unvocalized *qws*): Qaws, also called Qays, is among the best attested gods of ancient Arabia, where his worship appears to have continued until the coming of Islam. The Hebrew form of his name survives as that of the villages of Qūshah (*qšh*) in the southern Hijaz, and Qīshah (also *qšh*) in the southern parts of the Asir highlands. Different Arabian villages carry variant forms of his Arabic name. Among those is Āl Quways, in the Asir highlands south of Āl Hayah. Another is Āl Qays, in the Yamamah region of Central Arabia, not far from Urāṭ (or 'Ararat'), and close by 'Inān — the village of the cloud god (see above).

What follows, perhaps, is the secret of the Noah myth, as it was once understood by the initiates of the mystery cult of Yahweh long before he became the One God of latter-day Judaism and ultimately of Christianity:

At one time the cult of the god Yahweh coexisted peacefully with the cults of other gods, among them: Āl Nayīḥ, the god of human settlements; Āl Thābit, the god of stability; the cloud god Āl 'Inān, the god of torrential rain; and the rainbow god Āl Qays, apparently a god of the seasons, and hence of agricultural fertility. A great adversary of Yahweh, however, was Āl Bashar, the bull god of living flesh. This Āl Bashar had corrupted the earth, in the sense that he had a following greater than Yahweh was willing to tolerate. His followers were apparently vegetarians who abstained from eating meat — a practice which Yahweh abhorred. One might recall the otherwise inexplicable behaviour of Yahweh in the myth of Cain and Abel (pp. 37-39), where he accepted Abel's animal sacrifice, but refused Cain's vegetarian offering. The followers of Āl Bashar, moreover, in their regard for the sanctity of all flesh as a living manifestation of their god, did not punish murder with death. This must have resulted in considerable social disorganization, as issues involving murder were left to be settled by personal and tribal vendettas outside the pale of the law.

Now, Yahweh decided to put an end to the cult of Āl Bashar once and for all by a flood. For this purpose, he must have connived with the cloud god Āl 'Inān, the god of torrential rain. His intention, of course, was not to destroy 'all flesh', but only the cult of 'all flesh'; otherwise he would have been left with no one to follow him. Yahweh therefore devised a stratagem, for the execution of which he secured the willing co-operation of the two gods most interested in the survival of mankind and other living species: Āl Nayīḥ (Noah), the god of human settlements; and Āl Thābit (the 'ark'), the god of stability. Following Yahweh's instructions, Āl Nayīḥ built a huge ark, stored it with food and took aboard, with his own human 'household', paired samples of all living creatures. In effect, Āl Thābit was himself this 'ark' (as *tbt*) which floated on the surface of the waters and carried all those on board to a safe landing after the flood had abated. When the earth was dry and the passengers had disembarked, they immediately offered a varied animal sacrifice to Yahweh, and he was greatly pleased with its odour – naturally, as it symbolized his final triumph over the vegetarian cult of Āl Bashar. To assert his victory, Yahweh immediately abrogated Āl Bashar's ban on the eating of meat: 'Every moving thing that lives shall be food for you; as I gave you the green plants, I give you everything' (9:3). Āl Bashar's ban on capital punishment for murder was also reversed: 'Whoever sheds the blood of mankind, by mankind shall his blood be shed.' (9:6)

Āl Bashar, however, remained a god, albeit a defeated one, and some concession had to be made in recognition of his divinity. He was a god of 'living flesh', and the life in all flesh was conceived of as being its blood. Therefore, while Yahweh ordained the eating of all living creatures, he forbade the eating of 'flesh with its life, that is, its blood' (9:4). Animals had to be ritually butchered and drained of their blood, and so removed from the realm of Āl Bashar, before their flesh could be eaten. In short, people were not allowed to eat gods.

As it happened. Yahweh's triumph in the myth was not only over his adversary Āl Bashar. To ensure that he overcame this particular god, Yahweh had literally taken two other gods for a ride on the waters of the flood: Āl Nayīḥ, the god of human settlements, and Al Thābit, the god of stability. First, Yahweh had played a confidence trick on Āl Nayīḥ: he had taken him aside, warned him of the flood which he naturally feared, and persuaded him and his 'household' to 'go into the ark' (repeated twice, 7:1, 7), thereby surrendering his powers, temporarily, to Āl Thābit. True to his nature as the god of stability, Āl Thābit carried Āl Nayīḥ and his 'household' over the flood waters to a safe landing. Thereupon Yahweh told Āl Nayīḥ to 'go forth from the ark' (8:16), i.e. to abandon Āl Thābit, which he did (repeated three times for emphasis, 8:18; 9:10, 18). By this time, Āl Nayīḥ had been transformed from a god in his own right into the leader of a band of survivors who sacrificed to Yahweh. Abandoned by Āl Nayīḥ and his 'household', whom he rather than Yahweh had carried over the flood waters to safety, Āl Thābit suddenly found himself transformed from a god into the empty hulk of an ark, perched in the Tuwayq mountains of 'Ararat', or Urāṭ.

The beneficiary in both cases was none other than Yahweh, who now assumed the powers of the god of human settlements along with those of the god of stability. In the first capacity, he organized the survivors of the flood into a new settlement and gave them their law, commanding them to 'be fruitful, multiply, and fill the earth' (9:1). In the second capacity, he took it upon himself to regulate nature and the seasons, so that life on earth could continue forever on a stable basis (8:21-22). Having outlived their usefulness, Āl Nayīḥ and Āl Thābit were left to slip into oblivion. The available Arabian inscriptions which are believed to date from about 500 BC do not appear to make any mention of either of them.

Without the help of the cloud god Āl 'Inān, Yahweh could not have produced the flood from which he reaped all these benefits. Once the flood was over, however, Āl 'Inān also found his position compromised and his independent powers reduced. To secure the stability of nature and the regularity of the seasons, Yahweh had pitted against him the rainbow god of agriculture, Āl Qays — 'my bow' (*qšty*), as Yahweh possessively called him (9:13). By agreeing to moderate the natural ferocity of the rain god Āl 'Inān, Āl Qays, as the actual rainbow, became the mystic 'sign' of the covenant between Yahweh and the earth. At one time twin shrines for these two gods must have stood near the Tuwayq mountains in the Yamamah region, where the survivors of Yahweh's flood were believed to have emerged from the ark. The sites of these two shrines, as already observed, still carry the names of 'Inān and Āl Qays. In the same general vicinity lives the tribe of Thābit al-Basharī, still carrying a clear combination of the names of Āl Thābit and Āl Bashar. What survives on the site of this wonderful mythology is no more than this handful of names — perhaps also some archaeological remains, should the area one day be excavated.

Noah and his vineyard

The Noah who planted a vineyard and drank himself into a state of inebriation from its wine (9:20-24) was neither Noah the god nor Noah the community or dynasty. He was Noah of Adamah — a 'man of Adamah' (*'yš h-'dmh*, 9:20), as he is introduced in the story. He must have come from the village in the southern highlands of the Yemen called today al-Adamah, with the Arabic definite article (cf. *h-'dmh*, with the Hebrew definite article). This village is located in an area where excellent grapes are still grown. So far, the Hebrew *'yš h-'dmh* has been taken to mean 'man of the soil', in the sense of 'farmer' or 'cultivator'; the expression, however, is not attested elsewhere in the Bible in this sense, nor indeed in any other.

In the story about Noah of Adamah related by Genesis, we are told that he planted a vineyard; in idiomatic Hebrew, 'he began (*w-yḥl*) and planted (*w-yṭ'*) a vineyard.' In the idiomatic Arabic I speak, I would say, 'he got up and planted a vineyard.' The Hebrew 'began', like the Arabic 'got up', is here no more than an auxiliary verb emphasizing the initiative involved in the action. The complete sentence with which the story of Noah and his vineyard starts says nothing more than this: 'Noah, a man of Adamah, began and planted a vineyard' (*w-yḥl nḥ 'yš h-'dmh w-yṭ' krm*). The sentence does *not* say what the standing translations of the original Hebrew would have us believe: 'Noah was the first tiller of the soil; he planted a vineyard.' The Noah of Adamah was neither the first man to take up farming, nor the first man to plant a vineyard. Certainly this is not what the story about him says.

The complete story, in its original version, must have run more or less as follows: having planted a vineyard, Noah of Adamah became drunk from its wine, and lay naked and unconscious in his tent. His youngest son (9:24), on entering the tent, discovered him in this state and went and told his older brothers about it. The brothers, apparently scandalized, entered the tent in their turn, walking backwards (9:23), and without looking, covered their father's nakedness with a garment. When the man awoke from his drunkenness and learned what had happened, he railed curses against his youngest son for having seen him at his worst. Stories about men with a taste for drink who undertake the commercial manufacture of wines, brews or spirits, but end up as the chief consumers of their own produce, are fairly common. The original story of Noah of Adamah must have been a folk tale of this kind which was current in ancient Arabia.

Considering that the comic hero of this folk tale was called Noah, it was only natural that his identity came to be confused with that of the eponymous ancestor of the Noah people or dynasty — the legendary 'father' of the Shem, Ham and Japheth folk. At some point, an Israelite story-teller must have picked up this tale and developed it to explain why one branch of the Ham folk — the Canaanites — had come to be regarded as the social inferiors of other Noah peoples, notably those of the Shem and Japheth folk. It was the Israelites themselves, of course, who had reduced the Canaanites of West Arabia to a subject people by outright conquest, as Biblical history attests. For the Canaanites as an ancient people originally from West Arabia, I refer the reader to the relevant passages in *The Bible Came from Arabia*.

In the Israelite version of the story of Noah of Adamah, which is the only one we actually find in the Bible, what is said is the following: the Noah of Adamah who planted a vineyard and drank himself into inebriation from its wine was none other than the patriarchal Noah who was the father of Shem, Ham and Japheth. The son who saw his father lying drunk and naked in his tent, but did nothing about it, was Ham. Those who were discreet and covered the nakedness of their father without looking were Shem and Japheth. When Noah was sober again and discovered what *his youngest son* (understood here to refer to Ham) had done, he cursed Canaan, who was reportedly one of Ham's four 'sons' (10:6), pronouncing that he shall be 'a slave of slaves' to his kin — in particular to his 'brothers' (not 'uncles') Shem and Japheth. On the other hand he invoked God's blessings on Shem and Japheth.

This version of the story, as we read it in the standing text of Genesis, is definitely a doctored one. This is clearly indicated by one important omission: the failure to delete the expression *his youngest son* from the text of the original version. Wherever the three 'sons' of Noah are mentioned in Genesis, they are invariably listed as Shem, Ham and Japheth, the implication being that Japheth, not Ham, was the youngest of the three. Moreover, if Noah, as the 'father' of the three, cursed Canaan when 'he knew what *his youngest son* had done to him', the person who looked upon his nudity would have been his 'grandson' Canaan, not his 'son' Ham. Most probably Canaan had featured in the original version of the story, not as the eponymous ancestor of the Biblical Canaanites, but simply as the prankish *youngest son* of the wine-bibbing Noah of Adamah. Where the original version had probably said, 'Canaan saw the nakedness of his father, and told his brothers outside', a carefully doctored version should have made it read: 'Canaan saw the nakedness of his *grandfather* and told his *uncles* outside.' However, the version was clumsily changed to read: 'Ham, the father of Canaan, saw the nakedness of his father...' (9:22). The guilt here lies clearly with Ham, not with his 'son' Canaan, who was not his only son, but reportedly the last of four (10:6). Yet, in the carelessly redacted story, it was Canaan, not Ham, nor any of Ham's three other 'sons', who was cursed and condemned to eternal slavery by the man assumed to have been his grandfather, for a guilt which was his father's, not his own!

In any case the original story of Noah of Adamah must have ended as follows: 'When Noah awoke from his wine and knew what his youngest son had done, he said, "Cursed be Canaan!"' (9:24-25a). In the version immortalized in Genesis, this expression of playful anger, addressed by a father who knew he should have behaved better, to a son who was more amused than scandalized by his father's weakness for wine, was interpreted literally as a damnation. Hence Noah is made to say (9:25):

Cursed be Canaan:
He shall be a slave of slaves to his kin!

The Redactor here adds (9:26-27):

He said: 'The blessed of Yahweh, my God, is Shem;

Let Canaan be a slave to him!
May God be magnanimous (*ypt*, be spacious) to Japheth;
Let him dwell in the tents of Shem;
Let Canaan be a slave to him!'

Earlier in this chapter it was observed that the names of the 'sons' of the Noah of legend, Shem (*šm*) and Japheth (*ypt*), survive today in the southern hill country of the Yemen as those of the village of Shumm (*šm*) and the ridge of Jabal Wafīt (*wṕt*). Actually, Jabal Wafīt is located in the immediate vicinity of Shumm. The Japheth tribe of the mountain, and the Shem tribe of the village, must have been close neighbours, sharing what was, in effect, the same territory. Whoever made the final redaction of the story of Noah of Adamah and his vineyard, draining it of the last bit of its original humour, must have known this fact. In terms of the geography of the Yemen, Japheth, in a way, did live in the 'tents of Shem'!

3
The Tower of Babel

All the earth was one language;
  one set of words.
As they migrated from the east,
  they reached a plain in the land of Shinar
  and settled there.
They said to one another:
  'Come, let us make brick;
  let us fire it hard.'
  Brick was to them for stone,
  and bitumen to them was for coating.
They said: 'Come, let us build ourselves a city,
  and a tower with its top in the skies.
  Let us give ourselves a name,
  so we would not be dispersed in the world.'
Yahweh came down to see the city,
  and the tower which mankind had built.
Yahweh said: 'Here is one people;
  one language for all of them;
  and this is the beginning of their enterprise.
  Now nothing will be impossible for them
  of what they devise to make.
Come, let us go down there
  and confound their language,
  so they would not understand one another's speech.'

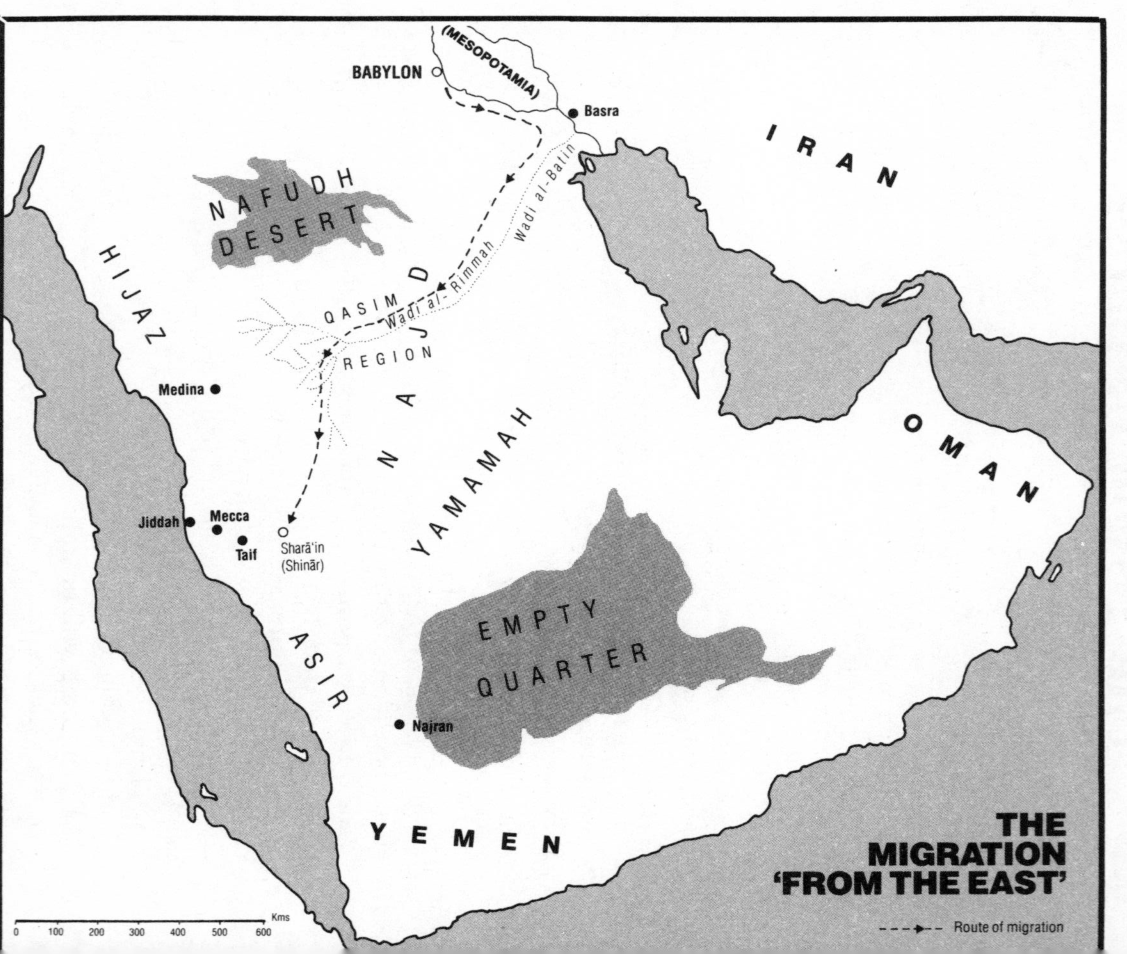
THE MIGRATION 'FROM THE EAST'
Route of migration
BABYLON
(MESOPOTAMIA)
Basra
IRAN
NAFUDH DESERT
HIJAZ
Wadi al-Batin
Wadi al-Rimmah
QASIM REGION
NAJD
Medina
YAMAMAH
OMAN
Jiddah
Mecca
Taif
Sharā'in (Shinār)
EMPTY QUARTER
ASIR
Najran
YEMEN
Kms
0 100 200 300 400 500 600

Yahweh dispersed them from there in the world,
    and they ceased building the city.
Therefore its name is called Babel (*bbl*),
    because Yahweh there confounded (*bll*)
        the language of the world;
    from there Yahweh dispersed them in the world.

I have taken the liberty of making my own translation of the Biblical story of the Tower of Babel (Genesis 11:1-9) not only to bring out the cadence of the original Hebrew verse, but also to highlight its nuances and reveal its composite structure. As I see it two different stories are fused together here. The first is a myth which explains why people in the world speak different languages. The second is a historical account of the migration of different peoples from the 'east' to a land called Shinar, where they set out to build a fortified city and organize themselves as a unified political community around it, but were dispersed before they were able to complete their work. Whoever put these two stories together was a skilled redactor, and for this reason the Biblical Tower of Babel story, as it stands, can easily pass for one story at first glance. It is only upon closer scrutiny that the seams between its two original component parts begin to show. Let us stop to consider where this is the case.

First, there is no direct logical connection between the two opening verses of the story. The first speaks of mankind on the earth in general, and the original unity of language among them; the second disregards the general and concentrates on the particular, to tell of the migration of a random grouping of people from one place to another. It is not indicated that this immigration involved all the people on earth.

Second, the people who migrated from the 'east' to settle in the land of Shinar are left unidentified. I imagine that something must have been said about their identity in the older text which spoke of their migration. From the third verse we learn that they came from a place where people were accustomed to building with brick and bitumen. In the fourth verse it is implied that the immigrants to the land of Shinar were not originally one unified tribe, as they had to devise for themselves a common name to keep them together in the territory where they arrived to settle. In the fifth verse, however, the builders of the 'city' and the 'tower' in the land of Shinar are simply called 'the sons of Adam' (*bny 'dm*) — another term for 'mankind'. From the particular and apparently historical, the Genesis story suddenly switches back to the general and the mythical, as in the opening verse.

Third, there is a serious and obvious linguistic flaw in the last verse, where a curiously inappropriate etymology is suggested for the place name 'Babel' (*bbl*, Akkadian *Bab-ili* or *bb 'l*, 'Gate of God'). This name is explained as a derivation from the Hebrew *bālal* (*bll*, 'confuse, confound'), which is an entirely different word. For the name of the place in question to mean 'confound', which is what the story indicates, it ought to have been something like Bālal (in any case, *bll*) rather than Babel. There must have been some reason, however, for the story to have cited the name as Babel. Perhaps Babel had featured in the original account of the migration from the 'east' to the land of Shinar. I shall assume that this is what actually happened and attempt a reconstruction of what was originally said of this migration as follows:

As *people from Babel* migrated from the east,
  they reached a plain in the land of Shinar
  and settled there.
They said to one another:
  'Come, let us make brick;
  let us fire it hard.'
  Brick was to them for stone,
  and bitumen was to them for coating.
They said: 'Come, let us build ourselves a city,
  and a tower with its top in the skies.
  Let us give ourselves a name,
  so we would not be dispersed in the world.'
Yahweh dispersed them from there in the world,
  and they ceased building the city.
  From there Yahweh dispersed them in the world.

On the other hand, here is what could have been the original text of the language myth which Genesis fuses with the above story:

All the earth was one language;

one set of words.
Yahweh said: 'Here is one people;
one language for all of them.
Now, nothing will be impossible for them
of what they devise to do.
Come, let us go down there
and confound their language,
so they would not understand one another's speech.'
Therefore *that place* is called Bālal (*bll*),
because Yahweh there confounded (*bll*)
the language of the world.

The two stories seem to me to be completely different, treating two different subjects. In the Genesis text the artificial fusion between them is introduced essentially by one intruding verse (9:5), introduced for the purpose by whoever first put the two stories together. It is, in fact, the same verse in which the switch in the com-posite text is made from the particular to the general, as observed above:

Yahweh came down to see the city,
and the tower which mankind had built.

To strengthen further the fusion between the two stories, some redactor, I believe, did three other things. First, he suppressed the name 'Babel' from the first verse of the first story (Genesis 11:2), and changed the name 'Bālal' to 'Babel' in the last verse of the second story (11:9). Next, he took the second verse of the second story (11:5) and interpolated in it an additional sentence: 'and this is the beginning of their enterprise', in reference to the building of the city and the tower by the immigrants to Shinar, which legitimately belongs to the first story. Finally, he took the last sentence of the last verse of the first story and attached it to the last verse of the second (11:9). This was the result, the attached sentence indicated in italics:

Therefore, its name is called Babel (*bbl*),
because Yahweh there confounded (*bll*)
the language of the world.
From there Yahweh dispersed them in the world.

Even if one were to insist that what is in question here is one story, not two, and that the city the story speaks of was called 'Babel', not 'Bālal', the fact remains that this 'Babel' could not have been the Babylon of ancient Mesopotamia – the city of the 'hanging gardens', one of the seven wonders of the ancient world, and whose ruins can still be seen near the modern town of Hillah, on the Euphrates river in southern Iraq.

Firstly, the land of Shinar, to which the immigrants from the 'east' arrived to start building a city, could not have been southern Iraq. According to the story, the immigrants 'reached a plain (*bq'h*) in the land of Shinar and settled there'. So far, Biblical scholars have firmly maintained that the Biblical Shinar (*šn'r*) was the Sumerian *Shingi-Uri* (*šngr*), and the Akkadian *Sha-an-kha-ra* (*šnḫr*), today the ridge of Jabal Sinjār (*snğr*), in northern Iraq, at a flying distance of no less than 540 kilometres from the site of ancient Babylon. What they suggest, and even affirm, is that the ancient Israelites took the Akkadian name of this Jabal Sinjār, transformed it into *Shīn'ār*, or 'Shinar', and applied it to the whole of Mesopotamia, including its southern parts, where ancient Babylon once stood. Apart from the fact that the identification of the Biblical *Shīn'ār* with the Akkadian *Sha-an-kha-ra* and the Sumerian *Shingi-Uri* is linguistically arguable, if not untenable, one has also to bear the following in mind: in southern Mesopotamia the immigrants to 'Shinar' would not have had to 'reach a plain' in which to settle. The whole country is a plain, as flat as flat can be. Obviously the 'Babel' of our story must have been located in a 'Shinar' of rugged highlands, where 'plains' for settlement had to be searched for. The territory of Babylon in southern Mesopotamia was no such place.

There follow two other matters to consider. First, the story makes a point of explaining that the immigrants who reached a plain in the land of Shinar and settled there, set out to build a city with brick instead of stone, specifically because they were accustomed to building with brick instead of stone. This implies that stone for building was not available in the country of the 'east' from which they emigrated, while it was available in the land of Shinar where they arrived to settle, yet they did not use it. In the alluvial land of southern Mesopotamia, stone is not readily available for building. Second, the Genesis story makes clear that the settlers in the land of Shinar were dispersed in the world before they had completed the building of their city. This alone, to me, argues strongly against the city in question being the Babylon of ancient Mesopotamia — one of the greatest cities of antiquity and twice the seat of powerful empires, whose construction could hardly be described as having been abandoned before completion, even in legend. In the days of the ancient Israelites, Babylon was a magnificent city by the standards of the time, standing there for all to see.

For the sake of argument, then, let us proceed on the assumption that in the Biblical story of the Tower of Babel we have a fusion of two different stories; we shall examine the content of each story separately.

The immigrant community of Shinar

The migration to the land of Shinar, the first story says, began 'from the east' (*m-qdm*, 11:2), where the emigrants were used to building with brick and bitumen (11:3b). This could point to Mesopotamia not as the land where the emigrants arrived to settle, but as their land of origin. As already indicated, the southern part of Mesopotamia is a land of alluvial deposits where no stone is available for building. There, also, natural seepages of bitumen have always been found at Hīt — a town on the Euphrates less than 200 kilometres upstream from the site of ancient Babylon. The immigrants, as I have already suggested, could have actually come from the vicinity of Babylon, which would explain the confusion between the names 'Babel' (*bbl*) and 'Bālal' (*bll*) in the Genesis text under consideration.

The emigrants to the land of Shinar definitely arrived 'from the east', although translators so far have taken the unwarranted liberty of taking the original Hebrew *m-qdm* in this story to mean 'eastwards', which in Hebrew would be *qdmh*. In the Hebrew *m-qdm*, the prefixed particle *m* (variant of *mn*) can only mean 'from', and cannot mean 'to' or 'towards'. If the emigrants originally came from the 'east', and their country of origin was lower Mesopotamia, it follows that the land of Shinar, where they arrived to settle, must have been located somewhere to the west of Iraq: either directly to the west, in Syria, or more to the south-west, in Arabia. On the map southern Iraq appears to be closer to Syria than to Arabia. Before the days of modern transport, however, it was not easy to cross the intervening desert directly. To reach southern Syria from southern Iraq, one would have had to take a long detour through North Arabia. On the other hand, the route from southern Iraq to the Hijaz, in West Arabia, is direct. From the banks of the Euphrates, south-east of Babylon, it follows the course of Wadi al-Batin, upstream through Wadi al-Rimmah, whose numerous tributaries lead further upstream to different points in the Hijaz, spanning the area between Medina and Taif (see map p. 64).

The connection between southern Iraq and the Hijaz has always existed historically. In Islamic times whatever happened in the Hijaz had immediate repercussions in southern Iraq; and the reverse was equally true. For uncounted centuries, tribes are known to have migrated from one area to the other, and such migrations are probably as old as time. In fact the west bank of the Euphrates may be described, in terms of historical geography, as the northern end of Arabia in the direction of the east. This could explain a number of things in the history of ancient Mesopotamia which remain uncertain. For example, the founder of the first Babylonian empire, Sargon the Great, is described in the Mesopotamian records as the king of 'Agade' — usually identified as the place name *Akkadi* or *Akkad* (*'kd*), which appears not only in the Babylonian records but also in the Bible (as *'kd*, vocalized *Akkad*, Genesis 10:10). So far, the location of this Agade, or Akkad, remains uncertain, and the fact that two different names are involved may well mean that Agade was one place, and Akkad another. One could reasonably entertain the possibility that Sargon's Agade (*'gd*) is today the village of Waqīd (*wqd*), in the Hail region of North Arabia, about 500 kilometres south of the site of Babylon; that Akkad or Akkadi (*'kd*), of the Hebrew Bible and the Babylonian records, an altogether different place, is today the village of Wākid (*wkd*), in the Taif highlands of the Hijaz. One would have to excavate there, however, before venturing to affirm such guesses.

In the Assyrian records, to take another example, Chaldea (*kaldu*, or *kld*) features as the name of a place or territory in the extreme south of Assyria (i.e. northern Iraq). It was allegedly the original home of the 'Chaldean' dynasty which ruled the second Babylonian empire. So far it has been assumed that Chaldea comprised those parts of southern Mesopotamia lying downstream from Babylon. Such a Chaldea, however, would lie south-east rather than south of Babylonia and Assyria. More directly to the south from there, one would arrive at the southern Hijaz and Asir, in West Arabia. Again, one would have to excavate before rejecting the seemingly outrageous suggestion that Chaldea (*kld*), rather than being in lower Mesopotamia, could have been the present village of Kalādā' (*kld'*, or *kld*), in the Taif highlands of the southern Hijaz. The names, certainly, are identical. Moreover, this suggestion is not as outrageous as it seems. As early as 1926 one scholar, B. Moritz, proposed that the Chaldeans could have come from South Arabia. More recently in 1952, W.F. Albright thought that they came from 'an undetermined part of East Arabia'. Then in 1968, J.A. Brinkman, writing on the Chaldeans, stated: 'What slim evidence is presently available suggests a West Semitic relationship for the Chaldeans and possibly some kinship with the Arameans.' West Arabia abounds in ancient Aramaic inscriptions; so my own suggestion that the Chaldeans of Mesopotamia could have taken their name from a place of origin called Kalādā' in the Hijaz is not so absurd after all.

Whatever the truth may be regarding the question of Agade, Akkad and Chaldea, I am convinced that the Biblical land of Shinar was nowhere in Iraq. It was in the same Taif highlands where Wākid (my suggested 'Akkad') and Kalādā' (my suggested 'Chaldea') are found. Here the name 'Shinar', which is actually Shīn'ār (*šn'r*), survives as Sharā'in (*šr'n*) — the name of one of the many villages of the fertile valley of Wadi Kilakh. This must have been the 'plain' which the Mesopotamian immigrants 'reached' after their long journey following the course of Wadi al-Rimmah 'from the east', and where they decided to 'settle' and build a city of 'brick' in the Mesopotamian manner. It is possible that they had intended to give this city the name of 'Babel', after the Mesopotamian Babel, or Babylon. We are distinctly told, however, that they were 'dispersed' by Yahweh before the construction of their city was completed. In the language of legend this would mean that their settlement in Wadi Kilakh, in the vicinity of a Shinar, today's Sharā'in, was attacked and destroyed by a people of the locality who happened to be Yahweh worshippers — perhaps the people of Āl Hawā' (*'l hw'*), in the Bani Malik highlands south of that valley, whose village still carries the name of the god Yahweh. In traditional societies, immigrants are rarely made welcome unless they establish themselves by force. In any case the Mesopotamian immigrants never completed the building of their city of 'Babel' in Wadi Kilakh. There is certainly no place by this name in the region today.

South of Sharā'in and Wadi Kilakh, however, in the same Bani Malik highlands where the village of Āl Hawā', or the 'God Yahweh', can be found, there is another village which is still called Āl Balāl (*bll*) — a name which, in Hebrew, would mean 'confusion', from *bll* as a verb meaning 'confound, confuse'. This brings us to our next story.

The language myth

The name of the village of Āl Balāl, in the Taif highlands, does not simply mean 'confusion'. As *'l bll*, it actually means 'god of confusion'. In Hebrew there are two words for 'language'. The one used in the story of the 'Tower of Babel' is *sāfāh* (*sph*, Arabic *shafah*, or *šph*, meaning 'lip'); and the other is *lāshōn* (*lšn*, or *lšwn*, Arabic *lisān*, or *lsn*, 'tongue'). In ancient West Arabia, there was a god of language as well as a god of confusion. While the second was called Āl Balāl, the first was called Āl Shāfī (*'l špy*, cf. *sph*), and also Āl Lisān (*'l lsn*, cf. *lšn*). His name in both its forms is carried to this day by two villages of the Asir highlands south of Taif. Add the god Yahweh and mankind to the god of language (I shall call him Āl Lisān) and the god of confusion (Āl Balāl), and we have the four characters of a fascinating myth.

The benevolent god of language, Āl Lisān, gives mankind one speech and one vocabulary, to enable the people of the earth to understand and co-operate with one another. Yahweh, ever anxious to consolidate his power over mankind and over the other gods, is alarmed by this. He particularly fears that mankind, united by one language, would be able to achieve all ends without his help, and so slip from his control. Yahweh therefore turns for help to Āl Balāl, the malevolent god of confusion, who confounds the language of mankind, so that the people of earth cease to understand one another. According to the myth, the place where this happened came to be called 'Bālal', which is today Āl Balāl in the Taif region

By pitting Āl Balāl against Āl Lisān and playing on the natural rivalry between them, Yahweh, of course, gained another benefit: he neutralized the antithetical powers of these two gods, for his own aggrandizement, triumphing yet again as a god over other gods in the Arabian pantheon.

So much for the story of the 'Tower of Babel' as myth; yet it contains an aspect which may be considered historical legend.

Ancient West Arabia, where the myth is set, was a highway connecting the civilizations of the Indian Ocean and Red Sea basins with the world of the eastern Mediterranean basin. The whole of peninsular Arabia, in fact, was a network of highways connecting different lands and cultures. As such it was a real crossroads of ancient nations and tongues, which converged by land or by sea from various directions: a fact reflected by the polyglot nature of the names of places and tribes in Arabia even today, particularly in West Arabia. These names have been left behind by the many peoples who lived side by side in the area at one time, some speaking Canaanite dialects such as Hebrew; others Aramaic, Akkadian, Arabic, ancient Egyptian, ancient South Arabian and Ethiopic, and perhaps other languages as well. Most of these tongues were closely related, yet mutually unintelligible. The vocabulary they shared was not only pronounced differently; it also included many words that had altered shades of meaning, ranging even to opposite, between one language or dialect and another. For example, the word for 'sit' in, say, Hebrew and ancient South Arabian meant (and still means) 'jump' in Arabic; the word for 'fall' in Hebrew and some dialects of Arabic meant 'rise', even 'soar', in other Arabic dialects.

This was a real confusion of tongues, and the myth at hand offers a genial explanation. At one time there was one language and one vocabulary for the world, which was the gift of the god Āl Lisān; but Yahweh did not wish it to remain that way. Therefore, he made the god Āl Balāl confound the language of mankind. The event took place in the Taif region of West Arabia, where main highways from every part of the peninsula met and crossed. Little wonder that the obscure village of Āl Balāl, which still carries the name of the forgotten god of confusion, survives in that same region as the principal clue to the myth.

4
The Abrams Who Were Not Abraham

To establish the identity of a person, name, ethnicity and place of normal residence are of primary importance. In the so-called patriarchal narratives of Genesis, Abraham goes by two names: he is first called Abram (11:27-17:5), then his name changes to Abraham. He is also spoken of as living in different places. People, of course, may change their names; they may also change their places of residence, more frequently if they happen to be nomadic. With ethnicity, however, it is a different matter; one cannot have two origins. Abraham could not have been a 'Hebrew' and an 'Aramean' at the same time.

The standing text of Genesis first introduces Abraham (under the name Abram) as a descendant of Eber (*'br*), the great-grandson of Shem (*šm*) (11:10-27); elsewhere, his great-grandfather Eber features as the eponymous ancestor of all the 'Eber people' (*bny 'br*, 10:21). In one instance Abraham (again as Abram) is distinctly identified as a 'Hebrew' (*'bry*, 14:13). At first glance this could mean simply that he belonged to the Eber (*'br*) folk. Abraham, however, both as 'Abram' and as 'Abraham', is said to have had a brother called Nahor, and the son and grandson of this Nahor are repeatedly described as being 'Aramean' (*'rmy*, RSV 25:20; 28:5; 31:20, 24); Nahor's grandson, in fact, is even made to utter two words of pure Aramaic (31:47).

Abraham, of course, could not have had a brother who was 'Aramean' unless he was an 'Aramean' himself. If that was the case, he could not also have been a 'Hebrew'. This means that the rambling

Genesis story of Abraham confuses at least two different strains of lore about two different characters, one 'Aramean', the other 'Hebrew'. In the composite story both characters begin as Abrams and end up as Abrahams.

To disentangle the different strains of the Abraham story, let us tag one of the Abrahams and find out in what parts of the story he fits. We can begin with Genesis 14, the only place where Abraham is distinctly called Abram the Hebrew, to determine what attributes are given to him in that particular text, and label him accordingly.

Abram the Hebrew

In Genesis 14, Abraham, as Abram the Hebrew, comes closest to being a historically plausible figure. He is a local or tribal chief who has a retinue of trained fighters (14:14); he leads them expertly in warfare (14:15) to vindicate his kin (14:13-16), and is solicitous of the interests of his allies (14:13, 24). He is magnanimous (14:24), but also wily and circumspect in political bargaining (14:21-23); people of high station treat him with honour and respect (14:17-20). Beyond the fact that he reveres the god El Elyon (*'l 'lywn*, frequently rendered 'God Most High', 14:22), he does not appear to have been a man of God in any special way.

I do not propose to retell the story of Genesis 14, which one may easily consult in the original (see also *The Bible Came from Arabia*, chapter 12). What is important for the purposes of our present experiment is that Abram the Hebrew, in this story, is given two distinct attributes by which he can be identified and labelled:

1. He lived in the wood of Mamre (*'lny mmr'*, 14:13). Mamre, it is explained, was his ally and confederate, known as Mamre the Amorite, brother of two other allies, Eshcol and Aner. This is the only place where these details about Mamre are given.

2. He has a nephew (*bn 'ḥ*, 'brother's son', 14:12) or 'kinsman' (*'ḥ*, 'brother, kinsman', 14:12, 16) called Lot, who lived in Sodom.

There are two other episodes in the Genesis story where Abraham (as Abram, or as Abraham) features as both a resident of Mamre, and as a man who is somehow closely associated with Lot. In Genesis 13:5-12, the story tells how Abram and Lot, who were at first living in close proximity, agreed to part company because of the strife between their respective herdsmen, Lot leaving Abram and going to settle in Sodom. At the end of the story we find Abram living in the wood of Mamre, which is identified as being located in Hebron (13:18). Here, for the first time, we meet Abram the Hebrew true to type. He is a political realist who is anxious to avoid conflict with his 'kinsman', so he takes the initiative in suggesting that they part company (13:8); he is also magnanimous, giving his kinsman the first choice of the land he wished to claim (13:9).

We have a further story told about Abram (this time as Abraham) in Genesis 18 and 19. The setting is again in the wood of Mamre (18:1). On this occasion Abraham is reportedly warned of Yahweh's anger against Sodom and Gomorrah (18:16-22), and becomes gravely concerned about the safety of Lot and his family in Sodom (18:22-33; 19:27-28). Here again we see Abram the Hebrew, solicitous about his kinsman, driving a hard bargain, this time reportedly with Yahweh, to secure Lot's well-being (18:23-32).

Abram, again as Abraham, is once more in the vicinity of Mamre in Genesis 23. His wife has recently died in Kiriath-arba, identified as Hebron, and Abraham is anxious to secure for her a decent burial. Again, true to type as the down-to-earth Abram the Hebrew, the man makes a great exhibition of his bargaining skills as he sets out to negotiate with the inhabitants of the area the purchase of the cave of Machpelah, east of Mamre, as a burial site for his family (23:3-18). When Abraham died, he was reportedly interred in the same place (25:9). Granting the historicity of the event, I would say that the Abraham who was buried in the cave of Machpelah, near Mamre, was none other than Abram the Hebrew.

In *The Bible Came from Arabia*, I identified the Biblical Mamre (*mmr'*) as being present-day Namirah (*nmr*), in the hinterland of the coastal town of Qunfudhah, in West Arabia. The Hebron (*ḥbrwn*) of that vicinity is called today Khirbān (*ḫrbn*). I would not have been so certain, had it not been for the existence of a Machpelah (*mkplh*) and a Kiriath-arba (*qryt 'rb'*, 'villages of four', or 'four villages') in the same vicinity, which I visited. Those are today Maqfalah (*mqṗlh*) and the 'four' (*'rb'*) villages (*qryt*) of Qaryat (*qryt*) Āl Sīlān, Qaryat al-Shiyāb, Qaryat 'Āsiyah, and Qaryat 'Āmir. No other cluster of 'four villages' with construct names, the first part of the name of each village being exactly *Qaryat*, is found anywhere else in the Near East. Nor have I been able to spot the name of Machpelah in any other Near Eastern region.

The geographical accuracy of this story apart, Abram the Hebrew need not have been a historical person; he could have been the eponymous hero of a Hebrew tribe called the Abram, who was made to act and speak consistently as a man by master story-tellers. Let us assume, for the moment, that this was actually the case. If he was a tribe, it is possible that his name (Biblical *'brm*) survives as that of the village of Burmah (*brm*), in the same Qundfudhah hinterland where 'Mamre', 'Hebron', 'Kiriath-arba' and 'Machpelah' are found. In that same region there is a valley called Wadi Hārūn (*hrn*). According to Genesis 11:27, 31, Lot's 'father', who was a 'brother' of Abram's, was called Haran (*hrn*), which is precisely the name of this valley. Lot's own name (Biblical *lwṭ*) survives in the same area as that of the village of Līṭ (*lyṭ*), near a Sodom (*śdm*) which still exists as present-day Sudūmah (*sdm*). This indicates that Lot was not so much a 'nephew' or 'kinsman' to Abram the Hebrew, but a tribe which was considered to be of the same stock as the Hebrew Abram tribe. Where Lot features as the nephew of Abram in episodes other than the two mentioned above, it is invariably in clumsy interpolations, such as 'and Lot went with him' (12:4), or 'and Lot with him' (13:1). Lot's 'father' Haran, who was the 'brother' of Abram the Hebrew only, and not of the other Abram or Abrams, had to be explained away in some manner. For this reason he is made to die at the beginning of the composite Genesis saga of Abraham (11:28), so that his continued presence would not raise awkward questions.

Abram the Aramean

As with the case of Abram the Hebrew, we have to tag Abram the Aramean to be able to spot him in the different episodes of the Abraham story. This task is more difficult because there is no specific passage in Genesis which actually speaks of 'Abram the Aramean'. However, we know that there was an Aramean Abram, because Nahor, who features as Abram's 'brother' in Genesis 11:27, had Aramean (even Aramaic-speaking) descendants. We may assume, therefore, that the Abram who features in the first episode of the Abraham story (Genesis 11 and 12) was Abram the Aramean. Here are his attributes:

1. He had a 'brother' called Nahor (11:27, 29).

2. He migrated with this 'father' and his 'brother' Nahor from their native Ur Kasdim with the intention of settling in the land of Canaan, but the family stopped in Haran (here *ḥrn*, not *hrn*) and settled there instead (11:31).

3. After the death of his 'father', Abram was commanded by Yahweh to part company with his folk and emigrate from Haran under his divine guidance (12:1), promising to make of him a great nation (12:2). As soon as he arrived in the 'land of Canaan' (12:5), he built an altar to Yahweh (12:7).

4. In the 'land of Canaan', initially he stopped at Shechem (12:6), then in the wood of Moreh (*'lwn mwrh*, 12:6), until he settled, 'in the mountain east of Bethel... with Bethel to the west and Ai to the east' (12:8).

5. From this last place, he journeyed on and went to the Negeb (12:9).

From this information we discover three labels by which we can identify the person of Abram the Aramean: first, he was the 'brother' of Nahor; second, he was a devotee of Yahweh, acting on his commands; third, the area where he finally arrived to settle included places called Shechem, Moreh, Bethel, Ai and the Negeb. Keeping the distinct attributes of Abram the Aramean in mind, we can proceed to observe where his person reappears in the Genesis story under consideration:

1. In Genesis 13:2-4, an Abram who is rich in 'cattle, in silver, and in gold' leaves the Negeb and returns to the place between Bethel and Ai where he had lived earlier; there he builds an altar and sacrifices to Yahweh. He is beyond doubt Abram the Aramean.

2. In Genesis 15:7, Yahweh reminds Abram that he had brought him out of Ur Kasdim. This statement, being irrelevant to the context in which it appears, could be an interpolation. The Abram of Genesis 15, as we shall subsequently discover, had nothing to do with Abram the Aramean. In any case, it was Abram's 'father', not Yahweh, who had led Abram the Aramean out of Ur Kasdim (11:31). Yahweh had only brought him out of Haran (12:1). In short, the conversion of this Abram to the cult of Yahweh must have occurred at Haran (see below).

3. In Genesis 22:20-24, in a passage which stands out as artificially attached to that preceding it, we are told that someone brought news to Abraham about the progeny of his 'brother' Nahor. The Abraham who reportedly received this news could only have been Abram the Aramean.

4. In Genesis 24:1-61, we are told how Abraham sent his most trusted servant to his 'country' and his 'kindred' to take a wife for his son. The servant reportedly proceeded to the Aram of Naharaim (see below), which was the city of Abraham's 'brother' Nahor, and took one of Nahor's grand-daughters as a wife for his master's son. Here also the Abraham who sent his servant on this perfectly understandable mission could only have been Abram the Aramean.

From Genesis 31:47, as already observed, we learn that Nahor's descendants spoke Aramaic, not Hebrew. From Genesis 31:19, 32, 35, we further learn that, unlike their kinsman Abram and his descendants, they were not worshippers of Yahweh, but had their own household gods, which were 'idols' (*trpym*). This may imply that Abram parted company with his 'country and kindred' following his conversion to the cult of Yahweh, apparently in Haran (see above). A change of religion is usually a good cause for migration; certainly it is an understandable one in a tribal society where common religion is an important bond.

But where did Abram the Aramean originally come from, and what were the actual stages of his migration? In Genesis he starts off with his 'father' from Ur Kasdim, then continues on his own from Haran. From there he moves to Shechem, then to the wood of Moreh, then to the 'mountain' between Bethel and Ai. His prospering cattle business takes him for a time to the Negeb, after which he returns to his former place of settlement between Bethel and Ai — apparently the one where he came to be domiciled. Regardless of my earlier identification of some of these places in *The Bible Came from Arabia*, let me now identify all of them, after further research, as follows (see map p. 128):

1. Ur (*'wr*), the native land of Abram the Aramean, must have been the fertile ridge of Jabal Awr (exactly *'wr*), sometimes referred to as Uwārah (also *'wr*), and called today Ayār (*'yr*), south of Medina in the central Hijaz. The different historical and present forms of the

name of the ridge are dialectal and merely a matter of pronunciation. In Genesis this Ur is identified as Ur Kasdim, traditionally rendered in translation as 'Ur of the Chaldees'. Actually, Kasdim (*ksdym*, which I would vocalize in this context as *Kasdāyim*, dual rather than plural of *ksd*) could only have been today's Qudsān (Arabic dual of *qds*, metathesis of *ksd*), the twin ridges which dominate the countryside south of Medina, where Jabal Awr, the Biblical 'Ur Kasdim', is located.

2. Haran (*ḥrn*), the first stop of Abram the Aramean after his departure with his 'father' and his 'brother' Nahor from their native Ur, or Jabal Awr, carries the same name as the present village of Khīrīn (*ḫrn*), south-west of Taif, along the main highway from Medina to the southern parts of the Hijaz.

3. Aram-naharaim (*'rm nhrym*, or the Aram of *nhrym*), where his 'brother' Nahor and his descendants stayed, is not 'Mesopotamia' as usually rendered, but the village of Nahārīn (*nhryn*), in the same Taif region.

4. Considering that the migration of Abram and his Aramean kin from Ur to Haran was apparently in a southerly direction, one might assume that Abram, when he parted company with his Aramean kin, proceeded to migrate further to the south. In this case, Moreh (*mwrh*), his first stop alone, could have been the present village of Marāwah (*mrwh*), in the Zahran highlands of the southern Hijaz south of Khīrīn.

5. Shechem (*škm*), Abram's next stop near Moreh, assuming that it is actually Marāwah, would have been the present village of Qisamah (*qsm*) in the Zahran highlands.

6. Bethel (*byt 'l*), in the same Zahran highlands, would undoubtedly be the present village of Buṭaylah (*bṭyl*), which controls one of the main passes across the escarpment between the inland and coastal parts of the Zahran region.

7. Ai (*h-'y*, with the Hebrew definite article) is none other than the present al-'Ūyā' (exactly *'y*, with the Arabic definite article) — a village of the Taif highlands, to the north-east of Buṭaylah, or Bethel, and separated from it by hill country — the 'mountain' (Hebrew *hr*, also meaning 'hill country') between Bethel and Ai.

8. The Negeb (*h-ngb*, again with the Hebrew definite article), in this particular region, must therefore be Jabal Janabah (the 'mountain' of *ğnb*, with the Arabic definite article), north of Buṭaylah,

or Bethel — a densely forested, evergreen ridge, with excellent pastures where the cattle of Abram the Aramean would have grazed.

Strangely enough the highlands of the Zahran region of the southern Hijaz adjacent to these places in the west are called to this day Jabal Ibrāhīm — the 'mountain of Abraham'. Folk tradition is often correct. In any case, at least from the point of view of topography, the story of the migrations of Abram the Aramean does seem to hold together convincingly in the setting of the Hijaz. Of course this Abram need not have been a historical character. Like Abram the Hebrew, he could have been the legendary eponymous hero of an Aramean Abram tribe, as distinct from another, Hebrew Abram tribe. Other explanations are also possible, as we shall find out. For the moment, however, let us pursue our investigation.

The Abram of Genesis 15

Of all the Abrams or Abrahams of Genesis, the Abram of Genesis 15 is the most enigmatic. He is no ordinary man as the Hebrew and Aramean Abrams are, but a brooding sacerdotal figure who dabbles with the occult and enters into a mysterious covenant with Yahweh. I strongly suspect that he was none other than the god Baram (*brm*, sometimes written *brn*, cf. Biblical *'brm*), whose name features in a number of ancient South Arabian inscriptions. What does the story say about him?

Yahweh, we are told, comes to this Abram in a 'vision' (*mḥzh*), and says to him: 'Fear not, Abram; I am your shield; your very great reward!' Abram answers that he has no use for anything that Yahweh could possibly give him as long as he continues childless, without a son to inherit from him. Actually Abram says more than this (15:2-3):

My Lord Yahweh, what will you give me,
  while I go childless, a man of continence (*w-bn mšq*),
  my house being the Dameseq of Eliezer (*byty dmsq 'ly'zr*)?
Behold, you have given me no seed!
  behold, the son of my house (*bn byty*) shall inherit me!

For readers familiar with Biblical Hebrew, who may challenge my translation of the words attributed to Abram in this passage of

Genesis, I owe some technical explanation. The Hebrew of the first verse is highly problematic and has been generally pronounced 'unclear'. The first part of the first verse, which presents no problem, reads: *'dny yhwh mh ttn ly w-'ny hwlk 'ryry* (clearly, 'My Lord Yahweh, what will you give me while I go childless'). In the second part, however, the original Hebrew says: *w-bn mšq* (problematic) *byty* (clearly 'my house') *dmsq 'ly'zr* (problematic). So far translators of the Bible have taken the first problematic expression, *w-bn mšq*, to mean 'steward', assuming it to be the subject of the second sentence in the verse, which would make it read: 'and the *steward* of my house is Dameseq Eliezer'. They generally admit, however, that the rendering of the Hebrew *bn mšq* as 'steward' is arbitrary. In Arabic, however, the root *msk*, which is equivalent to the obscure Hebrew *mšq*, gives the sense of 'continence, constipation, abstinence'. A *bn mšq*, hence, would be a 'son of continence', idiomatic for a 'man of continence' — a hermit practising sexual abstinence. Having arbitrarily assumed that the expression in question means 'steward', the translators have hitherto taken the next problematic expression in the verse, Dameseq Eliezer (*dmsq 'ly'zr*), to be the name of this steward, whom they call Eliezer of Damascus. Actually Biblical scholars have obligingly produced a considerable literature on the identity of this imagined Eliezer of Damascus, adopted as a slave in lieu of a son by the patriarch Abraham when he was still childless. The patriarch, it has been suggested, must have purchased this Eliezer in the Syrian city of Damascus while on his way from Iraq to Palestine; and there has also been recourse to surviving legal records from ancient Mesopotamia (the so-called Nuzi documents) to prove that a slave adopted as a son was entitled, by the traditions of the times, to inherit his master's property, if the master happened to be childless. However, while the Biblical place name *dmsq* is indeed identical with the historical and present name of Damascus (Dimashq, or *dmšq*), the capital of present-day Syria, Dameseq Eliezer, as a construct, cannot possibly mean 'Eliezer of Damascus'. If anything it would mean 'the Damascus of Eliezer'. Hence the standard translation of the assumed second part of the verse in question, 'and the steward of my house is Eliezer of Damascus', is untenable on all grounds. On the other hand, if the Hebrew *bn mšq* is understood to mean 'man of continence', by comparison with the Arabic *msk* which actually means 'continence', the original Hebrew of the verse begins to make perfect sense. In this case, *w-'ny hwlk 'ryry w-bn mšq*, in the first sentence of the verse, would mean 'while I go childless, a man of continence'. What follows would be an explanatory phrase, *byty dmsq 'ly'zr*, meaning 'my house *being* the Dameseq of Eliezer' (a construct of two place names). The question is, why was this explanatory phrase thrown in?

The only way to gain a complete understanding of what the Abram of Genesis 15 said to Yahweh on this occasion is to assume that this Abram was not merely a celibate hermit, but in fact a virgin god of sterility and sexual continence whose principal shrine (*byt*, 'house', in the accepted sense of 'temple') was at a place called Dameseq (*dmsq*, or *d-msq*, the 'one of continence'), near another place called Eliezer (parsed not *'ly 'zr*, but as *'l y'zr*, 'god of virginity'; cf. Arabic *'zr*, 'withhold', or *'ḏr*, the root of the standard Arabic word for 'virginity'). The name Abram itself, as a variant of *brm*, may denote this sense. In Arabic a *baram* (*brm*) is a 'miser', or a 'man who takes no risks'; most important, he is 'a man who keeps to himself and does not go along with others'. What better name could there be for a god of sexual abstinence — an Abram who was none other than the ancient South Arabian god Baram?

In the story under consideration, this god Abram or Baram blames Yahweh for his condition; Yahweh being frequently described in the Hebrew Bible as a God highly interested in fertility, always commanding his followers to 'multiply and fill the earth'. The god Abram actually complains to Yahweh that as long as he remains without 'seed' (Hebrew *zr'*), whatever he comes to possess will go to the 'man of his house', perhaps meaning the high priest in charge of his temple at Dameseq, near Eliezer. All this would have been mere speculation had it not been that both places still exist by name as neighbouring villages in the hill country of Rijal Alma' — the rugged parts of the maritime side of Asir which slope precipitously down to the coast of the Red Sea south-west of the present city of Abha. There the Biblical Dameseq (*d-msq*) still survives as the village of Dhat Misk (*dt-msk*), along with the Biblical Eliezer (*'l y'zr*) which is today the village of al-'Adhrā (*'l 'ḏr*). Also in the same vicinity lies the village of Sha'b al-Baram (the 'ravine' of the God Baram, *'l brm*), still carrying the name of the Abram of Genesis 15 as a god. In any case Genesis 15 gives no other setting for the story.

After these digressions into linguistic and topographical technicalities, we must now return to the actual Biblical narrative. In response to Abram's complaint about his continued sterility, Yahweh announces to him that he will, in fact, have a son to be his heir instead of the high priest of his temple; more than that, he would indeed have countless progeny. Abram asks how he can 'know' (*'d'*) this — in short, he asks for a cultic 'sign' to assure him of the truth of Yahweh's promise. Yahweh instructs him as to how he may 'know', and Abram follows the instructions, doing the following (15:9-11): he brings a heifer, a she-goat and a ram (all are three years old), and a turtledove and a pigeon. He cuts each animal in two, placing each half of an animal against the other, but leaves the birds uncut. When the birds of prey (*h-'yṭ*) come down to attack the carcasses, Abram drives them away. Then follows the great mystery (15:12, 15, 17-21):

> As the sun was going down, a deep sleep fell on Abram;
> and lo, a dread of great darkness fell upon him...
> [And Yahweh said to him]:
> 'You shall go to your fathers in peace;
> you shall be buried in a good old age...'
> When the sun had gone down and it was dark,
> behold, a smoking fire pot and a flaming torch
> passed between the pieces.
> On that day Yahweh made a covenant with Abram, saying:
> 'To your descendants I give this land,
> from the river of Mizraim to the great river,
> the river Perat —
> [the land] of the Kenites, the Kenizzites, the Kadmonites,
> the Hittites, the Perizzites, the Rephaim,
> the Amorites and the Canaanites,
> the Girgashites and the Jebusites.'

The secret of the mystery, as I see it, is this: in return for a promise of 'seed' advanced to him by Yahweh, the god Abram, or Baram, weary of his dismal continence and continued sterility, surrenders his divinity to Yahweh, having been assured of the veracity of Yahweh's promise by a mystic 'sign': the smoking fire pot and the flaming torch which miraculously appear before him, apparently to consume the ritual sacrifice he had prepared for Yahweh, according to given instructions. Along with his divinity, the god Abram also surrenders his immortality; he implicitly agrees to 'go to his fathers in peace', and 'be buried at a good old age' (15:15). In compensation for his personal immortality, he was to be satisfied with the immortality of his seed — his countless descendants, who were to populate a territory extending all the way from the 'river of Mizraim (*mṣrym*)' to the 'river Perat (*prt*)'. For a god previously condemned to eternal sexual abstinence and sterility, the bargain was perhaps worthwhile, especially when the territory promised to his descendants was to comprise the full stretch of the maritime side of the Asir highlands. In *The Bible Came from Arabia*, I identified the 'river of Mizraim' and the 'river Perat', respectively, as the valleys of Wadi Masram (*mṣrm*), in the extreme south of geographical Asir, and Wadi Aḍam, in the extreme north. The latter valley is referred to in the Bible as Perat (*prt*) after one of its villages, called Firt or Furāt (in both cases *ṕrt*). There I also identified the names of all the tribes of peoples mentioned by name in Yahweh's promise to Abram as ancient inhabitants of that same region and its broader West Arabian vicinity.

I suspect that the story told in Genesis 15 is continued in Genesis 17:10-11 (these two verses are followed by details which, it seems to me, have been added by a priestly redactor to the essence of the original). Here, I would suggest, the wording of Yahweh's 'covenant' with Abram, as quoted above, continues as follows:

> This is my covenant with you,
> which you shall keep between you and me,
> and you and your descendants after you:
> every male among you shall be circumcised.
> You shall be circumcised in the flesh of your foreskins,
> and it shall be a *sign* of the covenant
> between me and you.

Until recently, in the same picturesque hill country of Rijal Alma' where the god Abram or Baram was first robbed of his divinity and then circumcised, the most brutal form of circumcision used to be performed in public on young men reaching the age of marriage. Several years ago a ban had to be placed on the practice, which involved not only the removal of the foreskin, but the flaying of the whole skin between the navel and the thighs. Despite the ban it is said that some local tribes still follow the ancient practice in secret. Such, it seems, was the effect of Yahweh's command not only on the god Abram in his time, but on all later inhabitants of his home territory. The Greek geographer Strabo, writing about Arabia in the early decades of the Christian era, noted that the male inhabitants of the parts of the peninsula recognizable as Asir 'deprive themselves of the prepuce'. In any case linguistics remain constant; one word for 'circumcision' in Arabic is *'adhr* (*'ḏr*), which is derived from the same root as the Arabic word for 'virginity' (*'udhrah*, also *'ḏr*). The name of the village in Rijal Alma' called al-'Adhrā (Abram's 'Eliezer') is formed from the same root. To overcome his eternal 'virginity', it appears that the ancient god of sexual abstinence and infertility in Rijal Alma' had to surrender not only his divinity and immortality, but also his foreskin.

From the semantics of the root *'zr* and its variant *'ḏr*, in the two senses of 'virginity' and 'circumcision', we gain an interesting insight into the original significance of circumcision as a rite which prepares a young man for marriage — for the bridegroom, the equivalent of the breaking of the bridal hymen. We shall have occasion to elaborate further on this point in due course.

The story of the Abram of Genesis 15 is next picked up in Genesis 22, or so it appears to me. Here Abram, in the Biblical narrative, is already called Abraham, and the text is heavily edited. Significantly, what is usually taken to be 'God' in this story features in the original Hebrew in two forms: *Elōhīm* (*'lhym*), which means 'God', in reference to the Biblical God Yahweh; and *hā-elōhīm* (*h-'lhym*), with the prefixed definite article, which actually means 'the gods' (as in the opening passage from Genesis 6 translated on p. 33). Bearing this in mind the story that actually transpires from the Hebrew of Genesis 22:1-18 is the following:

The 'gods' (*h-'lhym*), apparently amazed at the ease with which their colleague Abram or Baram barters his divinity with Yahweh in return for fertility, decide to 'test, try' (*nśh*) Abram, perhaps to find out whether or not they can persuade him to break his covenant with Yahweh and return to their ranks. Abram, here called Abraham, already has a son, identified in the standing text as Isaac; he is an 'only son' (22:2, 12), and Abram naturally 'loves' him (22:2). From the preceding episodes of the Genesis story, we know that Abraham already has two sons, not one: Ishmael who was born to him from Hagar, and Isaac who was born to him from Sarah, Ishmael being more than thirteen years older than Isaac (17:25). If the 'Abraham' of this particular story was the same Abraham, he would not have had an 'only son', unless this son was Ishmael, before Isaac was born.

The story continues: the gods ask Abram to take his 'only son' and 'offer him as a burnt offering' at a place subsequently identified as the 'Yahweh of Yireh' (*yr'h*), in the land of Moriah (*mryh*). Today Yireh would be the village of Yarā' (*yr'*), in Rijal Alma', where Moriah also survives as the village of Marwah (*mrwh*). Abram, it seems, succumbs to the temptation. He takes his 'only son' to the place indicated, making the boy carry the wood with which his butchered body is to be burnt, while Abram himself carries the fire and the knife (22:6). The boy, who is unaware of the fact that he is to be sacrificed, wonders about the absence of the sacrificial 'lamb'. Abram answers, somewhat wryly: 'God (*'lhym*, not 'the gods', or *h-'lhym*) will provide himself the lamb for the burnt offering, my son' (22:8). As I see it, Abram here is clearly referring to the God Yahweh, who had already provided the 'lamb' for his intended burnt offering, by taking away his divinity and giving him instead the son he was now determined to sacrifice.

Having reached the appointed place, Abram builds an altar, lays the wood in order, binds his son, and stretches him over the wood on the altar. Then, as he takes out the knife to slaughter the boy in preparation for his ritual burning, Yahweh (mentioned for the first time by name, 22:11) suddenly intervenes to stop him. Yahweh diplomatically pretends to believe that Abram had intended to sacrifice his son to him: 'Do not lay your hands on the lad,' he says, 'or do anything to him; for now I know that you fear God (again *'lhym*, not *h-'lhym*), seeing that you have not withheld your son, your only son, from me' (22:12). Abram, caught at his game, yields to Yahweh's command, and Yahweh miraculously provides a ram for the sacrifice, which is now an ordinary animal sacrifice to himself. Abram thereupon gives up the last thought of breaking his covenant with Yahweh and dedicates the place of the sacrifice to him, calling it Yahweh Yireh (*yhwh yr'h*) — the Yahweh of Yarā' (22:14). The moral: once you have concluded a bargain with Yahweh, you cannot easily rescind it, no matter how sly or determined you may be, for he can always outwit you.

Of course one can interpret the above story in other ways. What is important, however, is that it appears to be clearly related to the Abram of Genesis 15, as distinct from Abram the Hebrew or Abram the Aramean, its setting being at Yarā', near Marwah, in the same region of Rijal Alma' where the story of Genesis 15 is set. This provides us with the first clue as to how the stories about the different Abrams of Genesis are confused. Abram the Aramean, as we have learnt, had made his home in the Zahran highlands of the southern Hijaz, between a Bethel which is today Buṭaylah, and an Ai which is now al-'Ūyā'. In Rijal Alma', there is another Bethel which is known today as the village of Batīlah (*btl*), and an Ai presently called Ghayy (*ġy*, cf. Biblical *'y*). All one has to do is place Abram the Aramean between the Bethel and Ai of Rijal Alma', instead of the Bethel and Ai of the Zahran region, and the story of the Abram of Genesis 15 and Genesis 16 can be made to apply to him. The identity of the Abram of Genesis 15, however, is specifically that of an infertile and childless god. To be identified with him, Abram the Aramean also has to be made initially childless; yet, as the legendary progenitor of a tribe, he cannot be made personally 'sterile' or 'continent'. Instead he can be provided, fictionally, with a 'barren' wife. To make this fiction credible it has to be introduced from the start, when Abram the Aramean still lived in his native land of Ur Kasdim. Thus, we are told at the beginning: 'Abram and Nahor took wives; the name of Abram's wife was Sarai... Now Sarai was barren; she had no child' (11:29, 30).

The Abram of Beersheba

Another Abram in Genesis (also featuring as Abraham) is identified with the childless Abram of Genesis 15 by fictionally being provided with a barren wife (again called Sarai, or *sry*, simply meaning 'lady'). This Abram 'dwelt in Beersheba' (22:19), where he had a plantation of tamarisk trees (21:33). Today tamarisks are valued for their ability to resist drought and soil salinity. They are planted on sea coasts or in desert areas, where the taller species may be used as windbreaks. In the Near East, however, one species of tamarisk (*Tamarisk mannifera*), when its stems are punctured by a particular parasite (*Coccus manniparus*), exudes an edible honey-like substance, traditionally relished as one of the many forms of manna. The Abram of Beersheba, as a cultivator of tamarisks, was apparently in the manna business.

In *The Bible Came from Arabia* I identified the Biblical Beersheba (*b'r šb'*, the 'well' of Sheba, or *šb'*) as the village of Shabā'ah (*šb'*), in upper Wadi Bishah in inland Asir. Today the village is part of the expanding city of Khamis Mushait. In the same area I identified one Biblical Gerar (*grr*) as being present Qarārah (*qrr*); also one of the several places which the Bible calls Mizraim (*mṣrym*) as the present village of Miṣrāmah (*mṣrm*). Further downstream in Wadi Bishah I located a Beer-lahai-roi (*b'r lḥy r'y*, the 'well of the ravine of *r'y*') as the present oasis of Rūyah (*rwy*). According to the Genesis story, this Beer-lahai-roi was the place where the angel of Yahweh came to the rescue of Abram's pregnant wife Hagar, who subsequently bore him his son Ishmael (16:15). It was also one of the places where Abraham's son Isaac was supposed to have lived (24:62; 25:11). Upstream from Khamis Mushait lie the highlands of Dhahrān al-Janūb (*ğnb*, Arabic for 'south'), which I believe to be the Negeb (*ngb*) of Abraham of Beersheba, as distinct from the Negeb of Abram the Aramean which was the ridge of Janabah (also *ğnb*), in the Zahran highlands of the southern Hijaz (see above). Having now tagged Abram of Beersheba geographically, as we have already done with Abram the Hebrew, Abram the Aramean and the Abram of Genesis 15, we may proceed to discover where he, rather than any of these other Abrams, features in the composite Genesis saga of Abraham.

First we have the story of Abram's sojourn in Mizraim (today Miṣrāmah), and the affair which his wife Sarai, passing for his sister, had with the local Pharaoh — the local potentate, or perhaps the local god (12:10-20). There is more to this story than meets the eye (see chapter 5).

Second, we have the story of Abram's other wife Hagar (16:1-15), whose setting appears to have been Wadi Bishah, considering that her Beer-lahai-roi (see above) is still there. This story leads us to assume that the Abram who was the father of Ishmael was Abram of Beersheba; also that this Ishmael, rather than Isaac, was the son of 'Abraham' who lived in Beer-lahai-roi (24:62; 25:11), considering that it was not Isaac's mother Sarah (originally Sarai), but Ishmael's mother Hagar who fled there when she was pregnant with him.

Third, we have the story of Abraham's sojourn in Gerar (today Qarārah), where his wife (now called Sarah), again passing for his sister, had an affair this time with the 'king of Gerar' (20:1-18). Here again we have Abram of Beersheba, not 'Abraham'.

Fourth, we have the story of Abraham's repudiation of Hagar, who takes her son Ishmael and wanders off with him into the 'wilderness of Beersheba' (21:9-20). At the end of this story, we are told that Ishmael, when he grew to manhood, lived in the wilderness of Paran (*p'rn*) — probably the Farān (*ṕrn*) which is the present ridge and oasis of the Zahran highlands at Wadi Ranyah, north of Wadi Bishah, rather than the Āl Farwān (*'l ṕrwn*) of the highlands south of Khamis Mushait, which features elsewhere in the Genesis story of Abraham as El Paran (*'l p'rn*, 14:6).

Fifth, we have the story of how Abraham (again Abram of Beersheba) persuades the 'king of Gerar' to recognize his possession of the well he had dug at Beersheba, then proceeds to plant his tamarisks (21:22-33).

Sixth, and last, it is possible that Abram of Beersheba was the 'Abraham' who took another wife by the name of Keturah (25:1-6), considering that this Keturah's sons and their descendants reportedly lived in the same 'east country' as Ishmael (25:6).

How did the redactors of Genesis manage to identify the Abraham who was actually Abram of Beersheba with the three other Abrams whose identities we have already established? The answer is simple:

1. To identify the prolific Abram of Beersheba with the initially childless Abram of Genesis 15, he was provided, fictionally, with a first wife who 'bore him no children' (16:1).

2. To identify him with Abram the Aramean, the report of his journey from Mizraim to the Negeb (13:1), i.e. from the present Miṣrāmah to the present Dhahrān al-Janūb in southern Asir, was combined with the report of the journey of Abram the Aramean from the Negeb towards Bethel (13:3), i.e. from the present Janabah to the present Buṭaylah in the southern Hijaz, without indicating that the first Negeb was one place and the second Negeb another, about 350 kilometres away.

3. To identify him, finally, with Abram the Hebrew, all one had to do was to make him 'come' (*yb'*) from Beersheba (22:19) to bury the wife of Abram the Hebrew in Hebron, which was the latter Abram's home. The deft interpolation of the verb 'come' here did the trick, enabling the Abram of Beersheba to take full charge of the burial of another man's wife.

Abram of the Yemen

Apart from the mythical Abram of Genesis 15, who was apparently a god, which of the remaining three Abrams was the descendant of Eber and Shem introduced in Genesis 11:27? Perhaps none. Abram the Eberite (if we may call him so) was definitely a tribe or folk. Projecting his name and the names of his ancestors against the map of Arabia, one finds that the Eberite Abrams must have been an ancient community of the Yemen.

In the southern highlands of the Yemen, as we have noted in the preceding chapter, the name of Shem (*šm*), allegedly the son of Noah, and the ancestor of 'all the Eber people' (Genesis 10:21), survives in the village of Shumm (exactly *šm*). It has also been observed that the same Shem features in the recorded lore of the Yemen as a national hero who was the founder of the city of Sanaa, the capital of modern North Yemen. The following are the names of Shem's descendants down to Abram, as they are listed in Genesis 11:10–26:

1. Shem's 'son' was Arpachshad (*'rpkšd*, or *'rp kšd*). His name appears to combine the name of the historical Yemenite tribe called the Yarfā (*yrṕ*) with that of the village of Kasād (*ksd*), in the northern Yemen highlands. This would make the name Arpachshad, linguistically, a construct meaning 'the Yarfā of Kasād'.
2. Arpachshad's 'son' was Shelah (*šlḥ*). His name is clearly that of the historical Yemenite tribe of the Salīḥ (*slḥ*), who ultimately migrated to Syria in the early centuries of the Christian era.
3. Shelah's 'son' was Eber (*'br*). His name is still carried by 'Ubrah (*'br*), a village of the southern Yemen highlands not far from Shumm, or 'Shem'.
4. Eber's 'son' was Peleg (*plg*), today the name of the valley of Wadi Falaqah (*ṕlq*), in the inland Jawf region of the northern Yemen.
5. Peleg's 'son' was Reu (*r'w*), remembered in the name of the historical Yemenite tribe of Ra'ā (*r'*), once the inhabitants of the present village of 'Arū (*'rw*), in the same Jawf region.
6. Reu's 'son' was Serug (*srwg*). This is probably in the name of the historically attested northern Yemenite village of Shawāriq (*šwrq*).
7. Serug's 'son' was Nahor (*nḥwr*). The name, today, is probably that of the village of Ḥawrān (*ḥwrn*, metathesis of *nḥwr*), near Shumm (Biblical 'Shem') and 'Ubrah (Biblical 'Eber'), in the southern Yemen highlands.

8. Nahor's 'son' was Terah (*trḥ*). The historically attested Yemenite village of Takhir (*tḫr*) carries a metathesis of this name.

9. Terah's 'son' was Abram (*'brm*), this one, the Abram of the Yemen. The name of this Abram still stands immortalized near Shumm ('Shem'), 'Ubrah ('Eber') and Ḥawrān ('Nahor'), in the southern Yemen highlands, as the village of Burm (*brm*).

In Genesis 11, Terah, 'father' of the Abram of the Yemen, was transformed into the 'father' of Abram the Aramean, and hence of the other Abrams of the Genesis story, by interpolating him into one verse: 'Terah took Abram, his son... from Ur Kasdim to go into the land of Canaan' (11:31). As I see it, Terah and his 'son' Abram of the Yemen are figures of an entirely different lore, deriving from a different place.

Why so many Abrams?

All five of these Abrams — the Hebrew, the Aramean, the one of Genesis 15, the men of Beersheba and the Yemen — could not have been 'Abrahams', because they were known by an altogether different name. The question of Abraham himself deserves to be discussed in a separate chapter. Here, however, one must ask: why are the stories of five different Abrams combined and narrated as one story in Genesis? The answer is anyone's guess, my own being the following:

The ancient Israelites, like most historical peoples, did not come from one stock. They were a confederation of different West Arabian tribes, traditionally reckoned to be twelve, some of whom were originally 'Hebrew' (e.g. Deuteronomy 15:12), while others were 'Aramean' (Deuteronomy 26:5). As these tribes developed into a historical nation, the cult of Yahweh, originally one of a countless number of Arabian folk cults, was developed among them into a monotheism which came to have many non-Israelite Arabian adherents, most notably among the tribes of the Wadi Bishah basin, and in the Yemen.

The 'Hebrew' Israelite tribes, who were established from an early time in the coastal hill country of the southern Hijaz and Asir, used to claim descent from a common ancestor whose home was in Hebron, today the village of Khirbān, in the Qunfudhah hinterland. To them, this ancestor was an 'exalted father', who in Hebrew as in Aramaic would be an *ab rām* (*'b* for 'father'; *rm* for 'exalted'). In legend this 'exalted father' was given his title as a personal name, Abram. The Aramean Israelite tribes also claimed for themselves an 'exalted father', or *ab rām*, whose original title was transformed by legend into the personal name Abram. The original home of this Aramean Abram was believed to be a place called Ur which is today Jabal Awr, south of Medina in the central Hijaz. Among the proto-Israelites of the Wadi Bishah basin there was a rich lore about another local 'exalted father' — the *ab rām*, or Abram of Beersheba, today Shabā'ah, in the vicinity of Khamis Mushait. In the southern Yemen there existed a tribe actually known as the Abram, whose name survives as that of the local village of Burm, along with the names of other related tribes.

Among the latter-day Israelites, all these different strains of tribal lore, being equally relevant to Israelite and Jewish Arabian society, were naturally fused into one. As this fusion of the lore was set in motion, it also absorbed the mythology of an attested South Arabian god called Burm — a god of celibacy and sexual chastity, whose cult involved ritual circumcision for young men reaching the age of marriage. Perhaps the mythology of this god Abram was fused with the composite folk legend of the common Israelite Abram because male circumcision, which may have been originally his special rite, was adopted by the Israelites and ultimately enjoined and standardized as regular and universal Jewish practice.

This is mere conjecture, but it may be useful for the time being to keep it in mind as we turn to consider other matters which may put its possible validity to the test.

5.
The Secret of the House of Abraham

In many passages of the Genesis story, as we have seen, Abraham is really 'Abram' under a different name: Abram the Hebrew, Abram the Aramean, Abram of Beersheba, Abram of the Yemen, or the Abram of Genesis 15. In other passages, however, Abraham is an altogether different person: like the Abram of Genesis 15, he is a figure of religious mythology rather than tribal legend — more a god in a world of gods than a man in a world of men. In the nineteenth century this was the wild guess of a number of eminent Biblical scholars, but it has since been abandoned in favour of more 'scientific' assessments on the historicity or non-historicity of Abraham. For the sake of argument let us assume that he was actually a god and examine the Genesis material about him accordingly. Perhaps the evidence we shall discover will restore some respectability to an old view which has long been condemned by modern 'Bible Science'.

The rain god Abū Ruhm

Much has been written about the etymology of the name 'Abraham', yet it has remained a puzzle. In Genesis 17:5, 'Abraham' (*'brhm*, parsed *'b rhm*) is taken to mean 'father of a multitude'. Certainly, the common Semitic *'b* does mean 'father', as in *'b rm*, or 'exalted father' — the name of 'Abram' (see preceding chapter). In Hebrew, *rhm* is not known to mean 'multitude', but in Arabic the same word, vocalized as *ruhām*, can mean 'great number'. With the same vocalization, the word in Arabic also means 'non-raptorial birds', i.e. those which are not birds of prey. Genesis 15 could have been preparing for the change of the name 'Abram' to 'Abraham' by suggesting the name in this second sense, where one verse (15:11) explained somewhat fortuitously: 'When the *birds of prey* came down on the carcasses, Abram drove them away' (see preceding chapter). The subtle hint offered here could have been that Abram came to deserve the change of his name to 'Abraham' (*'b rhm*, meaning 'father of the non-raptorial birds'), because he prevented birds of prey attacking the carcasses he had prepared for his mystery rite, which included two birds of particularly harmless breed: 'a turtledove and a young pigeon' (15:9).

However, there is another sense to the Arabic *rhm*. When vocalized as *rihām* or *ruhm*, it is best attested to mean 'rain' — not destructive torrential rain, but the 'gentle drizzle' which makes the soil arable and causes crops to grow. Arabic dictionaries give this sense to the term for the personal name Abū Ruhm (*'b rhm*, exactly as in the Biblical *'brhm*, for 'Abraham'). In Arabia this name was extremely common until the coming of Islam, when it suddenly vanished from existence. Literally it means 'father of rain', or the 'one of rain', which in idiomatic Arabic can mean 'generous, hospitable, magnanimous'. More likely, however, the original Abū Ruhm (or 'Abraham') was an ancient Arabian god of rain, and hence of dry-farming.

In Genesis 17 it is not Yahweh but 'God', under the name of El Shaddai (*'l šdy*, traditionally rendered 'God Almighty'), who changes the name of Abram to 'Abraham', or Abū Ruhm, thus transforming the sexually continent god of infertility of Genesis 15 into a god of rain, the prime giver of fertility. El Shaddai had good reason to do this. Judging by his name (Akkadian *shadu*, or *šdw*, 'mountain'; Arabic *sawd*, or *swd*, 'rocky mountainside'), he was the god of a 'mountain', keenly interested in securing rain to make his terraced slopes amenable to dry-farming. In West Arabia the name of the mountain god El Shaddai (*'l šdy*) survives as Āl Sādī (*'l sdy*) — the name of a village in the rugged highlands of Dhahrān al-Janūb, which was the 'Negeb' of Abram of Beersheba (see preceding chapter). In one way or another, the topography of West Arabia seems to fit the Genesis saga of Abraham at every level.

A marriage of convenience

In Genesis, Abram, the ancestor or 'exalted father' (*'b rm*) of different groups of Israelites, is the husband of Sarai (*sry*), whose name means simply 'lady'. In idiomatic Arabic 'lady' is the standard way to refer to a 'grandmother', or 'ancestress'. Thus, so to speak, Abram, personifying the 'ancestor', was married to Sarai, personifying the 'ancestress'. With Abraham as the rain god Abū Ruhm it was a different matter; his wife was not Sarai, but Sarah. In Hebrew, *Sārāh* (*srh*, in constructs *srt*) can also mean 'lady'. In Arabic, however, it is a collective noun meaning 'highlands'. In West Arabia, the *Sarāh* or *Sarāt*, identical with the biblical 'Sarah', is the name by which the highlands of the southern Hijaz, Asir and the Yemen have traditionally been known. Thus, allegorically, when Abram the god of infertility, at the bidding of the mountain god El Shaddai, agreed to become the prime agent of fertility as the rain god Abū Ruhm, or 'Abraham', he automatically became the 'husband', and hence the fertilizer, of the West Arabian highlands called until today the *Sarāh*. Even more likely, he became the husband of the goddess of these highlands, Āl Sarah (*'l srh*), whose name survives intact there as that of a village in the Asir highlands which flank Wadi Bishah from the west. Allegorically, Āl Sarah (Biblical 'Sarah') was 'barren' and 'had no child' until Abū Ruhm (Biblical 'Abraham') came forth to become her husband. Here, truly, was a marriage of convenience between a god of 'rain' and a goddess of the parched 'highlands'.

Such is the trust and intimacy that develop between 'Abraham' as the rain god Abū Ruhm, and 'Sarah' as the highland goddess Āl Sarah, that they can afford some dangerous pranks. In Mizraim (today Miṣrāmah), in Wadi Bishah, Pharaoh (*pr'h*) was apparently a local god of 'running streams'. At least, this is one sense that *pr'h* (as *far'*, or *ṕr'*) has in Arabic. Āl Fāri' (*'l ṕr'*, the 'god' *pr'*) and Āl Firā'ah (*'l ṕr'h*, the 'god' *ṕr'h*) still exist as place names in the Asir highlands — the first in Dhahrān al-Janūb, a short distance south of Miṣrāmah. This attests to the ancient worship of a god of 'running streams' in the region. When, according to Genesis, Abraham and Sarah go to Mizraim, Abraham surmises that Pharaoh would have an eye for his beautiful wife and instructs her to pretend that she is his sister. So Sarah goes to stay in Pharaoh's 'house' (*byt pr'h*, 12:15) — I would say, the god Āl Firā'ah's 'temple' (also *byt*). In this story Abraham is identified with the Abram of Beersheba, and Sarah features as this Abram's wife Sarai. The same story, however, is repeated in Genesis about Abraham and Sarah and the king of Gerar (20:2-18) which is today the village of Qarārah, in

Wadi Bishah; it is also retold about Abraham's son Isaac and his beautiful wife Rebekkah when they went, in their turn, to stay in the same Gerar (26:7-11). Rather than try to fathom the allegorical significance of this thrice-repeated story, I shall limit myself to recounting what the British explorer H. St.J.B. Philby experienced in the 1930s when he visited Wadi Bishah and its neighbourhood, where the Biblical Mizraim and Gerar are located (*Arabian Highlands*, Ithaca, N.Y., 1952, p.188):

> I espied a girl guiding a flock of goats in our direction, and [my guide] Halaf suggested that a draught of milk would be refreshing. I agreed, whereupon he raised his voice and shouted: *Ya ra'iyat al ghanam* — 'Oh, Shepherdess!' The girl came towards us and halted a little way off to milk one of her goats into a wooden bowl, which she brought to us with a confident smile — a nice-looking girl in picturesque rags which outlined the perfect lines of a young, well-made body with firm breasts and rounded haunches... I naturally wanted to know more about her... 'She is my sister,' explained Halaf, 'and not yet married.' The girl giggled in confirmation... Halaf, who was to accompany me on our next stage, made an excuse that he had certain instructions to give his sister, and I went... alone. By the time I got back to camp he had not come in, but his father was there... 'What have you done with my son?' he asked quizzically. 'I left him up there,' I replied, 'with his sister and her goats.' 'His sister!' he replied with a chuckle. 'Did he say she was his sister now? Why! She is his wife.' It seemed almost like an echo from the days of Abraham!

Is it conceivable that a piece of ancient West Arabian mythology about a god and his consort should have survived as a standard joke in the exact land of its origin?

The birth of the god of wells

The product of the marriage of Abraham and Sarah was Isaac — a somewhat shadowy figure who only comes to life twice in the Genesis narrative: first, as he goes out to meet his cousin Rebekkah, when she is brought to him as a bride from Aram-naharaim (24:62-67) (see p. 80); second, in blindness and old age, when he confuses the identities of his twin sons Esau and Jacob, and unknowingly grants the second the birthright of the first (27:1-40). In the first instance, Isaac is clearly the 'son' of Abram the Aramean, and the bride who is brought to him is allegedly the granddaughter of his Aramean uncle Nahor. The place where he meets her and brings her 'into his tent' is the 'Negeb' — in this case, the Janabah of the Zahran highlands in the southern Hijaz, in whose rich pastures Abram the Aramean's cattle used to graze. The identity of the place is beyond doubt. The topography provides the following evidence.

In translations, Genesis 24:63 says that Isaac 'went out' from the Negeb 'to meditate (*l-swḥ*) in the field (*b-sdh*) in the evening (*l-pnwt 'rb*)', then he lifted up his eyes to see Rebekkah arrive (RSV). What the original Hebrew actually means is that Isaac 'went out' from Janabah, 'to Sūaḥ (*l-swḥ*), in Sādeh (*b-sdh*) to the corners (environs, towers?) of 'Āreb (*l-pnwt 'rb*)', and it was there that he first set eyes on his bride. All three places — Sūaḥ, Sādeh and 'Āreb — are still found by name in the Zahran highlands, downhill from the ridge of Jabal Janabah, or the 'Negeb', towards the Red Sea coast. There 'Sūaḥ, in Sādeh' is today the village of Āl Sāḥah (*sḥ*, on one of the twin ridges of Jabal Shadā (*šd'*). Facing Āl Sāḥah to the north, on the other Shadā ridge, is the village of 'Arbā' (*'rb'*). The Isaac (*yṣḥq*, noun derivative from the verb *ṣḥq*) who was Abram the Aramean's 'son' had to go downhill from Jabal Janabah to meet his bride, who was being brought to him from Nahārīn (Biblical 'Naharaim'), in the Taif region, by way of the coastal road (see map p. 128). His own name survives in the same Zahran highlands as that of the mountain pass called 'Aqabat Mazḥak (*mzḥk*, noun derivative from *zḥk*, cf. the Biblical Hebrew *ṣḥq*), which crosses the rocky escarpment from the vicinity of Jabal Janabah to reach the coastlands of the Red Sea.

So the Isaac who lived in the 'Negeb', today Janabah, was the 'son' of Abram the Aramean, regardless of whether or not the bride who was brought to him was actually called Rebekkah. To identify him with the other Isaac who was the son of 'Abraham' and 'Sarah', Genesis had to explain how this other Isaac came to be living in Jabal Janabah in the Zahran highlands at the time of his marriage, since his home must have been not there, but in Wadi Bishah, where the story of his parents 'Abraham' and 'Sarah' is set. The explanation given is somewhat clumsy: 'Now, Isaac had come from Beer-lahai-roi (i.e. the oasis of Rūyah, in Wadi Bishah, see p. 90), and was dwelling in the Negeb (i.e. Janabah, in the Zahran highlands)' (24:62).

The second instance when Isaac comes to life in the Genesis story is when he appears to be the son of Abram the Hebrew of Hebron. This Isaac was the father of Esau and Jacob who are subsequently called Edom and Israel (another confusion of identities, as we shall see). Like his father Abram the Hebrew, the 'Isaac' who was the father of Edom and Israel, regardless of his actual name, must also have lived in Hebron (stated only in Genesis 35:27). His son Israel reportedly lived in the 'valley of Hebron' (37:14), in the 'land of Canaan' (37:1), and was finally buried in the nearby cave of Machpelah (49:30; 50:13), where his alleged grandfather Abram the Hebrew had been buried. It is significant that Genesis apparently makes a point of not specifying where the Isaac who was Israel's father was buried. He simply 'died at a ripe old age, and his sons Esau and Jacob buried him' (35:29). No mention is made of the cave of Machpelah as his place of burial. I suspect that there was no Isaac of Hebron who was the 'son' of Abram the Hebrew in the original lore from which the Genesis story of Abraham was composed.

If we accept that there was a Hebrew Isaac who lived in Hebron, to disentangle his character and that of the Aramean Isaac from the character of the Isaac who was the son of 'Abraham' and 'Sarah', in the confusion of the Genesis story, would make tedious reading. Therefore, I propose to concentrate instead on the most interesting of the three — the shadowy and elusive Isaac who was born to the rain god Abū Ruhm, or 'Abraham', by his consort Āl Sarah, or 'Sarah', the goddess of the Asir highlands.

To begin with, we must examine Isaac's name, *yṣḥq*, which in Genesis is taken to mean 'laughter' (substantive of *ṣḥq*, 'laugh'; Arabic *ḍḥk*, also 'laugh'; see Genesis 18:12-15; 21:3, 6). In Arabic, however, this word for 'laugh' also means 'overflow' (said of the water in a well). Laughter is figuratively an 'overflow' of cognizant emotion. Actually, the Arabic dictionaries give 'overflow' as the original meaning of *ḍḥk* (Hebrew *ṣḥq*), from which the sense of 'laugh' is derived. Thus the Arabic personal name *Ḍaḥḥāk*, which is the equivalent of the Hebrew *yṣḥk*, or 'Isaac', would have originally meant the 'overflowing one' — figuratively, a reference to generosity, or abundance of means, but literally, an 'overflowing well'. Where he is the son of Abū Ruhm, the god of rain, and Āl Sarah, the goddess of the highlands, I would venture to guess that Isaac was a well, or rather god of wells. Consider the following:

1. In the same chapter (Genesis 21) where the birth of Isaac is reported, we are told that it was Abraham who first dug the 'well' of Beersheba (21:30).

2. Abraham is actually credited with digging a number of wells in different places, all of which were subsequently stopped and filled with earth (26:15).

3. Isaac, it is said, 'dug again the wells of water which had been dug in the days of Abraham his father' (26:18). Four such wells are mentioned by name (26:19–23, 32–33), one of them being the well of Beersheba (*b'r šb'*), which Isaac reportedly called Shibah (*šb'h*, or 'abundance') — today Shabā'ah (*šb'h*), in upper Wadi Bishah, near Khamis Mushait.

4. Isaac, it is said, 'lived' in Beer-lahai-roi (*b'r lḥy r'y*) and in Beersheba (26:33; 28:10). Both places were 'wells' (singular *b'r*).

As a god of wells who actually 'lived' in wells, Isaac, the 'overflowing one', must have been one of three deities associated with a cult of fertility in ancient Wadi Bishah, the other two being his 'father', a god of rain, and his 'mother', a goddess of the highlands. In Wadi Bishah cultivation still depends partly on rain (Abraham), partly on wells (Isaac) — not to mention the local 'running streams' (Pharaoh). Here is how Philby describes the agriculture of upper Wadi Bishah, near Khamis Mushait, where the Genesis story of Abraham, Sarah and Isaac is set (*Arabian Highlands*, p. 132):

> The main industry in the area was the growing of cereal crops, chiefly wheat... and millet... and lucerne. The cornfields... covered a vast area on both sides of the Bisha channel and its local tributaries — being partly irrigated by the floods and partly from wells, which are for the most part wide-mouthed (in some cases twenty feet across) with a loose steening of stones to keep out the silt from the shaft, which after a few feet pierces the underlying granite to reach water at only three fathoms from the surface.

For a god of fertility, such as a god of wells, the natural 'sign' would have been his male prowess — his 'thigh' (Hebrew *pḥd*, Arabic *fakhdh*, also *p̄ẖd*), which, certainly in Arabic, is a standard euphemism for the phallus. In Genesis 31:42, Jacob, as the son of Isaac (see below), identifies the 'god of his father' as being the 'thigh of Isaac' (*pḥd yṣḥq*), meaning the 'phallus of Isaac'. In 31:53, it is by the same 'thigh' or phallus of his 'father Isaac' that he swears. In some modern translations this *pḥd yṣḥq* is rendered as the 'fear of Isaac' (from the Hebrew *pḥd* in the sense of 'tremble'), but this makes poor sense and is plainly incorrect.

El Roi and Ishmael

There is hardly a doubt that the Biblical Beer-lahai-roi (the 'well of the ravine of *r'y*') is actually the oasis of Rūyah (*rwy*) in lower Wadi Bishah. In Hebrew, a *r'y* is a 'seer' or 'one of vision', from the verb *r'h* (Arabic *r'y*), 'see'. In Arabic the word *rūyah* is a widely attested, dialectal pronunciation of *ru'yah* (*r'yh*), meaning 'vision'. According to Genesis, Beer-lahai-roi 'lies between Kadesh (*qdš*) and Bered (*brd*)' (16:14) — today Jadas (*ǧds*) and Baridah (*brd*), two other oases in the same area. It is also said to lie 'on the way to Shur (*šwr*)' (16:7) — apparently present Banī Sār (*sr*), on the inland side of the Zahran highlands to the west.

Apart from being mentioned in Genesis as one of the places in which Isaac dwelt, Beer-lahai-roi also features in the story of Hagar — the woman by whom Abram (I would say Abram of Beersheba) begot his son Ishmael (see preceding chapter). According to this story, it was the childless Sarai who instructed her husband Abram to have children by her maid Hagar, who is described as a *Mīṣrīt* (*mṣryt*, 16:3), traditionally taken to mean an 'Egyptian'. Actually, Miṣr (*mṣr*) still exists as a village in the Wadi Bishah basin; as a *Mīṣrīt*, or 'woman of Miṣr', Hagar would have come from there.

When Hagar became pregnant, so the story continues, she looked on her mistress with contempt; thereupon Sarai, with Abram's permission, proceeded to deal harshly with her, forcing her to flee into the wilderness. The angel of Yahweh (16:9-10), or Yahweh himself (16:13), found her by a water spring and told her that she would have a son whom she should call Ishmael. Hagar, however, did not recognize the god who spoke to her as being Yahweh, so she called him El Roi (*'l r'y*), the 'god of seeing' (16:13); hence the name of the spring where he found her, which was none other than Beer-lahai-roi, or the 'well of the ravine of Roi'. The Biblical form of the name Ishmael, which the god El Roi chose for her yet unborn son, is *yšm'l*, shortened form of *yšm' 'l* — 'god hears' or the 'hearing of god'. This was actually the name of an ancient West Arabian 'god of hearing' whose name survives in the villages of Āl Sham'ah (*'l šm'*) in the Taif region of the Hijaz, and also in the village of Āl Samī'ah (*'l sm'*) in Asir. There is, furthermore, a village called Āl Ismā'īl (literally, 'the god Ishmael') in the vicinity of Abha, which I visited.

How did this lore about El Roi, the god of seeing, and Ishmael, the god of hearing, become fused with the legend of Abram of Beersheba, and ultimately with the myth of Abraham or Abū Ruhm? In the highlands of Dhahrān al-Janūb (the 'Negeb' of Abram of Beersheba), there still exists a village called Banī Hājar (*hğr*), whose name literally means the 'Hagar folk'. At one time a tribe called the Hagar must have lived there, claiming descent from a Hagar who was allegedly the wife of Abram of Beersheba and who came originally from Miṣr in lower Wadi Bishah. Today, as a result of some ancient migration, the Hagar (or Banū Hājar) are to be found as a tribe of considerable size in the vicinity of another Dhahrān — today's oil capital of East Arabia. Among the many branches of these modern Banū Hājar are the Maṣārīr (*mṣryr*), or 'Miṣr (*mṣr*) folk', still known by the name of Hagar's alleged place of origin in lower Wadi Bishah. Another is that of the Shabā'īn (those of Shabā'ah, the Biblical Beersheba), still known by the name of the territory of their alleged ancestor Abram of Beersheba. Yet another branch, and an important one, is that of the Shamā'īl (*šm'l*), whose name is so obviously a corruption of the 'Ishmael' of the Bible. Apparently, one branch of the Hagar folk were originally called the Ishmael, possibly because of a special devotion to the 'god of hearing', or because they claimed an ancestor called after this god. Other Hagar folk, however, must have paid special veneration to El Roi, the 'god of seeing', whose main shrine was at Rūyah, the Biblical Beer-lahai-roi, in lower Wadi Bishah; hence the Biblical association of the story of Hagar with the place.

As Wadi Bishah was the setting for the mythology of the rain god (Abraham) and the god of wells (Isaac) on the one hand, and that of the god of seeing (El Roi) and the god of hearing (Ishmael) on the other, it was only natural that the two mythologies became fused. But let us return to the story of Isaac and his progeny.

Esau and Jacob

As the 'son' of Abram the Hebrew, Isaac (assuming this to be his actual name) was the 'father', or claimed common ancestor, of two peoples: the Hebrew Israelites (Israel) and the Edomites (Edom). As the god of wells and the product of the marriage between Abraham, the god of rain, and Sarah, the goddess of the Asir highlands, he was the father of two far more interesting figures: the twin brothers Esau and Jacob. First, Esau was born out of his mother's womb, then Jacob followed, his hand clutching at his brother's heel (25:25-26). The two were twins in more than one sense. Born to a god of wells, by whose 'thigh' or phallus people swore, they were twin gods of male prowess: the first, a god of unbridled male sexuality; the second, of domestic connubiality and concern for progeny. Being himself a god of masculinity, Isaac preferred Esau to Jacob. His wife Rebekkah, however, naturally preferred Jacob to Esau.

To begin with, let us consider the names and characters of the twin brothers, as described in Genesis. Esau's name (*'sw*), in Hebrew, means 'hairy'; on the other hand, judging by the surviving meaning of *'s* (vocalized *'īs*) in Arabic, it is more likely to have meant 'semen', for this is what the Arabic word actually means. Esau himself was the stereotype of nonchalant masculinity: a skilful hunter and a man of the outdoors (25:27) who 'despised his birthright' (25:34). Jacob's name (*y'qb*), of which the Arabic equivalent is 'Uqbah (*'qb*), comes from the verb *'qb* (Hebrew and Arabic, 'follow behind, succeed'), of which the transitive Arabic form *a'qaba* (*''qb*) means 'to have progeny'. As the archaic substantive of this verb, *y'qb*, or 'Jacob', would mean 'succession, progeny'. Unlike the reckless Esau, Jacob was a 'correct man' (*'yš tm*), a 'dweller in tents' (25:27). Setting high value on domestic prestige, he persuades his careless brother Esau to sell him his right of the firstborn for a meal of bread and boiled lentils (25:29-34), then tricks his father, Isaac, into confirming this arrangement, with the help of his wily mother Rebekkah (27:1-29).

There remains one unanswered question: was Rebekkah the wife of the Isaac who was the son of Abram the Aramean, or was she the consort of Isaac the god of wells? She could have been both, but she was certainly the second. Her name (Biblical *rbqh*), if read as the Arabic *rābighah* (*rbġh*), would mean 'fecund', which would make her personalize fecundity. If read as the Arabic *rābiqah* (*rbqh*), it would mean 'wily'. As a goddess personifying fecundity, Rebekkah would have been eminently suitable as a consort for the god of wells. As the personification of female guile, her role in the story of Esau and Jacob is clear: she taught the god of progeny and regular domestic life the stratagem by which he could triumph over the god of unbridled male sexuality and rob him of his 'right of the firstborn'. Genesis fully approves of the wiles of Rebekkah, and for a very good reason: without her manipulative talents, untamed masculinity would have succeeded to its birthright and made regular family life impossible; and without the institution of the family, where would civilization be?

The name of Isaac as a god perhaps survives topographically in West Arabia in a corrupted form in the village of Āl Ḥusaykah (*'l ḥsyk*), in the Asir highlands west of Wadi Bishah. The name of his consort Rebekkah — as Rābigh (*rbġ*), Rabqah (*rbqh*), and also in other recognizable forms — survives as a place name in various West Arabian regions, one of them being Āl Gharībah (*'l ġrbh*, the 'goddess' *ġrbh*, metathesis of *rbqh*), in lower Wadi Bishah, close to the oasis of Rūyah (Beer-lahai-roi). The name of Jacob as a god certainly survives there as the place name Āl 'Uqbah (*'l 'qb*). As for the name of Esau as a god, it is carried to this day by no less than seven villages called Āl 'Īsā (*'l 's*, 'god of the semen') in all parts of the Hijaz and Asir except Wadi Bishah. Rebekkah, we may suppose, succeeded in suppressing the cult of her sexually irresponsible son Esau in Wadi Bishah, in favour of the more domesticated cult of her son Jacob. Elsewhere in ancient West Arabia, however, the cult of Esau, judging by the topographical statistics, remained the more popular one.

Nevertheless, Jacob, as the god of domesticated masculinity, was no less potent than his wanton 'brother' Esau. The fact that Esau was a flamboyant, 'hairy man', while Jacob was a quietly sly 'smooth man' (27:11) did not make a great difference. In the cult of Jacob, his 'mighty one' (*'byr*), no different from the 'thigh' (*pkd*) of his 'father' Isaac, was credited with special significance (49:24). And for good reason; after all, the ultimate proof of genuine masculinity does not lie in outward and irresponsible demonstrations of male prowess, but in the regular siring of progeny.

Yet Esau, though defeated by his domesticated 'brother' Jacob, always remains ready to reassert his presence on the mythological scene at the first opportunity, with secret approval from his doting 'father' Isaac. According to the Genesis story, the smooth Jacob, wearing a kid's skin, approaches his blind father Isaac and deceives him into believing that he is the hairy Esau, and so secures from him the blessing reserved for the firstborn. Isaac, deceived, actually blesses Jacob instead of Esau. When Esau returns home to ask his father for the blessing that was his own birthright, Isaac can no longer give it, as it is already bestowed on Jacob. Yet Isaac does have a word of consolation left for the son he still secretly prefers (27:39-40):

> Behold, away from the fatness of the earth
>   shall your dwelling be,
>   and away from the dew of heaven on high.
> By your sword you shall live,
>   and you shall serve your brother;
>   *but when you break loose,*
>   *you shall break his yoke from your neck*!

6
Joseph and his Egypt

In the rugged highlands of Rijal Alma‘, south-west of Abha, the capital of the modern Saudi Arabian province of Asir, stands a tiny village called Khaṭm Ṭāwī (*ḫṭm ṭ'wy*). There is nothing especially significant about the place except its tell-tale name, which makes no sense except in ancient Egyptian. In that language, and only in that language, *Khaṭm Ṭāwī* means nothing less than 'Fortress of Egypt'. At one time, the ancient Egyptians must have maintained a military presence in the area. Their interest in West Arabia was quite natural. From there they imported frankincense and myrrh — products of South Arabia and the coastlands of the Horn of Africa, which were carried by land or sea to the towns of Asir and the Hijaz and marketed there.

Apart from frankincense and myrrh, the people of ancient Egypt doubtlessly had other interests in West Arabia, for here was a land just across the sea, where fine wood was available from the dense juniper and cypress forests of the Asir highlands, at a sailing distance of only one and a half days from the nearest harbour on the Nubian coast. There was also gold, copper and various precious stones from the areas further inland, as well as other products of the region: excellent butter, honey, cereals, nuts, vegetable dyes, aromatics for the manufacture of perfumes, plus a variety of other vegetable, animal and mineral resources. In addition to these local products, the rich trade of India reached East Arabia or South Arabia by sea, and was carried by caravan to the market towns of Asir and Hijaz for distribution to other lands. So far archaeologists have barely scratched

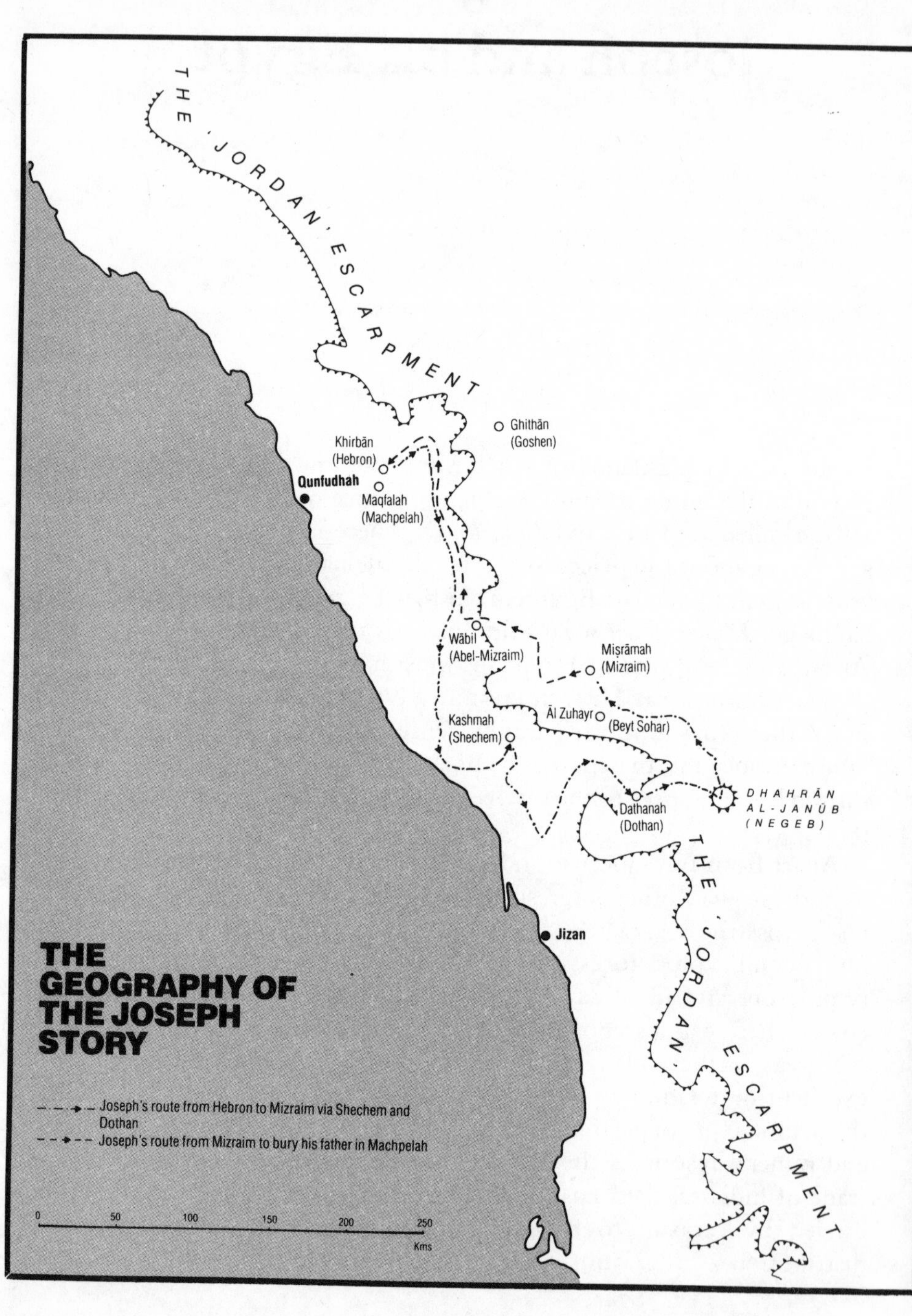
THE 'JORDAN' ESCARPMENT
Ghithān (Goshen)
Khirbān (Hebron)
Qunfudhah
Maqfalah (Machpelah)
Wābil (Abel-Mizraim)
Miṣrāmah (Mizraim)
Āl Zuhayr (Beyt Sohar)
Kashmah (Shechem)
DHAHRĀN AL-JANŪB (NEGEB)
Dathanah (Dothan)
THE 'JORDAN' ESCARPMENT
Jizan
THE GEOGRAPHY OF THE JOSEPH STORY
Joseph's route from Hebron to Mizraim via Shechem and Dothan
Joseph's route from Mizraim to bury his father in Machpelah
0 50 100 150 200 250
Kms

the surface of West Arabia, yet enough artefacts have been found to indicate an ancient Egyptian presence there. More indicative than these artefacts, however, are the countless place names of ancient Egyptian derivation in the area — names which only make sense in the language of ancient Egypt. Khaṭm Ṭāwī, in this respect, is by no means the sole example. West Arabian place names which are, in fact, simply the names of Egyptian gods make an impressive list. The following includes twenty of them, by no means all:

Yāsah (*yst*): the Egyptian goddess Isis (*'st*)
Āl Yasīr (*'l ysyr*): the Egyptian god Osiris (*wsyr*)
Āl Yamānī (*'l ymn*): the Egyptian god Amon (*imn*)
Yānif (*ynṕ*): the Egyptian god Anubis (*inpw*)
Āl Tūm (*'l tm*): the Egyptian god Atum (*itm*)
Wiṭn (*wṭn*): the Egyptian god Aton (*itn*)
'Anaqah (*'nqt*): the Egyptian goddess Anukis (*'nqt*)
Fātiḥ (*ṕtḥ*): the Egyptian god Ptah (*ptḥ*)
Minā (*mn'*): the Egyptian god Minu (*mnw*)
Āl Nfīrī (*'l nṕry*): the Egyptian god Nepri (*npri*)
Nakhbah (*nḫbt*): the Egyptian goddess Nekhbet (*nḫbt*)
Rā' (*r'*): the Egyptian god Ra (*r'*)
Āl Ḥarū and Āl Ḥarāh (*ḥr*): the Egyptian god Horus (*ḥr*)
Ḥarshaf (*ḥršṕ*): the Egyptian god Arsaphes (*ḥryšf*)
Āl Saqr (*ṣqr*): the Egyptian god Sokar (*sqr*)
Khinās (*ḫns*): the Egyptian god Khons (*ḫnsw*)
Subka (*sbk*): the Egyptian god Sobk (*sbk*)
Ṣafadah (*ṣṕd*): the Egyptian god Sopd (*spdw*)
Khāmin (*ḫmn*): the Egyptian god Chnum (*ḫnm*)
Āl Shāwiyah (*'l šwy*): the Egyptian god Shu (*šw*)

Place names of Egyptian extraction, such as those above, are found all over West Arabia, including no less than six which are essentially *Ṭāwī* (*ṭ'wy*), one name which the ancient Egyptians gave to their native land, Egypt. These Egyptian names, however, tend to be concentrated in some areas more than others, one being in the neighbourhood of Khamis Mushait in upper Wadi Bishah in inland Asir. Here the name of Egypt does not survive as the Egyptian Ṭāwī, which means the 'two lands' (dual of *ṭ'*), but as Miṣrāmah (*mṣrm*), the Arabicized form of the Biblical Mizraim (*mṣrym*), which also means the 'two lands' (dual of *mṣr*, vocalized Arabic *miṣr*, 'province, land'). This Mizraim, as already seen, was the 'Egypt' of Abraham. It was also the 'Egypt' of another more colourful hero of the Genesis narratives, Joseph. The reportedly brilliant career of this Joseph was certainly not in the Egypt of the Nile valley, where not a trace of him has been found. Rather, it was in the thriving Egyptian colony of Mizraim (as we shall henceforth call the present Miṣrāmah), in the Khamis Mushait highlands; a territory which must have included the whole of Wadi Bishah, possibly extending southwards as far as the valley of Wadi Najran, on the borders of what is today North Yemen. A preliminary archaeological report on that area, published in 1981, indicates a high concentration of archaeological sites around Khamis Mushait. The excavation of these sites, one day, may throw more light on the nature of the Egyptian colonization there.

In the Genesis story, the person of Joseph is a fusion of more than one character, as has been shown to be the case with other heroes of the Genesis lore. On the one hand there was a 'Hebrew' Joseph (39:14, 17; 41:12) whose brothers were 'Hebrews' (43:32): the son of Israel, grandson of Abram the Hebrew (14:13), who came from the same 'Hebron' (37:14), in the 'land of Canaan' (37:1), where his alleged great-grandfather Abram had lived. On the other hand, there was also the Joseph who was the son of the wily Jacob, worthy heir of his father's unusual gifts for trickery. The first Joseph is clearly a figure of legend — the eponymous ancestor claimed by an Israelite tribe called the Joseph. The second, I strongly suspect, took after his own family: like his father Jacob and his uncle Esau, his grandparents Isaac and Rebekkah, and his great-grandparents Abraham and Sarah, he was a god. What kind of god? His name, Joseph (*ywsp*), gives the secret away. It is the archaic substantive of the Hebrew *ysp*, 'add, continue, increase' (cf. Arabic *wsṕ*, 'grow fat'), which means that he was a god of 'continuity, increase, fatness' — in short, of worldly success.

As the name of a tribe, 'Joseph' survives as the name of the Banū Yūsuf (*ywsṕ*) who inhabit the vicinity of Khirbān (the 'Hebron' of Genesis), in the same Qunfudhah hinterland of the coastal parts of the southern Hijaz and Asir which was the Biblical 'land of Canaan', where Abram the Hebrew had lived (chapter 4). Joseph, reportedly, had two sons, Manasseh and Ephraim (41:51-52), who became the eponymous ancestors of the two branches of the Hebrew Israelite tribe of Joseph. Today the tribe of the Banū Yūsuf in West Arabia is also called *al-Far'ayn*, which literally means 'the two branches'. The same *al-Far'ayn*, read as the dual of the Biblical *pr'h*, can also mean 'the two pharaohs'. This may explain how the legendary personality of Joseph the Hebrew came to be confused with the mythical personality of Joseph the god, and possibly also with the personality of another, quasi-historical or historical Joseph of 'Egypt'. This Joseph's historicity comes into better focus if we consider that his 'Egypt' was the West Arabian Egyptian colony of Mizraim rather than the Egypt of the Nile valley, where no trace of his career has been found (see below).

As the name of a god, 'Joseph' survives as Āl Yūsif (*'l ywsṕ*), the name of a village in the Asir highlands fringing Wadi Bishah from the west. It also survives, in Arabic translation, as Āl Yazīd (*'l yzyd*, from the verb *zyd*, 'add, increase'): the name of no less than five villages in different parts of Asir, one of them near Āl 'Uqbah (the 'god Jacob'), in lower Wadi Bishah. Here the name of Joseph stands immortalized near that of his father, both in the Arabic form. There is also epigraphic proof of the existence of an ancient West Arabian god called Joseph, which will be considered in due course.

In the Genesis story, Joseph the man (or tribe) and Joseph the god are continually confused (chapters 37, 39-50). This is clear from the fact that the father of 'Joseph', in every episode, is called 'Jacob' in one sentence, and 'Israel' in the following. For the moment we shall leave aside the other confusion between these two Josephs on the one hand, and the third Joseph of Mizraim on the other. The Genesis story of Joseph, for example, begins with the announcement: 'Joseph dwelt in... the land of Canaan. This is the progeny of *Jacob*' (37:1-2). Next we are told that '*Israel* loved Joseph more than all his sons' (37:3). It is the same *Israel* who sends Joseph to inquire about his brothers who are out with their flocks (37:13); but it is *Jacob*, not *Israel*, who 'rends his garments, and puts sackcloth upon his loins, and mourns for his son for many days' (37:34), when he is made to believe that a wild beast has devoured him. At the end of the story, it is *Jacob* who 'draws his feet into the bed, and breathes his last, and is gathered to his people' (49:33); but it is *Israel* who is subsequently 'embalmed' (50:2) and mourned, then carried to the 'land of Canaan' to be buried there with his fathers in the cave of Machpelah (50:13).

As I see it, this regular alternation between calling Joseph's father 'Jacob', then 'Israel', and in some cases 'Israel', then 'Jacob', was deliberately intended by the redactors of Genesis to blur the difference in identity between the two Josephs on the one hand, and Jacob and Israel on the other. Their interest, it seems to me, was to transform the legendary Joseph son of Israel into the hero of the entertaining story of the mythological god Joseph the son of Jacob. To begin with, a summary of the story:

The Joseph story

As a youth of seventeen, Joseph went out to herd the family flocks with some of his brothers, and came back to his father with 'an ill report of them'. This action caused great unpopularity with his brothers, which compounded their envy of Joseph as their father's favourite. Worse still, Joseph repeated to his brothers two dreams in which he obviously saw himself, under different guises, as the one member of the family to whom all the others would one day pay deference. His father rebuked him for having these dreams, but was secretly happy with what they implied (37:10-11). The brothers' resentment of Joseph turned into positive hatred when his doting and discriminating father presented him alone with a festive tunic (37:3) of the sort that was later worn by the virgin daughters of kings (2 Samuel 13:18-19).

One day, at the request of his father, Joseph left Hebron, wearing the same tunic, to enquire about his elder brothers, who were herding the family flocks in distant Shechem. Failing to find them there, he pursued his older siblings to Dothan, where he was told they had gone. As they saw him approach, his brothers decided to kill him; so they seized him as soon as he arrived, stripped him of his festive tunic, and cast him into a waterless pit. Caravaneers happened to be passing through Dothan on their way to Mizraim, carrying 'gum, balm and myrrh' (37:25). Rather than leave Joseph to die of thirst in the pit, the brothers decided to make some money by selling him to the caravaneers for twenty shekels of silver. Then they took his tunic, slaughtered a kid, and dipped the tunic in its blood. When their father saw the blood-stained tunic brought to him, he naturally concluded that his favourite son had been devoured by a wild beast and became prostrate with grief.

In Mizraim the caravaneers who had bought Joseph from his

brothers sold him to a local Egyptian official of Pharaoh called Potiphar. This Potiphar was so pleased with the boy that he made him the chief steward of his household, seeing how 'successful' (39:2) he was in all he did. Joseph's youthful good looks, however, attracted Potiphar's wife, who tried time and again to get the boy to take her to bed, but without success. One day, when she found him alone, she caught him by his garment; but Joseph fled, leaving his garment in her hand. The woman now became vengeful and announced to everyone that Joseph had tried to rape her, but had run away when she cried out, leaving his garment behind as proof of his guilt. She told the same story to her husband when he came home. So Potiphar sent Joseph to the prison of the king of Mizraim. Here he was later joined by the butler and the baker of the king, who had been condemned to prison because they had somehow offended their master.

In prison Joseph won the favour of the warden, who put him in charge of all the prisoners, among them the king's butler and baker. One night these two had disturbing dreams, which Joseph volunteered to interpret. The butler's dream, according to Joseph, indicated that he would be released from prison and restored to his former position in court in three days. The baker's dream, however, meant that the unfortunate man would be taken out and hanged in three days. Joseph asked the butler to intercede for him with Pharaoh after his release, which actually followed in three days; but the butler forgot to do so. As for the baker, he was actually taken out after three days and hanged.

Two years later Pharaoh had two disturbing dreams in succession during the course of one night, and no one could interpret them. Then the butler remembered Joseph and his skill at dream interpretation, and told Pharaoh about him; so Joseph was brought out of prison to interpret the two dreams. He told Pharaoh that his two dreams were essentially one in meaning. They were a warning that the land of Mizraim was going to enjoy seven years of plenty, followed by seven years of famine. Joseph advised Pharaoh to appoint a man to store sufficient provisions from the seven years of plenty, to take care of the seven years of famine that were bound to follow. Impressed by the discretion of Joseph, who was thirty years old at the time, Pharaoh decided to adopt his suggestion and appoint him as the man responsible for storing the necessary provisions for the impending years of famine. He also gave him an Egyptian name and the daughter of an Egyptian priest in marriage. Thus Joseph became, after Pharaoh, the most important man in Mizraim.

When the seven years of plenty were over, a terrible famine struck throughout the area. Only in Mizraim was there sufficient bread from Joseph's stores. From the land of Canaan came the sons of Israel, sent by their father to buy grain. When they arrived in Mizraim, they appeared before Joseph. He recognized them, but they did not recognize him. He accused them of being spies, put them in prison for three days, then released them and sold them the grain they wanted, on condition that they returned to him shortly with their youngest brother Benjamin, who was Joseph's only full brother. As a security, Joseph kept one of the men with him. As the others were returning home, they discovered that the money each man had paid for his grain had been put back in the mouth of his sack. This greatly alarmed them, for they thought that on their return to Mizraim they would be accused of theft.

Back home, Israel would not be persuaded to send his youngest son Benjamin with his brothers to Mizraim, as Joseph had requested, until all the grain they had bought had been consumed and they were forced to return for more. This time they took with them double the amount of money, to make up for the silver which had somehow remained with them the first time. They also carried with them a present of some of the products of their land: 'some balm, some honey, gum, myrrh, pistachio nuts and almonds' (43:11). Joseph received them gracefully, enquired about the health of their father (who was also, of course, his own father), and had food sent to them from his own table. When they came to leave, he not only had each man's money put in the mouth of his sack as before, but also had his own silver cup placed in the mouth of Benjamin's sack. The brothers were hardly out of Mizraim when Joseph's guards followed them to search their sacks for the silver cup. They naturally found it where it had been placed, in Benjamin's sack, and the men were taken back to Mizraim to be charged with theft.

Joseph had every intention of continuing with this game; but when his brothers were brought before him again, this time humbled and abject with apology, he was so overpowered with emotion that he finally told them who he really was. He insisted that they go back to the land of Canaan and return with their father. When they did, arriving with their father Israel in Beersheba, Joseph had Pharaoh send wagons to Beersheba to carry Israel and the women and children of the family to Mizraim (46:5). Joseph arranged for all of them to settle in the land of Goshen, which belonged to Mizraim; then Joseph went up by chariot to Goshen to meet his father. In time, when Israel died, his son Joseph had him embalmed, and carried him back to the land of Canaan, where he was duly buried in the cave of his ancestors at Machpelah.

The Arabian setting of the story

Topographically, the story of Joseph fits into West Arabia in nearly every detail (see map p. 128). It starts in the 'valley of Hebron', the home of Joseph's father Israel, in the 'land of Canaan' — today Khirbān, in the hinterland of the coastal town of Qunfudhah (chapter 4). From there, Joseph first goes to seek his brothers in Shechem (*škm*), this particular Shechem being today Kashmah (*kšm*), in Rijal Alma', about 140 kilometres south of Khirbān. When he does not find them there, he pursues them to Dothan (*dtn*), today Dathanah (*dṯn*), in Jabal Faifa, about 100 kilometres south-east of Rijal Alma'. Here, at Jabal Faifa, the mountain road winds inland, proceeding about 100 kilometres in the direction of the north-west to reach Khamis Mushait. After buying Joseph from his brothers at Dothan, the caravaneers take him by this road to sell him to Potiphar in the Egyptian colony of Mizraim (or Miṣrāmah) near Khamis Mushait. Beersheba, where Israel stops before actually reaching Mizraim, is today Shabā'ah, within the precincts of modern Khamis Mushait (see p. 90). As for Goshen (*gšn*), where Joseph settled his father and brothers, it is today Ghithān (*ġṯn*), in the Balqarn hill country which flanks the lower course of Wadi Bishah from the west. With Goshen being located above Wadi Bishah in that direction, it was only natural that Joseph had to 'go up' (*y'l*, 46:29) to the place to meet his father.

Genesis also tells us how the body of Israel was carried from Mizraim for burial in the cave of Machpelah (present-day Maqfalah, (see p. 77), in the land of Hebron (Khirbān). From Mizraim in upper Wadi Bishah, it was taken 'up' to the 'threshing floor' (*grn*) of Atad (*h-'ṭd*), which is beyond the Jordan (*'br h-yrdn*)' (50:10), that place being called Abel-mizraim (*'bl mṣrym* 50:11) — thus according to the hitherto accepted translations of the Hebrew original. In *The Bible Came from Arabia*, I explained at length why the 'Jordan' (*h-yrdn*) of the Hebrew Bible must have been a term denoting the great West Arabian escarpment, rather than the name of the Jordan river in Palestine. One thing I did not point out is that the Egyptian records, citing the name of the Biblical 'Jordan' as *irdn*, provide it with the ideogram for 'hill country' rather than the one for 'water' or 'river', a further indication that this 'Jordan' was not a river.

From Miṣrāmah, near Khamis Mushait, Joseph and his party, who were taking Israel's body for burial in Maqfalah in the Qunfudhah hinterland, on the maritime side of Asir, would first have proceeded uphill in the direction of the west, to reach the Asir highlands running along the edge of the escarpment, which are called locally al-Ṭūd (*ṭd*, with the definite article; cf. Biblical *h-'ṭd* for 'Atad'). To descend to the Qunfudhah hinterland, they would have crossed the 'Jordan' or escarpment, in the so-called Ballasmar region, to reach not a 'threshing-floor' (*grn*), but a place called Qarn (*qrn*), one of many known by this name in the vicinity. From there they would have followed the course of the local wadi to the coast. Near Qarn on the peak of Jabal Dirim (the particular 'Atad' of Genesis 50), there is also a village called Wābil (*wbl*) — apparently the Biblical 'Abel', or *'bl*, once called 'Abel-mizraim', because it belonged to the Egyptian colony at Mizraim. There is definitely no 'threshing floor of Atad, which is beyond the Jordan' in question.

It is not the place names alone that indicate a West Arabian setting for the Joseph story; matters of ecology are also important. The land of Mizraim in upper Wadi Bishah is a land of grain (see p. 101); not so the land of the Qunfudhah hinterland, which is mainly devoted to pastoralism. Israel and his sons came from this region and were shepherds. In the hill country on the maritime side of Asir, which I contend was the Biblical land of Canaan, trees producing gum and balm are to be found, the gum trees peculiar to the area and its broader neighbourhood being the *Commiphora mukul*, which produces the prized 'Meccan balsam'. Almonds and terebinths also grow there, one type of terebinth (*Pistacia terebinthus*) producing an edible nut — in cultivation, the pistachio nut. The myrrh tree, moreover, is found in those hills, as elsewhere in South-West Arabia. From the rocks of the same rugged country, bedouins still extract an excellent honey, which they form into large cakes and sell in the local markets. Today this honey is sold to the rich at fabulous prices as it is considered a potent male aphrodisiac. When Israel sent his sons to Mizraim for the second time, he made them carry a present for Joseph of the typical products of their native region: 'some balm, some honey, gum, myrrh, pistachio nuts and almonds'. Of these products, certainly the myrrh and the gum could not have come from Palestine.

Likewise, judging by the cargo they carried, the caravaneers who passed through Dothan, bought Joseph and took him on to Mizraim, could only have come from South Arabia. They arrived from 'Gilead' (*gl'd*, 37:25) — this one al-Ja'diyyah (*'l-ğ'dy*, in South Yemen) — carrying 'gum, balm and myrrh', again, typical South Arabian products. The 'gum' in question must have been the frankincense gum, the best quality of which comes from the coastlands of the Arabian Sea. It was mainly to secure the precious frankincense and myrrh of South Arabia that Egyptian colonies such as Mizraim in Wadi Bishah had come to be established in the Arabian lands across the Red Sea. Certainly, no gum and myrrh are produced in the 'Gilead' of the Transjordanian highlands, today called Jilla'ad (*ğl'd*), even if this is the original name of the place, and not one given by later pilgrims. In any case, the etymological dictionaries of Biblical Hebrew cite *al-Ja'd* (*'l-ğ'd*), and hence al-Ja'diyyah, as the accepted Arabic form of the Biblical 'Gilead' (*gl'd*).

Furthermore, the Khamis Mushait area of upper Wadi Bishah is still the main bread-basket of Asir. At all times, even without famine, people must have travelled there from neighbouring regions to buy grain. In the Genesis story, Joseph is credited with having stored the grain of the area in the years of plenty to provide for years of famine. The area's actual ecology fits the story very well.

The Joseph of Israelite legend

At one level the Genesis story of Joseph sets out to explain how the Hebrew Israelites came to be living, at one time, in the territory of Mizraim — more specifically, in the land of Goshen — in lower Wadi Bishah, rather than in their original 'land of Canaan', on the maritime side of Asir. The explanation given is perfectly plausible: they were made to settle in the area, and were provided with every facility for the purpose, by a Hebrew kinsman (Joseph) who happened to have risen to a position of great power among the ancient Egyptian colonists at Mizraim. There is no reason why this should not have been, at least partly, the case.

The story recalls some interesting details about the 'Joseph' in question, which all but completely establish his historicity. Regardless of his original Hebrew name, he had assumed an Egyptian name, Zaphenath-paneah (*ṣpnt p'nḥ*, 41:45), which has been interpreted as the corruption of an Egyptian original, meaning 'the god speaks and he lives'. Like the Egyptians, he was clean-shaven (41:14). He first rose to public office in Mizraim when he was thirty (41:46), and was married to an Egyptian woman called Asenath (41:45, 50), whose father, Potiphera, was the priest of On (*'n*, 41:45) — possibly a shortened form of the Egyptian *wnn-nfrw*, or 'Onnophris', the name given to the resurrected Osiris. A village called Dhū Awān (the 'god' *'wn*, or 'On') in the Medina region of the Hijaz still carries the name of this Egyptian deity. Such detail, which the story offers fortuitously, must be authentic; it is not the sort of detail normally invented.

It is also possible, as Genesis seeks to explain, that the Hebrews, who were a shepherd folk living at first in the woodlands of coastal Asir, should have migrated at one time to the grain land of Wadi Bishah to escape a famine, and somehow have settled there. Famines can occur in coastal Asir, not only because of the periodic droughts that hit other parts of West Arabia, but also because the deep gorges of that particular area provide an excellent breeding ground for locusts — a fact which geographers of the region rarely fail to note.

It is also plausible that the Hebrew shepherds of the Qunfudhah hinterland of coastal Asir should have led their flocks to graze on the mountainsides of Rijal Alma' and Jabal Faifa, 150 and 250 kilometres to the south. In pastoral regions shepherds frequently cover such distances in search of good pasture. What is not plausible, however, is that a youth of seventeen, at the request of his doting father, should have gone running these long distances, across wild and rugged country, in search of his brothers, alone, and clad in his best festive tunic. Here my own doubts, at least, begin.

Joseph's garment

A 'coat of many colours', say the older translations (e.g. AV); a 'long robe with sleeves', say the more recent ones (e.g. RSV); the plain fact is that the meaning of the Hebrew *ktnt pśyś* remains a matter of conjecture, because no one really knows what the Hebrew *pśyś* actually means. I am convinced it is the equivalent of the Arabic *faṣīṣ* (*pṣyṣ*), which means 'studded with precious stones' (from *faṣṣ*, or *pṣ*, 'precious stone, gem'). As a word meaning 'tunic', the Hebrew *ktnt* is attested no less than fourteen times in the Bible as the dress of a priest, but only three times as the dress of a man, and no more than once as the dress of a woman. As for the expression *ktnt pśyś*, it is used in the Bible only to describe two garments: the tunic of the youthful Joseph and the tunic traditionally worn by the virgin daughters of kings. Had his garment been a simple *ktnt*, Joseph, more likely than not, would have been a priest, or perhaps a youth destined for priesthood. Considering that it is repeatedly described as a *ktnt pśyś*, or 'gem-studded tunic', the least he could have been is a high priest, if not a god.

In the opening chapter of the Genesis story, Joseph's 'gem-studded tunic' features with particular prominence. First, we are told that his father, who preferred him to all his brothers, made it for him as a sign of his special love (37:3). Second, we are told that when he caught up with his brothers at Dothan, they first stripped him of the tunic (37:23), then cast him into the waterless pit, before selling him as a slave for twenty shekels of silver. Third, we are told that Joseph's tunic was dipped into the blood of a slaughtered kid, then sent to his father, to deceive him into believing that his favourite son had been eaten by a wild beast (37:31f.). Then we have the story of Joseph in Mizraim, where he starts from humble beginnings to achieve great prominence. This tale is remarkably reminiscent of other stories told about the fertility gods of the ancient Near East (e.g. Adonis, Osiris) who die or who are taken to have died in one place, only to reappear again, alive and triumphant, elsewhere. What is involved, it seems to me, is a passion story, in a way much like that of Jesus, who was betrayed by one of his own disciples for thirty pieces of silver; who was made to wear the purple robe of a king before his trial; and whose 'garments' were subsequently divided by casting lots among those who were charged with his crucifixion.

Fine garments, one might say, make fine gods. Joseph's 'garment' features again in the story of his problem with Potiphar's wife, which ended with his long imprisonment — his second passion. This time it is a *bgd*, which can be any kind of garment, from the rags of a leper to the ceremonial robes of kings or priests. Potiphar's wife, in this story, seizes Joseph by his 'garment', which remains in her hand when he flees her adulterous advances; she uses the same 'garment' to charge him with attempted rape, and so have him thrown into prison.

The myth of the god Joseph

In the Genesis story, as I see it, the Joseph who was the eponymous ancestor of an Israelite tribe is identified, first, with the Egyptianized Hebrew Zaphenath-paneah, who was the benefactor of his fellow Hebrew settlers in the territory of Mizraim; second, with a god called Joseph who personified worldly wisdom and success — the god whose name survives in the Asir highlands as that of the village of Āl Yūsif (literally, 'god Joseph'). Judging by his name, this Āl Yūsif (*ywsṕ*, or *ysṕ*) could have been none other than the historically attested Arabian god Asaf (*'sṕ*), who was still revered as an idol in the Hijaz and other parts of the peninsula before the triumph of Islam. In Genesis, the attributes given to Joseph could have been those of a superior man, but they are especially suited for a god:

1. He was 'beautiful in form, and beautiful in appearance' (*yph t'r w-yph mr'h*, 39:6).
2. He was especially favoured: first, as a son by his father; second, as a purchased slave by his master; third, as a prisoner by the warden of the prison; fourth, as a public official by a powerful king.
3. He caused all those who favoured him to prosper.
4. He had an unfailing, uncanny ability to achieve personal success out of adversity.
5. He claimed the power of divination (44:15), and used the special silver cup in which he normally drank for that purpose (44:5).
6. He was a 'dreamer' (37:9) and an expert interpreter of dreams (40:5-22; 41:1-32; 42:9), and repeatedly declared the proper interpretation of dreams to be a divine prerogative (40:8; 41:16, 32).
7. He was unusually far-sighted, wily and resourceful.

These seem to me to be the attributes of the Biblical Joseph as Āl Yūsif, the ancient West Arabian god of good management and success. As a 'dreamer' and an interpreter of dreams, this god Joseph could have been revered in his time as an oracle, whose pronouncements were sought on problematic questions. Considering that he was the son of 'Jacob', or Āl 'Uqbah, the god of progeny; the nephew of Esau, or Āl 'Īsā, the god of masculinity; the grandson of Isaac, or Āl Ḥusaykah, the god of wells; and the great-grandson of Abraham, or Abū Ruhm, the god of rain (chapter 5), one may assume that Joseph, as Āl Yūsif, was the central figure in an ancient cult of worldly success which formed part of a broader West Arabian cult of fertility. His special 'sign', it seems, was his brilliant raiment — his *ktnt pśyś*, or 'gem-studded tunic', which no other male figure in the Hebrew Bible wears. Another of his special 'signs', perhaps, was his special 'silver cup' by which he divined.

To disentangle the story of this particular god from the mixed Genesis lore of Joseph, one must follow the Joseph with the first special 'sign' — the brilliant raiment. He first appears as the son of a doting father who presents him with his 'gem-studded tunic'. As I understand it, the god of responsible masculinity, and hence of progeny (Jacob), makes his main investment in a 'son' who is a god of 'increase', hence of prosperity and success (Joseph). This arouses the envy of the 'brothers' of the god Joseph, and they decide to kill him. These 'brothers' are not really the sons of Israel and therefore the eponymous ancestors of the different tribes of Israel. Rather, they are other gods of the West Arabian pantheon, jealous of the privileges enjoyed by Joseph as a god of success. In the Genesis version of the story, the 'brothers' do not kill Joseph; instead they only make him appear to have been eaten by a wild beast, while they actually sell him as a slave. In the original story, as I imagine it, the 'brothers' of the young and handsome god, after stripping him of his brilliant raiment, actually arrange for him to be mauled and killed (and perhaps eaten) by a wild beast, just as the young and handsome Adonis, in another ancient Near Eastern myth, is mauled and killed by a wild boar. I also suspect that in the original story, Joseph's godly raiment was not dipped in the blood of a freshly slaughtered kid, but drenched in the god's own youthful blood. Other stories are told about the blood of various gods who die and rise from the dead: the blood which flowed from the wounded feet of Adonis was immortalized by the red flower of the anemone; the blood flowing from the wounded side of the crucified Jesus became the wine of the Christian eucharist.

In my opinion, the fact that the 'brothers' first throw Joseph into a waterless pit is also significant. The waterless pit was a dry well; Isaac, the grandfather of the god Joseph, was the god of 'overflowing wells' (chapter 5). This episode of the Joseph myth must have been deliberately intended to underline the passion of the young god. Traditionally, Eastern Christians, in mourning the death of Jesus on Good Friday, have sung: 'Today he was suspended on a wooden pole, he who has suspended the world on water!' Perhaps, at one time, the devotees of the god Joseph, in mourning his passion, used to sing: 'Today he was cast in a waterless pit, he whose grandfather was the god of overflowing wells!'

In the next episode of the myth, the god Joseph reappears alive and well in Mizraim, where Genesis begins to confuse his story with that of the Egyptianized Hebrew Zaphenath-paneah. While this Zaphenath-paneah, in the Egyptian colony of Mizraim, was the chancellor of Pharaoh as the local 'king', wearing his 'signet ring' (41:42), the god Joseph, as the god of success, becomes the associate and chief agent of Pharaoh as Āl Fāri' or Āl Firā'ah, the god of 'running streams', hence of irrigation (see p. 97). Among the ancient Egyptians, it was common to regard the 'person' of a ruler, or his 'essence' (Egyptian *ka*, or *qi*, 'form, image') as a god. This special Egyptian term survives in two West Arabian place names, Qaw and Qawah (both *qw*); and perhaps the god of 'running streams', Āl Fāri' or 'Pharaoh', was regarded as the *ka* of the 'king' or viceroy of Egypt's West Arabian raj, long before the kings of Egypt itself came to be called Pharaoh (Egyptian *pr '*) in about 1550 at the earliest, but more definitely after about 950 BC.

Before his special gift for the prudent management of agricultural resources came to the attention of Pharaoh as a god of irrigation, the god Joseph in the guise of a slave had been in the service of Potiphar, who was a 'eunuch' (*śryś*, cf. Arabic *srys*, 'impotent or sterile male') of Pharaoh (37:36) — I would say one of the castrated priests of Pharaoh as a god; as indicated by his name (*pwtypr*, Egyptian *p't pr*, 'bread-offering of the house', i.e. of the 'temple'). Translations of Genesis describe him as 'captain of the guard', the Hebrew original (*sr h-ṭbḥym*) yielding more readily the sense of 'lord of the butchers'. I believe he was, quite simply, the 'lord (high priest) of Baṭḥān (*bṭḥn*)' — one of two villages by this name in the hill country of the Jizan hinterland, south of Khamis Mushait, and hence of Miṣrāmah, the Biblical Mizraim. As a slave of the castrated high priest, Joseph is amorously pursued by the high priest's frustrated wife. When she fails to persuade the handsome young god to seduce her, she tears his 'garment' from him, trumps up against him a charge of attempted rape, and uses the possession of his 'garment' to support her charge. Still disguised as a slave, the young god is condemned to prison.

It is at this stage, more than anywhere else, that the confusion between the myth of the god Joseph and the apparently historical career of the Egyptianized Hebrew Zaphenath-paneah begins to stand out in the original Hebrew text of the Genesis story (39:20 - 40:23). At some point in his career, Zaphenath-paneah, it seems, who was the historical 'Joseph', had actually spent some time in a penal colony called Beyt ha-Sōhar (*byt h-śhr*, the 'temple' of Sōhar, first mentioned 39:20) — today the village of Āl Zuhayr (the 'god' Zuhayr, or *zhyr*), a short distance to the south of Khamis Mushait. This village carries the name of a moon god, the Arabic *shr* (as *sāhūr*) and its variant *zhr* (as *zahr* and its diminutive *zuhayr*) being attested epithets for the 'moon'. In translation the Biblical *śhr* has been taken to mean 'prison' (from *shr* in the Arabic sense of 'watch, guard'), which would make the expression *byt h-śhr* mean 'the house of the prison', not simply 'the prison'. According to Genesis, Beyt ha-Sōhar (the present village of Āl Zuhayr) was 'a place where the king's prisoners were kept' (39:20). The unnamed 'lord' or 'master' (*'dn*, 39:20) who sent the historical Joseph to this penal colony must have been none other than the ruler of Mizraim whom he served. There the historical Joseph was placed in a 'pit' (*bwr*, 41:14) — presumably, a dungeon — until he was finally released (ibid.) and restored to the service of Pharaoh, as 'king of Mizraim' (41:46).

In the myth, the god Joseph, who is an entirely different figure, is also imprisoned, but in a different place — not Beyt ha-Sōhar, which was a place reserved for political prisoners, but the 'temple of the high priest of Baṭḥān' (*byt sr ṭbḥym*, 40:3-4), who was none other than the castrated priest Potiphar. The redactors of Genesis, alert to the fact that two different prisons were involved, made a point of identifying the 'temple of the high priest of Baṭḥān', upon first mention (40:3) as being the same as Beyt ha-Sōhar, thus strengthening the fusion between the identities of Joseph the god and the historical Zaphenath-paneah.

I shall not further labour the point here, but it is certainly one to be kept in mind. There are two prisons in question; hence, what we have must be a fusion of two different stories: one about the imprisonment of the historical 'Joseph' in the dungeons of Pharaoh as the king of Mizraim; the other about the imprisonment of the god Joseph in the temple of the god Pharaoh at Baṭḥān, which was kept by the high priest Potiphar. Now to return to the story:

In the prison of Potiphar's temple, Joseph becomes acquainted not with the 'butler' (*mšqh*) and the 'baker' (*'ph*) of the king of Mizraim (40:1), but with two other high priests of the god Pharaoh, both of them, like Potiphar, his 'eunuchs' (*śryśyw*, 40:2; *śryśy pr'h*, 40:7), who had angered him by their mismanagement of affairs. The first was the 'high priest of the Masqā community' (*sr h-mšqym*, 40:9); the other was the 'high priest of the Wafiyah community' (*sr h-'pym*, 40:16). To this day, both Masqā (*msq*) and Wafiyah (*wṕy*) are villages of the Khamis Mushait vicinity, near Miṣrāmah or Mizraim. In Hebrew, the names of these two villages would mean, respectively, 'butler' (or 'well-irrigated') and 'baker' (or 'baking'). Joseph reveals to both these high priests his supernatural ability to interpret dreams.

Of these two high priests, the one of Wafiyah (or 'baking'), responsible for grain production and storage for bread, has mismanaged the affairs of the god Pharaoh so badly that he is put to death. But the life of the high priest of Masqā, who apparently has charge of the god Pharaoh's 'irrigation' schemes, is spared; he is released and restored to his post. It is this high priest of Masqā who, reportedly, tells Pharaoh about the unusual talents of Joseph. Thereupon Pharaoh, as the god of irrigation, orders the release of the young god from prison, arrays him in 'garments of fine linen' (41:42), and entrusts to him the management of his grain resources — formerly the function of the discredited high priest of Wafiyah, whose execution the god Joseph himself had prophesied (and perhaps arranged). In one verse of the story, there is a subtle hint that Pharaoh recognized Joseph as a fellow god: 'a man who has the spirit of god in him' (*'yš 'šr rwḥ 'lhym bw*, 41:38). Perhaps he adopted him as an associate god, to take full charge of the prosperity of the realm under his paramount jurisdiction.

As the resourceful god of success, Joseph, or Āl Yūsif, appears to have been credited in ancient West Arabian mythology with the institution of grain storage; perhaps with the invention of the silo. He was also credited with instituting the royal monopoly of agricultural land (47:13-25), which became standard Egyptian practice (47:26) — not only in the Egyptian colony of Mizraim in inland Asir, but also in Egypt itself, as is known from Egyptian records.

Do I overinterpret the Joseph story here? Perhaps I do. The fact remains, however, that the names of Joseph (Āl Yūsif) and Pharaoh (Āl Fāri', or Āl Firā'ah) do survive on the map of West Arabia to this day as the names of gods, introduced by the Semitic *'l*, or *Ēl* (Arabicized as *Āl*), for 'god'. Add to this the undoubted fact that the story of Joseph's imprisonment is clearly a fusion of two stories, as demonstrated above. Yet a further matter to keep in mind is that the language of mythology is highly figurative and allegorical. Literally, it says one thing; cryptically, something else. In a typical myth, the explicit is expected to entertain the layman; the esoteric is to instruct the initiate in the mystery religion or cult to which the myth relates. One may join the laity and read the beautiful story of Joseph, as explicitly told in Genesis, for pure entertainment. To understand its esoteric content, as it was originally expounded in the closed circles of cult initiates, one has no choice but to look within.

7
The Wandering Aramean

The densely woven tapestry of Genesis ought to be unwoven thread by thread. In the two preceding chapters, I distinguished between two 'Jacobs' in the Genesis narrative: one who was actually a Jacob, and another who was not. The first I identified as being the god of 'progeny' Āl 'Uqbah; the second, as Israel of Hebron — like Abram the Hebrew of Hebron (chapter 4), a claimed ancestor of the Hebrew Israelite tribes of the region. In drawing the distinction between these two Biblical 'Jacobs', I limited myself to essentials in order not to clutter the text with too much detail. I also avoided mentioning a third Jacob, who is better dealt with separately. He is the Jacob who first appears as a distinct character in Genesis 28, where he can easily be identified and labelled according to his special attributes. His person can then be tracked down in the chapters that follow, where his story is blended, episode by episode, and even verse by verse, with the story of Jacob the god, and more particularly with the story of Israel.

This particular Jacob is an Aramean; he is depicted in Genesis 28 as the son of the Isaac who was the son of Abram the Aramean. When the time comes for him to marry, his father sends him to Paddan-aram (*pdn 'rm*, or 'the Paddan of Aram'), to take a wife from among his Aramean kin. Instead of one, he takes two, Leah and Rachel, who are the daughters of his maternal uncle Laban — 'Laban the Aramean' (*lbn h-'rmy*, 25:20; 28:5; 31:20, 24), who actually speaks Aramaic (31:47). Jacob stays for many years in Paddan-aram with his uncle, tending his cattle and flocks, and reportedly siring eleven

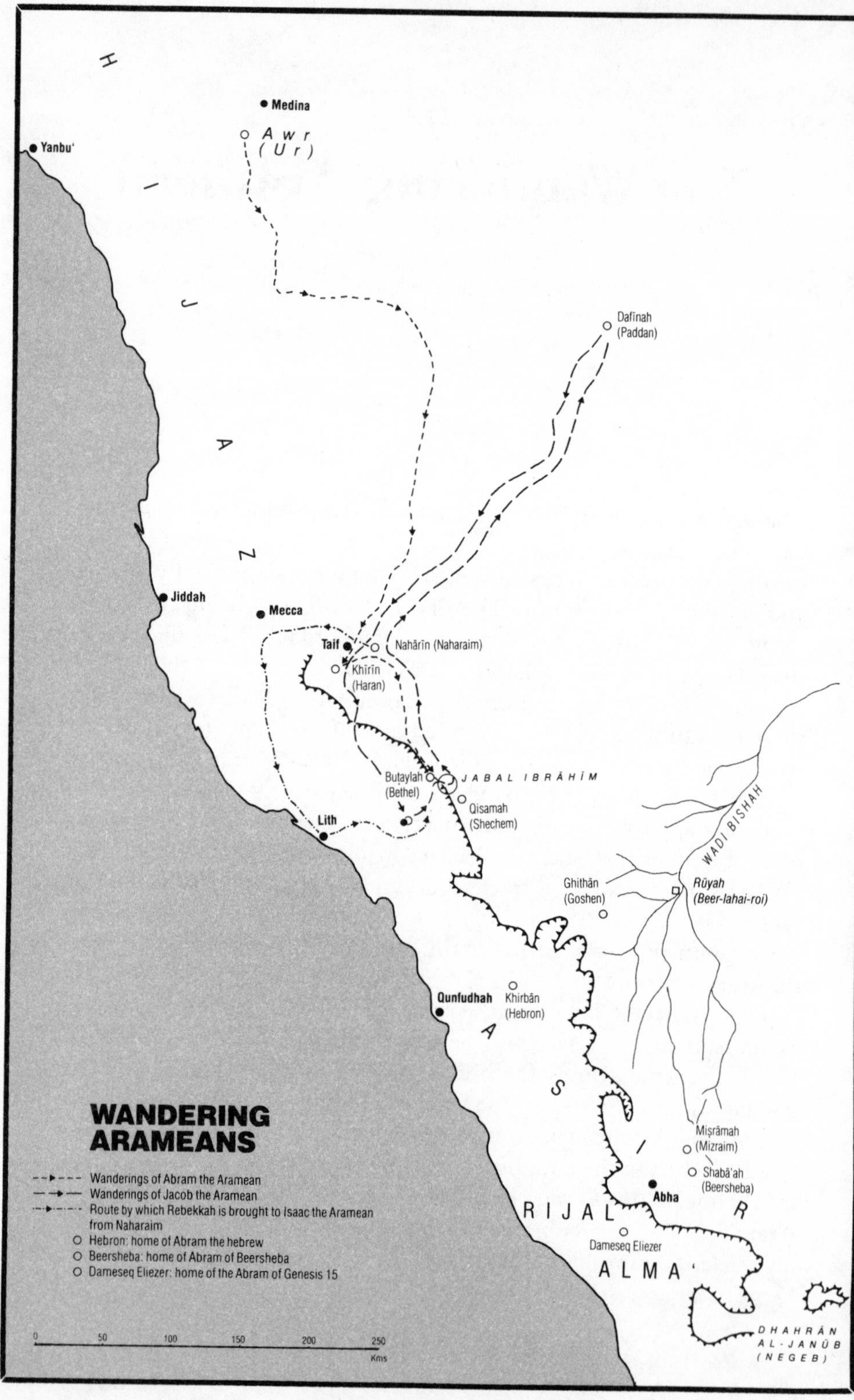
H I J A Z
Medina
Awr
(Ur)
Yanbu'
Dafīnah
(Paddan)
Jiddah
Mecca
Taif
Nahārīn (Naharaim)
Khīrīn
(Haran)
Buṭaylah
(Bethel)
JABAL IBRĀHĪM
Qisamah
(Shechem)
Lith
WADI BISHAH
Ghithān
(Goshen)
Rūyah
(Beer-lahai-roi)
Qunfudhah
Khirbān
(Hebron)
A S I R
Miṣrāmah
(Mizraim)
Shabā'ah
(Beersheba)
Abha
RIJAL
ALMA'
Dameseq Eliezer
DHAHRĀN
AL-JANŪB
(NEGEB)
WANDERING ARAMEANS
Wanderings of Abram the Aramean
Wanderings of Jacob the Aramean
Route by which Rebekkah is brought to Isaac the Aramean from Naharaim
Hebron: home of Abram the hebrew
Beersheba: home of Abram of Beersheba
Dameseq Eliezer: home of the Abram of Genesis 15
0
50
100
150
200
250
Kms

sons and a daughter by his two wives and their respective maids, Zilphah and Bilhah; then he falls out with his uncle and returns with his family to his original homeland — apparently to Shechem (35:4), the Qisamah of the Zahran highlands in the southern Hijaz, where his alleged grandfather Abram the Aramean had once lived. More a figure of legend than of history, the Jacob in question appears to have personified an Aramean folk of that region bearing that name.

In the Genesis story, Jacob the Aramean is not left to stop at his Shechem, in the Zahran highlands; instead, he is made to proceed further south 'to the land of Canaan' (31:18): the maritime highlands of Asir in the hinterland of the coastal town of Qunfudhah, where Israel the Hebrew of Hebron (today Khirbān) used to live (chapter 6). To reach the area, he allegedly crosses the 'pass' (*m'br*) of Jabbok (*ybq*), today Waqbah (*wqb*), near 'Hebron', or Khirbān, after which his movements become intricately confused with those of Israel, with whom he is now definitely identified. It is precisely at this point that Genesis comes forward with a special story to explain how Jacob had his name changed to Israel (32:22-29):

That same night he arose and took his two wives,
  his two maids, and his eleven children
  and crossed the pass of Jabbok.
He took them and sent them across the valley (*h-nḥl*),
  and likewise everything that he had.
And Jacob was left alone;
  and a man wrestled with him until the breaking of the day.
When the man saw that he did not prevail against Jacob,
  he touched the hollow of his hip;
  and Jacob's hip was put out of joint
  as he wrestled with him.
Then he said, 'Let me go, for the day is breaking.'
  But he said, 'I will not let you go,
  unless you bless me.'
And he said to him, 'What is your name?'
  And he said, 'Jacob.'
Then he said, 'Your name shall no more be called Jacob,
  but Israel (*ysr'l*),
  for you have striven (verb *srh*) with God (*'l*)
  and with men, and have prevailed '

This Genesis version, of what must have been an older story, is not only intended to identify Jacob the Aramean with Israel the Hebrew, but also to elaborate on a folk etymology of the name Israel (for my own suggested etymology of the name, see *The Bible Came from Arabia*, p.124). The original story, as I see it, must have been part of the mythology of the god Jacob (Āl 'Uqbah) and his strife with Yahweh, who only manages to disable him as a god of progeny by putting his hip out of joint, leaving him limping (32:31). One must bear in mind here that the male role in the production of progeny involves movements of the 'hip' which, no less than the 'thigh', can be symbolic of masculine prowess. Genesis goes on to explain in the story that the Israelites do not eat the sciatic muscle of animals (the 'sinew of the hip') because 'Jacob' (not 'Israel') was struck on this muscle (32:32). In the cult of Jacob as Āl 'Uqbah, the god of progeny, it is possible that the 'sinew of the hip' was originally not eaten because it was considered sacred, being a symbol of the generative powers of that god. This ritual abstention from eating the sciatic muscle of animals was perhaps inherited by the ancient Yahweh cult of the Israelites from the older cult of the god Jacob, which it otherwise obliterated. Once denuded of his divinity, the god Jacob came to be identified with the legendary figure of Israel as the eponymous ancestor of the Israelites. Hence, as in the Genesis story quoted above, 'Jacob', after the god Yahweh had disabled him by putting his hip out of joint, becomes 'Israel'.

The wanderings of Jacob the Aramean

Our concern in the present chapter is not with Jacob the god, but with Jacob the Aramean. Before he is made to proceed toward the 'land of Canaan' to become fused with Israel, this particular Jacob holds together very well. To begin with let us consider his name.

In its consonantal structure, the name of Jacob the Aramean (*y'qb*) is identical with that of Jacob the god, or Āl 'Uqbah. In Hebrew, however, as in Arabic, the verb *'qb*, as already indicated, has different meanings. As the substantive of it, 'Jacob', as *y'qb*, can mean 'progeny' (see p. 104); but it can also mean 'steep ground' (as in the Hebrew *'āqōb*), or 'difficult ascent, mountain pass, defile' (as in the Arabic *'aqabah*). In the highlands of the southern Hijaz, a number of mountain passes (Arabic *'iqāb*, plural of *'aqabah*) run across the great West Arabian escarpment (the *yrdn* or 'Jordan' of the Hebrew

Bible) to connect the highlands with the coastal lowlands. A modern gazetteer of the Zahran region lists the names of thirty-four such passes in that area alone. The author of the same gazetteer dwells on the ecological importance of these mountain passes or *'iqāb*, in the southern Hijaz. Here the local folk have traditionally practised transhumance, moving their residence between the highlands and the coastal lowlands according to the seasons. The Jacob (or *y'qb*) folk, as the people of the 'mountain passes' of that area, probably received their name from this pattern of living. Their name actually survives there in the village of al-Ya'āqīb (exactly *y'qb*), whose name, with its present Arabic vocalization, literally means 'the Jacob folk', i.e. 'the people of the mountain passes'.

In Genesis 28 a lame attempt is made to identify Jacob the Aramean as a descendant of Abram of Beersheba (chapter 4), by making him set out on his wanderings from the same Beersheba (28:10). As he was actually of the same stock as Abram the Aramean, this Jacob must, in fact, have started his wanderings from the Zahran highlands — possibly from Qisamah, or 'Shechem' (see above). From there, Jacob 'went towards Haran (*ḥrn*)' (28:10), already identified as Khīrīn (*ḫrn*), in the Taif highlands, north of the Zahran region (see p. 81). Next, he proceeded 'toward the land of Beney Qedem' (*'rṣh bny qdm*, 29:1) — not 'the land of the people of the east', as it is usually taken to mean, but that of the Bani Jadhmā (*bny ǧdm*) folk — according to the Arabic records, the ancient inhabitants of the Medina region and its environs in the central Hijaz. The exact place where he arrived was Paddan (*pdn*), today the large village of Dafīnah (*dṗn*), about 230 kilometres north-east of Taif, and roughly the same distance south-east of Medina. The local people told him they were originally from Haran (29:4), home territory of Abram the Aramean's folk.

As he first journeyed from the Zahran highlands towards Haran, Jacob reportedly stopped to sleep at a place called Bethel (*byt 'l*), where he had a curious dream: he saw a ladder set up between the earth and heaven, with Yahweh standing above the ladder, while his angels ascended and descended on it (28:12-15). At this place, we are further told, there used to be a city called Luz (*lwz*, 28:19), while 'below Bethel' there was a 'wood' (*'lwn*, usually rendered 'oak', or 'terebinth') called Allon-bakuth (*'lwn bkwt*). With these given coordinates, the position of the Bethel of the dream of 'Jacob's ladder' can be fixed with complete precision. It was not the Buṭaylah of the Zahran highlands (see p. 81), but the barren ridge of Jabal Batīlah (*btl*), east of Taif. In the same area there is a village called Alyānah al-Ḍūl (*'lyn ḍwl*), whose name combines what is clearly the Hebrew word for 'wood, forest' (*'lwn*) and a corruption of the name Luz (*lwz*). Nearby, also, is a tract of basaltic wilderness with thorn trees, called to this day Bakāwiyyāt (*bkwyt*). This, beyond doubt, was the Biblical Allon-bakuth, or 'wood' of Bakūth (*bkwt*). The whole setting is quite bleak. When Jacob awoke from his dream he reportedly exclaimed: 'How awesome is this place!' (28:17).

On his return journey from Paddan-aram with his wives and children, cattle and sheep, Jacob the Aramean 'crossed the river' (*h-nhr*) which is the great valley of Wadi Aḍam, south-east of Taif, then proceeded in the direction of Mount Gilead (*hr h-gl'd*, 31:21) — the coastal slopes of the Zahran highlands which end at the present village of al-Ja'dah (*'l-ǧ'd*). There he reached a place called Mahanaim (*mḥnym*, 32:2, plural or dual of *mḥn*) — today the village of Maḥnā (*mḥn*). To reach the coastal slopes of the Zahran highlands from the Taif region, which lies inland, Jacob had to cross the 'Jordan' (*yrdn*), or 'escarpment', to Wadi Aḍam. According to Genesis 32:10b, he says in his own words after making this crossing:

> At Maqlī I crossed this escarpment,
> until I was in Sheney from Ḥanōth.

This indicates that Jacob started his journey homeward from Ḥanōth (*ḥnwt*), which is today the oasis of Ḥanīṭ (*hnyṭ*), in the Qasim region east of Dafīnah — the Biblical Paddan-aram. From there he set out southwards to cross the escarpment (*h-yrdn*, the Biblical 'Jordan') at Maqlī (*mqly*) — today Maqālā (*mql'*), in upper Wadi Aḍam, directly west of the escarpment south of Taif. Finally, he reached Sheney (*šny*), which is today the village of Shayān (*šyn*) in the same Wadi Aḍam. So far, the words attributed to Jacob on the occasion have been misinterpreted by translators to mean the following: 'With only my staff I crossed this Jordan (*b-mqly 'brty 't h-yrdn hzh*); and now I have become two companies (*w-'th hyyty l-šny m-ḥnwt*)' (RSV). The confusion arose by taking *l-šny* to mean 'into two', and misreading the original *m-ḥnwt*, or 'from *ḥnwt*', as *mḥnwt*, plural of *mḥnh*, to mean 'companies' Incidentally, the expression for 'two companies' in Biblical Hebrew would be *šny mḥntym* in the dual, not *šny mḥnwt* in the plural.

It was actually the redactors of Genesis who first took the expression *l-šny mḥnwt* to mean 'into two companies'. In fact, they built a story around it. Their intent was to complete the identification of the person of Jacob the Aramean with that of Israel the Hebrew. To be the same person as Israel, who had a brother called Edom (the Edom confused with Esau, see chapter 5), Jacob had to be the brother of this same Edom. So the following story was invented (32:3-8):

When Jacob reached Mahanaim, he sent word to his brother 'Esau in the land of Edom' to notify him of his arrival in his neighbourhood. But Jacob feared his brother Esau, with whom he had once parted on bad terms. Therefore, he divided his family and retinue into 'two companies', so that if they encountered his brother Esau (or rather Edom), and he destroyed one company, the other one would be able to escape. As it ultimately turned out, the reunion between the two brothers was a cordial one (33:1-15). What is important though is not the story, but the purpose it was invented to serve. It identified Jacob the Aramean as the brother of Edom, who was actually the brother of Israel the Hebrew, and so gave this Jacob another of the distinguishing attributes of Israel.

Where did Jacob the Aramean finally settle?

After the arrival of Jacob the Aramean at 'Mahanaim' or Maḥnā, in the Zahran region, his story becomes confused at every point with that of Israel the Hebrew of Hebron. We are actually told that God changed his name from Jacob to Israel not once, but twice (32:28; 35:10) — no doubt for added emphasis. Whoever fused the stories of these two legendary figures into one had considerable explaining to do. From now on Israel is sometimes called Jacob, as well as Jacob being called Israel, which adds to the confusion. To determine who is who at every step, all we have to rely on are the geographical indicators preserved in the Genesis text, bearing in mind that the same person cannot be in two different places at the same time.

Upon his return from Paddan-aram, Jacob the Aramean did not go to the 'land of Canaan', in the Qunfudhah hinterland, to cross to the valley of 'Jabbok' (Waqbah) there (see above). This was the territory of Israel the Hebrew. From Maḥnā, on the maritime slopes of the Zahran region, he simply 'went up' (*'lh*) to 'Bethel' (35:1) —

this one the present Buṭaylah, right on the escarpment, in the highlands of the same region. In short, at the end of his wanderings, he returned to the same area where his alleged forebears, Abram the Aramean and his son Isaac, had been settled. In the text of Genesis 35, this 'Bethel' is taken to be Jabal Batīlah, at 'Luz' (35:6), where Jacob had his dream about the ladder (see above). To confuse matters further, the place is said to be located in the 'land of Canaan' (35:6), apparently in reference to the village also called Batīlah in Rijal Alma', in the southern reaches of Asir (see p. 89). One can tell, however, that the 'Bethel' in question was none other than the Buṭaylah of the Zahran highlands, because Jacob could readily get from there to the nearby Qisamah, or 'Shechem' (35:4). Moreover, the barren ridge of Jabal Batīlah is hardly a place where anyone would choose to settle of his own free will.

Like the present inhabitants of the Zahran highlands, in antiquity the Aramean folk of the same region also practised transhumance, moving down into the valleys to the west according to the season. Thus we find Jacob descending to Wadi Aḍam with his pregnant wife Rachel, in the direction of 'Ephrath' (*'prt*), today the village of Furāt (*ṕrt*), in the lower course of that valley. On the way, Rachel died in childbirth, and was buried at 'Bethlehem' (*byt lḥm*, the 'temple of *lḥm*') (35:19), today the village called Umm Laḥm (*'m lḥm*, the 'goddess *lḥm*'), near Furāt, in the same valley. The identification of this Umm Laḥm as being the 'Bethlehem' of the Hebrew Bible has been considered in more detail in *The Bible Came from Arabia.*

The question of Judah

The historical Israelites were a confederation of different West Arabian tribes and folk, some of Hebrew stock, others Aramean. The fact that there was an Aramean element among them, of enough importance to claim attention, is disclosed by the confession the Israelites were enjoined to make before Yahweh in Deuteronomy 26:5: 'A wandering Aramean is my father; and he went down to Mizraim with a small number; and there he became a great nation, great, mighty and populous'. As far as we can tell, Jacob the Aramean never went to Mizraim; it was Israel, the eponymous ancestor of the Hebrew Israelites, who at one time migrated there (chapter 6). In a tribal confederation, however, the myth of a common ancestor is of vital importance, because it makes for solidarity; without it, the confederation can easily fall apart. Thus, in Deuteronomy, Jacob, who is no doubt the 'wandering Aramean', is made to go to Mizraim (which he probably never did) in order to become the same person as Israel, and thereby the ancestor of the Hebrew as well as of the Aramaic elements in the confederation of Israel. In Genesis, as already noted, the identification of Jacob with Israel is carried out more elaborately by a fusion of their originally different stories into one, episode by episode. The question is, who were originally the Aramean folk, as distinct from the Hebrew folk, who ultimately joined the confederation of Israel?

In Genesis, Jacob (as Jacob, or as Israel) is depicted as the father of twelve sons whose descendants were the twelve tribes of Israel. In one instance, however, Judah is isolated from his brothers — he 'goes down' from them — and a special story is told about him (38:1-30). Here is a synopsis of the story, set against its West Arabian topography:

1. Judah 'went down' to a man from Adullam (*'dlm*) whose name was Hirah (*ḥyrh*), and he met the daughter of a man called Shua (*šw'*), whom he married (38:1-2). The three names cited here survive as place names in the Taif region, downhill from the Zahran highlands to the north: they are those of the villages of Da'ālimah (*d'lm*), Ḥīrah (*ḥyrh*) and Sha'yah (*š'y*), all three in close proximity.

2. Shua's daughter bore Judah three sons: Er (*'r*), Onan (*'wnn*) and Shelah (*šlh*); when she gave birth to the last one, she was in Chezib (*kzyb*, 38:3-5). The names of the brothers are recorded in the two valleys of Wadi 'Iyār (*'yr*) and Wadi Nawān (*nwn*), on the maritime slopes of the Zahran highlands, and the village of Shawlah (*šwlh*), uphill from these two valleys. Chezib, where Shelah was allegedly born, is today a village of the Zahran lowlands called Abū Qaṣīb (*qṣyb*, cf. Biblical *kzyb*).

3. Judah had his firstborn, Er, married to Tamar (*tmr*, 38:6), today Tamār (*tmr*), the name of a mountain pass north of Taif.

4. Er was a wicked man, and Yahweh slew him before Tamar bore him any children. Judah asked his second son, Onan, to have intercourse with Tamar on behalf of his dead brother, so she would bear offspring to his name; and Onan did so, but his performance was a wilful failure: 'he ejaculated on the ground, lest he should give offspring to his brother.' Yahweh was so angered by his refusal to

raise seed for his brother that he slew him, as he had slain his brother before him (38:8–10).

5. Judah sent Tamar back to her father's house, asking her to wait until his youngest son Shelah was old enough to perform the brother-in-law's duty to her (38:11).

6. Judah became widowed before Shelah grew to sexual maturity. One day he went to Timnah (*tmnh*), where his sheep were being sheared, and Tamar decided to seize the opportunity to have a child by him, considering that he was her dead husband's father, whose seed would be the same as the seed of his son. Dressed and veiled as a harlot, she waited for him at the entrance of Enaim (*'ynym*), where Judah saw her and 'went in to her', making her pregnant. He promised to send her a kid in payment, but she insisted on keeping his signet, his cord and his rod as a pledge. When Judah sent someone back to her with the kid, she could not be found anywhere in Enaim, where Judah had met her (38:12-23). Here it must be noted that the Timnah in the story is today Tumnā (*tmn'*), and Enaim is Ghunnam (*ġnm*), both villages of the Taif region.

7. When Judah heard that his daughter-in-law Tamar was pregnant, he had her brought before him to be burned as a harlot. Before she arrived, however, she had his signet, cord and rod sent to him, with a message saying that the man who was the owner of those objects was the one who had made her pregnant. Judah thereupon realized what he had done, and he decided to forget the matter. Tamar subsequently gave birth to twin boys, Perez (*prṣ*) and Zerah (*zrḥ*) (38:24-30) — the eponymous ancestors of the two main branches of the tribe of Judah. Today, Perez is the name of the village of Farḍah (*ṕrḍ*), and Zerah that of the village of Ṣarḥah (*ṣrḥ*), both in Wadi Aḍam.

Needless to say, this story is an entertaining legend which summarizes the early alliances and proliferations of the tribe of Judah — a tribe which always stood distinct from the other tribes of Israel. From the topographical identification of the names in the story, it is clear that it is set not in Asir, but in the southern Hijaz: the Zahran and Taif regions and the valley of Wadi Aḍam, where the story of Jacob the Aramean also takes place. As we have just seen, the names of Judah's two sons by his daughter-in-law — Perez and Zerah — are today those of two villages in Wadi Aḍam. From other Biblical passages, we learn that 'Bethlehem' and 'Ephrathah' (Micah 5:2) were towns of the 'land of Judah'. Both of these still exist as villages of Wadi Aḍam — Umm Laḥm and Furāt (see above) — indicating that the original territory of Judah was centred around Wadi Aḍam. In the Zahran highlands to the south of this valley, it appears that the local Judah folk did not survive for long. The story summarized above hints at this where it mentions that Judah's two older sons, Er (Wadi 'Iyār) and Onan (Wadi Nawān), both died childless at an early age. As for the branch of the Judah tribe called the Shelah, after Judah's youngest son by his own wife, there is reference to 'ancient traditions' concerning them elsewhere in the Bible, where they are described as linen-weavers and potters of yore (1 Chronicles 4:21-23) — a forgotten humble folk of the same region, who once inhabited places such as 'Chozeba' (variant of 'Chezib') and 'Bethlehem'.

Further detailed analysis of the story is not necessary for our purposes. What remains important is that its hero, Judah, lived in the same territories of the southern Hijaz as his alleged forebears Jacob the Aramean, Isaac the Aramean and Abram the Aramean. This means that Judah was an Aramean himself: that is to say, the tribe of Judah was Aramean in origin, unlike the other tribes of the later confederation of Israel, which were of Hebrew stock, claiming descent from Israel of Hebron. It must have been this significant difference in ethnic origin which kept the Judah separate from the other tribes of Israel, as is clear from the historical accounts of the Bible.

At this point it would be relevant to recall what I demonstrated in chapter 3, when I analysed the myth of the original confusion of tongues in the composite story of the Tower of Babel and suggested that the setting of this myth was the Taif region of the southern Hijaz. This indicates that more than one language was spoken in that part of West Arabia at some period of antiquity — including, no doubt, the Aramaic of the north and the Hebrew of the south. In the Genesis story of Jacob the Aramean, as we have seen, his uncle Laban is made to utter words in Aramaic; Jacob, on the other hand, is made to utter the same words in Hebrew (31:47). Yet when Jacob went to Paddan-aram, according to the same story, he readily communicated with his Aramean kinsfolk. This implies that he — or rather the Aramean Jacob folk he personifies in the story — were bilingual, as are most borderland peoples. By the time the Aramean Judah folk, who claimed Jacob the Aramean as an ancestor, had merged with the Hebrew Israelites from the lands further south, their language, most probably, had become mostly Hebrew. Nevertheless, they remembered their Aramean origin, and at least some of them continued to speak Aramaic as well as Hebrew (see p. 175). It was probably they, among the Israelites, who originally confessed before Yahweh, lest they should forget: 'A wandering Aramean is my father' — *aramī ōbēd ābī.*

8
The Search for the Historical Moses

There was a historical Moses who led the exodus of the Hebrew Israelites from the West Arabian land of Mizraim in about 1440 BC — according to the Bible (1 Kings 6:1), 480 years before Solomon began building his temple in Jerusalem in about 960 BC. Modern scholars have doubted this date for the exodus, mainly because Egyptian records and archaeological findings in Egypt, Sinai and Palestine do not confirm it. I can think of no good reason why this date should not be correct, considering that it relates, in my view, to an event which took place entirely in peninsular Arabia, and nowhere outside Arabia.

The dating of the history of the Biblical monarchies can be computed, accepting a small margin for error, from a number of synchronisms with Egyptian and Mesopotamian history, where the historical material in the Bible refers to Egyptian, Assyrian, Babylonian or Persian rulers by name. From this, the date 960 BC can be estimated for the commencement of the work on the construction of the temple in Jerusalem (which I contend was the original Jerusalem of West Arabia rather than the one of Palestine, see *The Bible Came from Arabia*, pp. 110-123). Adding 480 to this date, we arrive at 1440 BC — the start of the exodus.

Biblical archaeology discovered nothing to justify another date for the event. Yet modern Biblical scholars argue that the Hebrew Israelites must have left 'Egypt' (the standard identification of the Biblical 'Mizraim') in about 1290, not 1440 BC. By doing so, they inadvertently rob Moses of the distinction of being the first

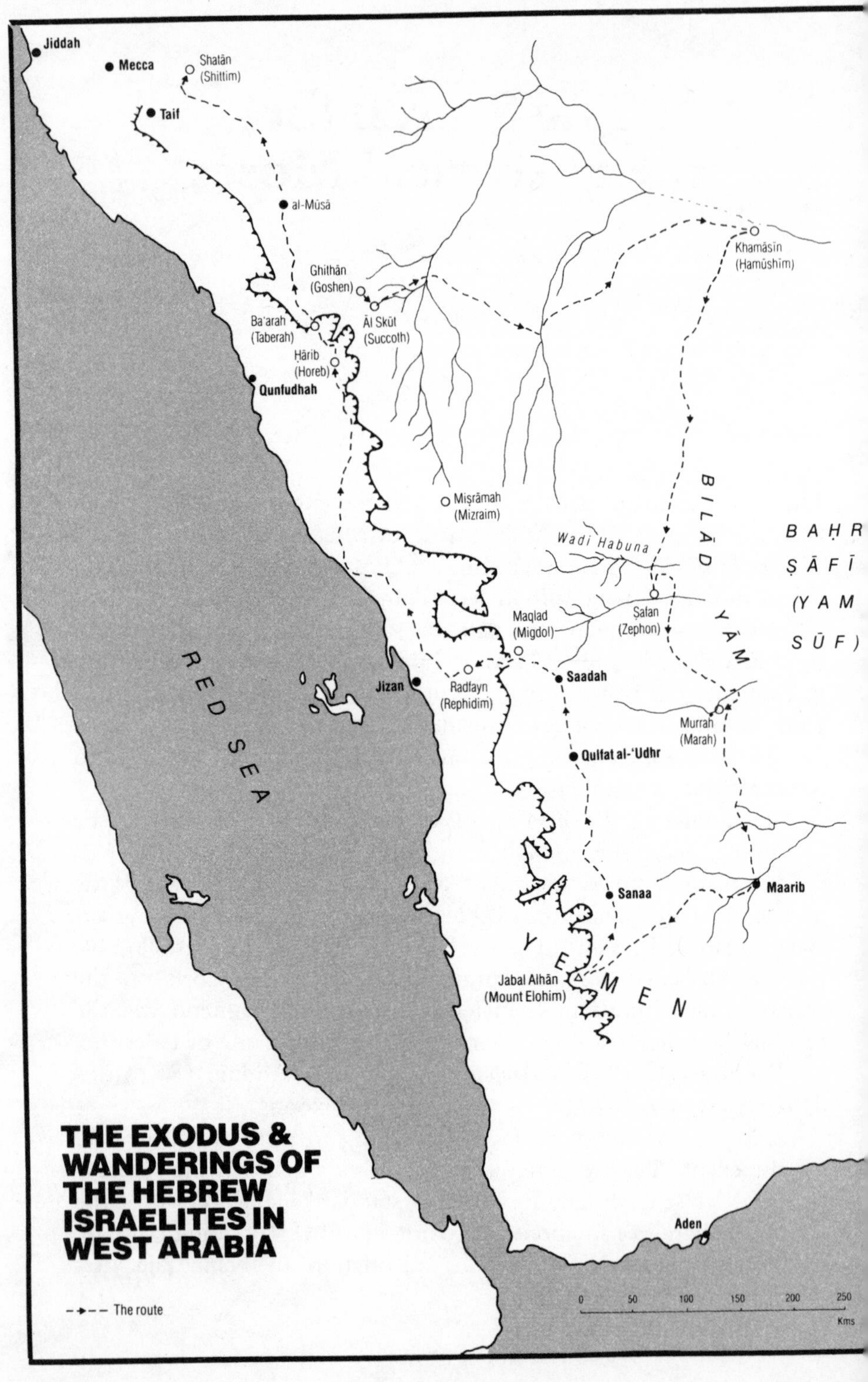

THE EXODUS & WANDERINGS OF THE HEBREW ISRAELITES IN WEST ARABIA

advocate of monotheism in recorded history, according this honour instead to the Egyptian king Akhenaton (1379-1362 BC). This has given rise to speculations (one from Sigmund Freud) that the Israelites first became monotheists under an Egyptian influence — speculations which remain entirely unsubstantiated.

More likely than not, it was the Egyptian king Akhenaton who was influenced by the monotheism of the Israelites of West Arabia, rather than the reverse. There are certainly traces of his special brand of monotheism in West Arabia, where the ancient Egyptians maintained colonies for a long time (chapter 6). What Akhenaton did was to identify all the gods of the Egyptian pantheon with his one sun-disc god Aton (*itn*). Two clusters of West Arabian villages, in Wadi Najran and Rijal Alma', carry construct names which couple the name of Aton (as Wiṭn, or *wṭn*) with those of other Egyptian gods: for example, Wiṭn Ḥarshaf (Aton Arsaphes); or Wiṭn Āl Ḥarah (Aton Horus). This makes one wonder: is it possible that the identification of the different Egyptian gods with the sun-disc Aton began as a heresy among the ancient Egyptian colonists in West Arabia, under a local monotheistic influence, before this heresy was made the official theology of Egypt by Akhenaton? Is it for this reason that the construct Aton place names survive in separate clusters in two secluded parts of West Arabia, while they are not found in Egypt, where the monotheism of Akhenaton was effectively disestablished almost immediately following his death?

As I see it, the career of the historical Moses preceded that of the Egyptian king Akhenaton by the better part of a century. His story can be salvaged mainly from the books of Exodus and Numbers, where it is fused with other material, mainly ancient myths. The teachings and discourses attributed to him form the main body of the books of Leviticus and Deuteronomy. Of the composition of these four books and their authorship and redaction, enough has already been said in the Introduction. What I propose to do here is to tackle the problem of the mixed identity of Moses in the Bible, in an attempt to discover who the historical Moses really was.

For a start we must establish the special attributes of the historical Moses, then track him down through the book of Exodus and the book of Numbers, and the narrative pieces in the book of Deuteronomy, where his story is fused with other lore about different figures who are also called Moses. There was, in fact, more than one Moses, as is made clear by a passage of the book of Exodus which interrupts the narrative, at a point where it has already become confused, to announce the following (Exodus 6:20, 26-27):

> Amram took to wife Jochabed… and she bore him Aaron and Moses… *These* are the Aaron and Moses (*hw' 'hrn w-mšh*) to whom Yahweh said: 'Bring out the people of Israel from the land of Mizraim…' *It was they* who spoke to Pharaoh (*hm h-mdbrym 'l pr'h*), king of Mizraim, about bringing the people of Israel out of Mizraim — *this* Moses and Aaron (*hw' mšh w-'hrn*).

Why should Israelite tradition, at one time, have recognized more than one Moses, so that the book of Exodus had to hint so broadly at a distinction between *this* Moses — the one who actually led the exodus — and others? The secret may lie in the etymology of the name 'Moses' (*Mōsheh*, vocalized as the active participle of *mšh*, 'draw out'; cf. Arabic *masā*, 'retrieve dirt manually from the uterus of a she-camel, cow, etc.'; Aramaic *mshā*, or *mš'*, 'cleanse'). If we turn to Exodus, we find a story which explains how Moses got his name. Pharaoh's daughter goes to a river to bathe, and there she finds a Hebrew baby in a basket among the reeds; so she decides to adopt him and call him Moses, because she 'drew him out' (*mšh*) of the water (2:10). Today Biblical scholars doubt this Biblically suggested etymology for the name 'Moses'. They suggest instead that it is the ancient Egyptian word *mes* (*ms*), or *mesū* (*msw*), meaning 'child, son' — from the verb *msi*, 'bear, give birth', which features as a suffix in such Egyptian personal names as Ahmose or Thutmose. I disagree. For once, the etymology suggested for a name in a Biblical text is correct. 'Moses', as the Hebrew *Mōsheh*, means 'the one who draws out': the 'deliverer', 'retriever', or 'redeemer'. In Psalms 18:16-17 (as in 2 Samuel 22:17-18), which is the only Biblical text other than Exodus 2:10 where the Hebrew *mšh* is attested as a verb, again meaning 'draw out', the verb is also equated with the idea of 'deliverance'.

> He drew me out (*ymšny*, from *mšh*) of many waters;
> He delivered me (*yṣylny*) from my strong enemy…

As I see it, 'Moses', in the sense of 'deliverer', or better 'redeemer', was not the actual name of the man who 'delivered' or 'redeemed' the Hebrew Israelites from the bondage into which they had fallen in the land of Mizraim. It was, rather, the honorific title by which he was historically remembered. Before the emergence of the tribal confederation of Israel, the Hebrew and Aramean tribes which formed this confederation had claimed different ancestors, all of whom were called Abram (*'b rm*), or 'exalted father' (see pp. 93-4). In the text of Genesis, all these different 'exalted fathers' were fused into one Abram, who was presented as the common ancestor of all the Israelites. It also appears that the same Hebrew and Aramean tribes who came together to form the confederation of Israel had originally revered different tribal 'redeemers', each of them, in Hebrew, a *Mōsheh*, or 'Moses'. As the book of Genesis collated the different 'exalted fathers' of these tribes, so the books of Exodus and Numbers collated their different 'redeemers': they were all fused into one *Mōsheh*, as each of them in turn was identified with the historical Moses of the exodus.

One day, perhaps, someone with monumental patience will unravel the Biblical story of Moses according to the above suggestion down to the last detail. In the meantime I shall limit myself to some cursory observations.

The man from Elohim

The historical Moses who led the Hebrew exodus from the land of Mizraim would probably have come from that place. Let us assume he did. In Exodus 2, such a Moses is presented as the Hebrew boy who grew up in Mizraim in the care of Pharaoh's daughter. He is depicted as a man who was socially privileged and accustomed to being high-handed: first, he kills an Egyptian whom he sees beating a Hebrew; second, he tries to impose himself as arbiter in a quarrel between two Hebrews (2:11-14). The story indicates to us that Pharaoh sought the death of Moses because he had killed an Egyptian, so Moses fled to the land of Midian, where he married a young lady whose father was called Reuel (2:15-21). He returned to Mizraim only after the death of Pharaoh (2:23), and after 'all the men who were seeking [his] life' were dead (4:19). So, it was not only Pharaoh who wanted to kill Moses; there were other men too, all of whom died after their master. The matter invites close scrutiny, as it clearly involves politics. We shall come back to it. Meanwhile, take note of the Moses whom the Pharaoh in question and his political supporters had wanted to kill. He is the man we are really after — the historical Moses of the exodus.

From the Mizraim which is today Miṣrāmah, near Khamis Mushait in upper Wadi Bishah, the Moses of Exodus 2 fled to Midian (*mdyn*) which is today the village of Madīnah (*mdyn*), in Wadi Tathlith, about 100 kilometres east of Khamis Mushait. Here he married a woman, allegedly Zipporah (2:21), who was the daughter of Reuel (2:18), the priest of Midian (2:16), and whom he first met with her sisters as he was sitting by a well (2:15). In Exodus 3 and 4, a new Moses is introduced into the narrative, whose wife is called Zipporah (4:25) and whose father is the 'priest of Midian' (3:1), except that the father here has a different name: he is not Reuel, but Jethro (3:1; 4:18). As the father-in-law of Moses, Reuel now vanishes completely from the scene, giving way to Jethro. He only reappears once again — not in Exodus, but in Numbers 10:29, where he is reintroduced briefly as 'Reuel the Midianite, Moses' father-in-law', with no indication that he was a priest. When someone's father-in-law, who is supposed to be the father of the same wife, suddenly undergoes a change of name, it is reasonable to suspect that two different sets of persons are being confused. The best way to unravel the mystery is to consider that there is more than one Moses in question. For a start, we may safely identify the Moses of Exodus 3 as the son-in-law of Jethro (which is initially the only attribute by which he can be distinguished) and follow his person through the composite story.

The Moses whose father-in-law was Jethro, priest of Midian, first appears in Exodus 3:1 as a shepherd in Jethro's employment, leading his flock across the wilderness from Midian 'to the mountain of the gods, towards Horeb' (my translation of *'l hr h-'lhym ḥrbh*). Here 'the angel of Yahweh appeared to him in a flame of fire out of the midst of a bush' which 'was burning, yet it was not consumed' (3:2). The Hebrew of the original indicates that 'Horeb' (*ḥrb*, featuring here in the locative case as *ḥrbh*, or 'towards Horeb') was simply the general direction in which the 'mountain of the gods' was located in relation to Midian (the Madīnah of Wadi Tathlith mentioned in Exodus 2), rather than the actual name of the mountain. In *The Bible Came from Arabia*, I identified the 'Horeb' of Moses as the present village of Ḥārib (*ḥrb*), at the foot of Jabal Hādī on the western slopes of Asir. As we shall subsequently discover, the historical Moses certainly stopped at this particular 'Horeb' at one point in his career. The 'Horeb' indicated in Exodus 3:1 as in the general direction of the 'mountain of the gods', however, was a different place. It was either of the two towns still called Ḥārib (also *ḥrb*) in the Yemen, roughly to the east of Sanaa, as will be shown below. Most likely, it was the one closer to Sanaa, called Ḥārib al-Gharāmīsh. I suggest this is the case because Moses, according to Exodus (2:22), had a son called Gershom (*gršm*) — essentially the same name as Gharāmīsh (*ġrmš*). At this point, the following is to be noted:

1. Horeb, which features as the sacred mountain of Moses no less than three times in Exodus and nine times in Deuteronomy, is nowhere actually called *Har hā-Elōhīm* (*hr h-'lhym*), the 'mountain of the gods (not the 'mountain of God', as in the usual translations, which would be *Har Elōhīm*, leaving *'lhym* without the definite article; cf. pp. 33, 87). Apart from the association between the two places in Exodus 3:1, which has just been discussed, the only Biblical passage in which the 'mountain of the gods' is actually called Horeb is not in the books of the Torah, but in 1 Kings 19:8. Here, the two places, lying in the same general direction from a given point in Asir, to the north, could have been telescoped into one place. On the other hand, *Har hā-Elōhīm*, the 'mountain of the gods', is mentioned three more times in Exodus in connection with Moses, without being identified or in any way associated with Horeb (4:27; 18:5; 24:13).

2. Wherever Jethro the priest of Midian features in Exodus (and he features nowhere else) in the story of Moses, *Har hā-Elōhīm* (we might call it more simply Mount Elohim) also appears. In 3:1, Moses leads Jethro's flock to Mount Elohim. In 4:27, Moses has left Jethro in Midian (4:18, 19), and is reportedly on his way back to Mizraim when Aaron meets him at Mount Elohim. In 18:5, Jethro pays his son-in-law Moses a visit in his camp at Mount Elohim.

3. In three independent Biblical passages, Moses is spoken of as *Īsh hā-Elōhīm* (*'yš h-'lhym*, Psalms 90:1; Ezra 3:2; 1 Chronicles 23:14). Had he been called here, or anywhere else, *Īsh Elōhīm* (*'š 'lhym*), it would have meant 'man of God', as the expression has traditionally been translated. The plain fact, however, is that he is actually called in these passages *Īsh hā-Elōhīm*, not *Īsh Elōhīm*. Taken as an ordinary Hebrew expression, *Īsh hā-Elōhīm* would not mean 'man of God', but 'man of the gods' — a singularly inappropriate way to designate

the man who is probably the first monotheist in recorded history. Perhaps the expression simply means 'the man of Elohim', to describe a Moses who came from the vicinity of Mount Elohim.

All this would have been mere speculation, had not diverse places called 'Elohim' actually existed in different parts of peninsular Arabia. In West Arabia, one of them is the historically attested village of al-Lahīm (*'l lhym*, a clear corruption of *'lhym*), in the Medina region of the central Hijaz. Another is the present al-Lihām (*'l lhm*, also a clear corruption of *'lhym*), in the Taif region of the southern Hijaz. The Moses who was the 'man of Elohim' could have come from either place. In northern Yemen, however, some distance west of the 'Horeb' which is the local Ḥārib or Ḥārib al-Gharāmīsh (see above), there is a mountain called Jabal Alhān (*'lhn*), whose name is an Arabicized form of the Biblical *Elōhīm* (*'lhym*). In Hebrew, this place would be called *Har Elōhīm*, or *Har hā-Elōhīm*. It is an inhabited mountain with many villages on its slopes, and a Moses who was a 'man of Elohim' could easily have come from there. Moreover, Jabal Alhān is located in a highly volcanic part of Arabia — the region of *Nār al-Yaman*, the 'Fire of the Yemen', south-west of the city of Sanaa, where volcanoes are well known to have been active in historical times. It is just the sort of place to come across fires that appeared supernatural because they did not seem to consume their fuel — 'the bush was burning, yet it was not consumed'. Then, consider the following:

1. In northern Yemen, there is a 'Midian' other than the Madīnah of Wadi Tathlith to which the historical Moses fled from Mizraim, and where he married the daughter of the man called Reuel. This Yemenite 'Midian' is called Maydān (*mydn*), and the Arabic geographical literature notes that it claims a famous historical well. It could have been at this well that the Moses of Elohim (not the historical Moses), as the story has it, met the daughter of Jethro of Maydān (not of Reuel of Madīnah), and decided to take her for a wife (see above).

2. In the same part of northern Yemen, there is a place called Adamah (*'dmh*), and another called Qadas (*qds*). The name of Adamah, in Hebrew, means 'soil, ground'. That of Qadas (as in the Hebrew *qōdesh*, or *qdš*) means 'holy'; no doubt, the Qadas in question

must have been, at one time, the site of a sacred shrine. When Yahweh reportedly called Moses out of the burning bush at Mount Elohim, he told him: 'Do not come near; put off your shoes from your feet, for the place on which you are standing is *'dmt qdš'* (traditionally taken to mean 'holy ground'). The expression for 'holy ground' in Hebrew would actually be *'dmh qdšh*, not *'dmt qdš*, which is a construct of two nouns, not a noun followed by an adjective. The construct can mean 'the ground of holiness'. More readily, however, it would mean 'the ground of Qadas'; even better, 'the Adamah of Qadas' (Arabic *Adamat Qadas*; or *'dmt qds*). What is indicated is not the abstract concept of 'holy ground', but the particular sanctity of the actual site of Qadas, or of the Adamah of Qadas, near Jabal Alhān, in the northern Yemen.

3. Again in the same area of the Yemen, there is a large village called Milyān (*mlyn*). According to Exodus 4:24, Moses, on his way from Midian (4:19) to Mount Elohim (4:27), passed or stopped at what Biblical translations take to have been a 'lodging place' (*mlwn*, traditionally vocalized *mālōn*) (RSV). As a term, *mlwn* in Hebrew can mean a 'lodging place'. Here, however, it seems to be none other than the present village of Milyān, in the Yemen, between Maydān, or 'Midian', and Jabal Alhān, or 'Mount Elohim'.

In Exodus 3 and 4, as elsewhere, the story of Moses of Elohim is fused at every step with the story of the historical Moses of Mizraim. When Yahweh spoke to Moses of Elohim out of the burning bush at Mount Elohim, in what I take to be the original version of this story, he said nothing to him about the deliverance of the people of Israel from their affliction and sufferings in Mizraim (the interpolated passages in 3:7-12, 16-22; 4:1f.). All he did was to introduce himself by name (3:14), saying '*Ehyeh* is what I am' (*'hyh 'šr 'hyh*) (traditionally taken to mean 'I am what I am'), and distinctly asking to be called *Ehyeh* (*'hyh*). This *Ehyeh*, rather than being the ordinary Hebrew for 'I am' was apparently a local, South Arabian variant of the name of Yahweh (*yhwh*), surviving to this day as the name of the village of Hiyāy (*hyy*), in the southernmost parts of the Asir highlands, close to the present Yemen border. The response of Moses of Elohim to Yahweh, when he called him out of the 'burning bush' at Jabal Alhān, must have been negative, for the 'anger' of Yahweh was reportedly 'kindled' against him forthwith (4:14). Then, as the Moses of the same story was travelling between Midian (Maydān) and Mount Elohim (Jabal Alhān), something very strange happened to him at Malon (Milyān) (4:24-26):

On the way, at Malon,
  Yahweh met him and sought to kill him.
Then Zipporah took a flint and cut off her son's foreskin,
  and reached to his feet (*w-tgʿ l-rglyw*)
  and said: 'Surely then,
  you are a bridegroom of two bloods (*htn dmym*) to me.'
So he let him alone.
  Then it was that she said:
  'You are my bridegroom of two bloods (*ḥtn dmym*)
  for circumcisions (*l-mlwt*).'

Does this story make any sense in the context of the career of historical, human and rational Moses? As I see it, the story is pure mythology, in which not just Yahweh, but all the characters are gods. The myth involved, which is related to the rite of circumcision, is not unlike that of the Abram of Genesis 15 (chapter 4). Moses of Elohim was apparently a 'redeemer' god of some ancient South Arabian mystery cult, and Zipporah, originally his virgin mother rather than his wife, was also a goddess. As in other mystery cults of the ancient Near East, the consort of a god can be his mother or sister who subsequently becomes his wife. In Christianity, the Virgin Mary is miraculously fertilized by God, so that she becomes essentially the wife of God, and also the mother of God (as the man Jesus) at the same time. At one time, it appears, the cult of the 'redeemer' Moses and his virgin mother Zipporah was not unlike that of Jesus and his virgin mother Mary, before it was suppressed and absorbed into the cult of Yahweh.

In the story we have salvaged out of the confused text of Exodus 3 and 4, Yahweh calls to the god Moses out of a volcano at Mount Elohim and apparently demands from him the surrender of his divinity, which he refuses. So the anger of Yahweh is kindled against him, and he seeks to kill him. Thereupon his virgin mother Zipporah intervenes to allay the wrath of Yahweh by sacrificing to him the foreskin of the recalcitrant 'redeemer' god who is her son. Having done this, she then crawls to her son's feet and recognizes him as her 'bridegroom', by virtue of the blood of his circumcision which she had personally performed, and which is the allegorical equivalent of the blood of her bridal hymen (hence the term *dmym* in the myth, which makes the best sense in context as the dual rather than the plural of *dm*, 'blood'). Having lost her hymen and become an ordinary 'bride', Zipporah ceases to be a goddess. Likewise, having lost his foreskin and become an ordinary 'bridegroom', Moses of Elohim ceases to be a god. So Yahweh leaves the two of them in peace. From being a god in his own right, Moses is now reduced to an agent of Yahweh. It is as an ordinary mortal, an agent of Yahweh, that his character comes to be fused with that of the historical Moses in the text of Exodus.

As usual, topographical evidence from West Arabia exists to underline the Biblical myth. In the same highlands of Asir, by the borders of the Yemen, where the name of Yahweh survives in the village of Hiyāy, there is another village, close by, called al-Mūsh (*'l-mwš*), the 'god Moses', not to mention a number of other villages called al-Mūsā or Āl Mūsā (*'l mws'*, also the 'god Moses') in regions further to the north. In the same vicinity as al-Mūsh there is the village of Āl Dammām (*'l dmm*, cf. Hebrew *dmym*), indicating a 'god of two bloods'; also the village of Āl Maylah (*'l mylh*, cf. Hebrew *mwlh*, 'circumcision'), whose name stands for a 'god of circumcision'. Not far to the south-east, in the valley of Wadi Najran, the village of Āl Ẓafīrah (*'l zṕrh*) still carries the name of the 'goddess Zipporah' (Biblical *ṣprh*). The conjunction of these topographical names in the same area cannot be pure coincidence. Moreover, uncanny as it may seem, it is possible to fix in the Yemen the exact site of the myth of the circumcision of the god Moses, and the loss of his virginity to the goddess who had formerly been his virgin mother. It is the village called to this day Qulfat al-'Udhr: literally, the 'foreskin of virginity', also meaning the 'foreskin of circumcision'. You can find the site and read the name for yourself on the Bartholomew World Travel Map of the Arabian peninsula. It is located along the main road between Sanaa and Saadah.

Moses of Elohim appears once again in the tangled text of Exodus (24:13, 15-18), where a Mount Sinai (*hr syny*) is mentioned side by side with Mount Elohim (*hr h-'lhym*). The Mount Sinai in question could not have been in the Egyptian Sinai peninsula, because this Sinai is not volcanic, whereas the Mount Sinai of Exodus definitely was (see below). No doubt it was the mountain ridge at the upper reaches of Ẉadi Sayān (*syn*), in the northern Yemen, at Jabal Alhān or Mount Elohim. Here is what happened:

> Moses rose up...
> and Moses went up into Mount Elohim...
> Moses went up into the mountain,
> and a cloud covered the mountain.
> The glory of Yahweh settled on Mount Sinai,
> and the cloud covered it six days;
> and on the seventh day he called to Moses
> out of the midst of the cloud.
> Now the appearance of the glory of Yahweh
> was as a devouring fire on top of the mountain...
> Moses entered the cloud, and went up on the mountain;
> and Moses was on the mountain forty days
> and forty nights.

It appears that Yahweh, at least according to one tradition, was originally the god of the volcanic fire of *Nār al-Yaman*. Here is another account of him as a volcanic phenomenon in Exodus (excerpted from 19:10-20):

> Yahweh said to Moses: 'Go to the people and sanctify them today and tomorrow... for on the third day Yahweh will come down in the sight of all the people on Mount Sinai. You shall set bounds to the people round about... for whoever touches the mountain shall be put to death. No hand will touch him; but he will surely be stoned or shot through. Whether beast or man, it shall not live....' And on the third day, in the morning, there were thunders and lightnings, and a thick cloud on the mountain.... Mount Sinai was all in smoke, because Yahweh had descended on it in fire; and its smoke rose as the smoke of a furnace, and the whole mountain quaked greatly.... Yahweh came down on Mount Sinai, on the top of the mountain....

From another passage in Exodus (24:10), we learn that the volcano god Yahweh, the 'devouring fire on top of the mountain', was actually represented there by an idol: 'under its feet, as it were, a paved work of sapphire stone, as clear as the sky'. When the local volcano was quiet and the site was approachable, the privileged initiates of the Yahweh cult could visit the idol, 'see' this god (24:10) without being harmed, and even 'eat and drink' in his presence (24:11).

Once he had ceased to be a god in his own right, Moses of Elohim came to be recognized as the 'redeemer' of his people from the unpredictable and destructive wrath of Yahweh. As the 'man of Elohim', he reportedly persuaded Yahweh, with whom he alone could speak 'face to face' (33:11), to abandon his original home in the terrible volcanic crater at Jabal Alhān and establish a residence for himself among his followers. According to Exodus (25:8 - 27:19), Yahweh agreed to this, provided a special 'sanctuary' — a 'tabernacle' — was reserved for him outside the main encampment of the people, with a special retinue of priests to guard him. To his new sanctuary among his folk, however, Yahweh brought his special 'sign' to recall his volcanic past. It was the 'pillar of smoke' which always stood at the entrance to the 'tabernacle' (33:9-10).

Could it be that Moses, the 'man of Elohim', was originally a high priest of the cult of the volcano god Yahweh in the northern Yemen, who came to be recognized for some time by a heresy of that cult as a 'redeemer' god in his own right? This could well have been the case, considering that Jethro, the alleged father of his consort Zipporah, was a priest — perhaps his mentor in the Yahweh cult. From Exodus 34:33-35, we learn that Moses used to wear a veil to cover his face from the people, and only remove his veil when alone in the presence of Yahweh. According to the Arab historians of early Islamic times, some of the high priests of Arabia before Islam were regularly veiled. Among them was the high priest of Yamamah, Maslamah Ibn Habib, better remembered as Musaylamah, who was a contemporary of the prophet Muhammad. He definitely covered his face with a veil, as Moses of Elohim reportedly did in his own time.

In the book of Psalms there is the text of a prayer (*tplh*) attributed to 'Moses the man of Elohim' (Psalm 90) which could well have been his own work, or one composed at an early time in the highlands of the northern Yemen, where the worship of Yahweh as a local volcano *'l*, or 'god', had originated:

Lord, you have been a support (*m'wn*) to us
from generation to generation.
Before the mountains were born,
or you had formed the earth and the world —
from ever and for ever you are a god (*'th 'l*).
You turn people to dust and say:
'Return, O mankind!'
For a thousand years in your eyes
are as yesterday that passes,
and as a watch in the night...
Who knows the power of your anger?
Your wrath is as your awe.
Teach us, therefore, to keep count of our days,
that we may become wise...

The son of Amram

We shall leave Moses of Elohim at this point and turn to another Moses, the 'son' of Amram and the 'brother' of Aaron who, contrary to the claim made in Exodus 6:26-27 (see above) was certainly not the historical Moses who redeemed the Hebrew Israelites from their bondage in Mizraim. According to Numbers 26:59, this Moses also had a sister called Miriam. The same Miriam is referred to in Exodus 15:20 as a 'prophetess' and a sister of Aaron, with no mention of Moses as her brother. While the Moses of Elohim represents a South Arabian tradition and belongs in the Yemen, the Moses who was the 'son' of Amram and the 'brother' of Aaron and Miriam, was a Moses of the Taif and Zahran regions of the Hijaz — the homeland of Abram the Aramean and his alleged descendants who were Isaac, Jacob and Judah. Most probably, he was originally revered there as a 'redeemer' by the local Aramean folk who later joined the confederation of Israel. The topographical survival of his own name in that territory, along with that of his 'father', his 'brother' and his 'sister', suggests that all four of them were originally gods:

1. Amram (*'mrm*, Koranic 'Umrān, or *'mrn*): Āl 'Amrīn (*'l 'mrn*, the 'god' *'mrn*), the name of two villages in the Taif region.
2. Aaron (*'hrn*): the village of Hawrān (*hwrn*), on the maritime slopes of the Zahran region.
3. Miriam (*mrym*): the village of Āl Maryam (*'l mrym*, the 'goddess

Miriam'), near Hawrān, or 'Aaron', in the same valley of the Zahran region.

4. Moses (*mšh*): the village of al-Mūsā (*'l mws'*, the 'god Moses', with the regular Arabic form of the name), in the Zahran highlands, uphill from Hawrān and Āl Maryam.

In the Biblical story of Moses, Aaron is introduced at every stage, and Miriam at some stages, with the purpose of identifying their 'brother', Moses son of Amram, with the historical Moses of Mizraim. Where Exodus starts to relate the story of the historical Moses, his father and mother are left unnamed (2:1). There is a brief reference to the fact that he had an older 'sister' (2:4, 7), who could have been merely a 'kinswoman' (the word in Hebrew is the same); but she is also left unnamed. On the other hand, no mention is made of a 'brother'.

It is only in Exodus 4:14 that Aaron is first introduced as the 'brother' of Moses, who was to serve as his 'mouth' and speak for him, as Moses himself was reportedly 'not eloquent', and 'slow of speech and tongue' (4:10f.). At this point in the Exodus narrative, the historical Moses is already confused with Moses of Elohim and Moses the son of Amram, both of whom were gods. In gnostic religions it is not uncommon to distinguish between the silent god, whose existence can only be inferred, and a subordinate speaking god, in whose person the transcendental reality of the silent god becomes manifest. In Islam there are esoteric sects which to this day distinguish between 'silent' prophets, of whom Moses is considered the prototype, and 'speaking' prophets, of whom the prototype is taken to be Aaron. In West Arabia, this distinction between 'silent' and 'speaking' gods or prophets must have been a gnostic concept of immemorial antiquity.

There were actually two Aarons, not one, who came to be identified in the Hebrew Bible as the 'brother' of the historical Moses. First, the Aaron who died on the top of Mount Hor (*hr h-hr*, Numbers 20:23f.), today Jabal Harrah (*hr*) in the Zahran highlands. Second, the Aaron who died in Moserah (*mwśrh*), near the 'wells of the people of Jaakan' (*b'rt bny y'qn*, Deuteronomy 10:6) — today Maysiriyyah (*mysryh*), near Wujay'an (*wǧy'n*), in the Qasim region north-east of Taif. The fact that there was more than one Aaron is implied in Exodus 6:26–27 (see above) which does not only specify '*this* Moses', but also '*this* Aaron', to distinguish them from others.

Here are some interesting details to consider: in the Biblical story of the exodus as it stands, Aaron, as one person, is depicted as the second-in-command to the historical Moses and also as the founder of the Israelite priesthood. He comports himself throughout with a sacerdotal dignity befitting his high priestly status, except on one occasion, when he reportedly yields to popular pressure in the temporary absence of Moses, and fashions a golden calf, summoning the people of Israel to worship it (Exodus 32:1-35). In Deuteronomy 10:6, it is said that when Aaron died at Moserah, or Maysiriyyah in the Qasim region, he was buried there, and his son Eleazer succeeded him as priest. The Aaron who died there must have been Aaron the priest, and it was he, not the one who died on Mount Hor, who was mourned 'by all the house of Israel' for thirty days (Numbers 20:29, see below). This Aaron had never fashioned a golden calf for the people of Israel to worship: it was not in his character to do so. The Aaron who died on Mount Hor must have been the recalcitrant one who seized the opportunity of the absence of Moses to order the worship of the golden calf. Of this Aaron, and of his equally recalcitrant 'sister' Miriam, the following story is told (Numbers 12:1-15):

Miriam and Aaron criticize Moses for having married a 'Cushite woman' (none other than the daughter of Reuel of Midian, see below). Thereupon Yahweh summons them, upbraids them strongly for having 'done foolishly' and 'sinned', and punishes Miriam by striking her with leprosy. Aaron pleads with Moses for leniency to his sister, but to no avail. As a leper, Miriam is 'shut up outside the camp seven days'. We are told subsequently that she died and was buried, but no public mourning over her death is reported (Numbers 20:1).

Aaron, like Miriam, was punished for his 'foolishness' and 'sin' in due time. Upon the command of Yahweh, who denounced him as a rebel (Numbers 20:24), he was seized by Moses and led up to the top of Mount Hor (Jabal Harrah, in the Zahran highlands) in the sight of all the people of Israel. There Moses had him stripped of his garments, after which 'he died' (20:23-28). There is no mention of his having been buried. When people are stripped of their clothes, they do not automatically die. I would say Moses put the rebel Aaron to death and left his body to rot unburied on the top of Mount Hor.

The Aaron who met such a violent and ignominious end could hardly have been the dignified priest who was mourned by 'all the house of Israel' for thirty days (20:29). The book of Numbers simply confuses him with the priest who happened to be his namesake. Who was he then? Who was his 'sister' Miriam? And what was the real 'sin' for which both of them received such terrible punishments?

My guess is that the offspring of Amram — Aaron, Miriam and the Moses who was their 'brother' — were originally central figures in related cults which rivalled the cult of Yahweh among the Aramean folk of the Taif and Zahran regions of the southern Hijaz. In the cult of Aaron the deity was worshipped as a golden calf. In time, the cult of Moses, among the three, was somehow absorbed into the cult of Yahweh, which ultimately facilitated the Biblical identification of this Moses with the historical Moses of the exodus. The outcome was a clash between the cult of Moses, in association with that of Yahweh, on the one hand, and those of Aaron and Miriam, who refused to be absorbed into the cult of Yahweh, on the other. This ancient clash between rival religious cults of the southern Hijaz was telescoped by the local folk memory into a myth, which was later edited and fused into the Biblical story of the historical Moses.

In the original myth, Aaron and Miriam did not criticize their 'brother' Moses for marrying a 'Cushite woman'. They must have criticized him for something far more serious: yielding his divinity so readily to Yahweh. This, I would suggest, was their grievous 'foolishness' and 'sin', for which Miriam was punished with leprosy and ostracism, and died unmourned, and for which her 'brother' Aaron was stripped naked on top of Mount Hor and put to death.

In Numbers 33:38, we are told that Aaron died on Mount Hor on the first day of the fifth month of the fortieth year of the exodus of the people of Israel from the land of Mizraim. Such accuracy in dating can only relate to a historical event. To my mind, however, this was not the date of the execution of the mythical Aaron on Mount Hor. Rather, it was that of the death of the historical Aaron at Moserah — the priest who was the associate of the historical Moses, without necessarily being his actual brother. Or was he an independent historical figure whose person somehow came to be associated in legend with the figure of the historical Moses? The truth of this matter is difficult to establish.

The historical Moses

Moses the man of Elohim and Moses the son of Amram were probably not the only tribal 'redeemers' whose mythology is fused in the Bible with the story of the historical Moses. With an effort, one may be able to discover others and detect, in detail, how the fusion was made. In the meantime let us turn to the historical Moses. Who was he? How can we ascertain his historicity?

The historical Moses was born in the land of Mizraim, possibly in the city itself (Exodus 2:1f.). He was of undetermined Hebrew parentage and was apparently brought up as an Egyptian of high status (2:10); he also seems to have retained a strong sense of his Hebrew ethnicity (2:11-12). The indications are that in time he came to be deeply involved in the politics of the Egyptian colony of Mizraim. On one occasion the Pharaoh in power and a large faction sought the young man's death for political reasons, forcing him to take flight. He was only able to return to Mizraim when this particular Pharaoh, his mortal enemy, 'died', and a new Pharaoh took over. I would say that the former Pharaoh did not die a natural death, but was overthrown and killed, after which his partisans were seized and executed: how else could 'all the men' who were seeking the life of Moses (4:19) have died at the same time?

During his exile Moses stayed in the 'Midian' which is today Madīnah, in Wadi Tathlith, at a safe distance, but close enough to be able to watch the political developments in Mizraim. He married the daughter of a local notable called Reuel. She appears to have been his only wife. Her brother Hobab, properly identified as the son of Reuel of Midian, is introduced as the brother-in-law of Moses at what must have been a much later stage in his career (Numbers 10:29-33). Originally, Reuel, the father-in-law, had come from Kūthah (*kwṯ*, cf. *kwš*, Biblical 'Cush'), near Mizraim, in upper Wadi Bishah, close by Khamis Mushait. This explains why his daughter, as the wife of Moses, is described as a 'Cushite woman' in Numbers 12:1. That this 'Cushite woman' was none other than the daughter of Reuel of Midian is implicit from the recognition of Reuel's son Hobab in the text of Numbers, as the brother-in-law of Moses, shortly before the 'Cushite woman' is spoken of as his wife. I very much doubt that this woman, like the consort of Moses of Elohim, was called Zipporah (see above); yet the coincidence cannot be entirely ruled out.

Moses, though a Hebrew, was a man of political prominence in Mizraim, as is clear from his behaviour after his return from Midian. He had ready access to Pharaoh, spoke freely in his presence, bargained with him from a position of power, and used strong language in his presence with impunity (Exodus, chapters 4-11 *passim*). He even had the privilege of walking out from interviews with Pharaoh 'in hot anger' (*b-ḥry 'p*, 11:8). Bearing in mind that Pharaoh was the ruler of the Egyptian colony of Mizraim, and that Moses was a politically privileged and ambitious Hebrew whose people lived in that colony under Pharaoh's rule, what were the arguments between the two men actually about?

After the setback he had experienced under the preceding Pharaoh, which had forced him to go into temporary exile in Midian, Moses, it seems, had been turning more and more to his own Hebrew folk in the territory of Mizraim for political support. Because he was of Hebrew origin, his chances for political advancement in Mizraim were limited. The best he could hope for was to become the second man in the colony after the Egyptian Pharaoh. So he decided to lead his Hebrew folk out of the land of Mizraim to establish a new political community elsewhere which would be Hebrew, not Egyptian, and of which he would be the independent ruler. Pharaoh might have opposed the idea in principle, for fear that his territory might in consequence become critically underpopulated. As I see it, however, Pharaoh was also concerned about the direction in which the Hebrews, under the leadership of Moses, proposed to go. The retranslation of a few passages from Exodus, in the light of the topography of West Arabia, illustrates this with the utmost clarity:

1. In the accepted translations, Yahweh says to Moses in Exodus 3:19 (AV): 'I am sure that the king of Egypt (Mizraim) will not let you go, no, not *by a mighty hand* (*w-l' b-yd ḥzqh*).' Here *yd ḥzqh* (vocalized *yād ḥazāqāh*) does not mean 'mighty hand'. Rather, it indicates the 'valley (Hebrew *yd*, Arabic *wādī*, or *wd*) of Ḥazāqāh'. The reference here is to the valley of Wadi Habuna, north of Wadi Najran, where a village called Ḥazqah (exactly *ḥzqh*) is still to be found. The village must originally have given this valley its name. The valley in question is one of the main natural outlets from the southern highlands of Asir into the Yamamah — a stretch of oases in the Arabian interior bordering the plateau of Najd from the south.

A Hebrew community established in Yamamah, in Central Arabia, would have been in a position to control the main caravan route between East and West Arabia, and so gain a stranglehold over the trans-Arabian trade of the Egyptian colony in Mizraim. It must be noted that the Hebrew *yād* is recognized by scholars as being the equivalent of the Arabic *wādī*, or 'valley', in addition to meaning 'hand' (Arabic *yad*). I would translate the Hebrew *w-l' b-yd ḥzqh* to mean '*not even* by Wadi Hazqah'. There are outlets from the Asir highlands into Central Arabia other than Wadi Habuna which are actually more direct (see below).

2. For Exodus 6:26, the accepted translations say: 'These are the Aaron and Moses to whom the Lord (i.e. Yahweh) said, "Bring out the people of Israel from the land of Egypt (Mizraim) *by their hosts* (*'l ṣb'tm*)"'(RSV). To begin with, the Hebrew preposition *'l* means 'on, over, above, onto', but not 'by', which in Hebrew would be *b*. As for *ṣb'tm* (traditionally vocalized *ṣīb'ōthām*), which can mean 'their hosts', it appears to me to indicate the oasis in Central Arabia, north of the Yamamah valley, known today as Ḍabaṭayn (*ḍbṭyn*). What is suggested is a more direct outlet from Wadi Bishah to Central Arabia by way of Wadi al-Dawasir north of Wadi Habuna (see above). My translation here: 'Bring out the people of Israel from the land of Mizraim on to Ḍabaṭayn (*'l ṣb'tm*).'

3. In the accepted translation of Exodus 13:17-18 (RSV), we are told: 'When Pharaoh let the people go, God did not lead them by way of the land of the Philistines (*'rṣ plštym*), although that was near... But God led the people round by way of the wilderness toward the Red Sea (*ym śwp*). And the people of Israel went up out of the land of Egypt (Mizraim) *equipped for battle* (*w-ḥmšym 'lw bny ysr'l m-'rṣ mṣrym*).' Here *ḥmšym* (traditionally vocalized *ḥamūshīm*) has been taken to mean 'equipped for battle'. I am convinced it refers to what is today Khamasīn (exactly *ḫmsyn*), the principal village of Wadi al-Dawasir (see above), which leads directly from inland Asir to the Yamamah and other parts of Central Arabia. Therefore I would retranslate the sentence: 'And the people of Israel went up to Khamāsīn from the land of Mizraim'. The Israelites, apparently warned against proceeding directly from there to Central Arabia, could have turned southwards to the 'valley of Ḥazqah' (*yd ḥzqh*), today Wadi Habuna (see above), close by the desert of Baḥr Ṣāfī, (*ṣṕ*; Biblical *śwp*): literally, in Arabic, the 'sea of Ṣāfī' (cf. Hebrew

ym śwp, vocalized *Yam Sūf*). A Lebanese secondary school teacher was the first to draw my attention to the fact that the Biblical *Yam Sūf* could only have been the Arabian *Baḥr Ṣāfī*. The pastoral fringes of the desert there are still called Bilād Yām (exactly, *ym*, a common Semitic word for 'sea'). Geologically, the area there abounds in ancient lake deposits, which is not surprising. All the valleys of the inland Yemen and Asir drain into it.

4. In connection with the same passage of Exodus, there remains the question of the 'way of the land of the Philistines' (*drk 'rṣ plštym*), which the Israelites avoided taking in their exodus from the land of Mizraim, although it was 'near' (*qrwb*). The 'Philistines' (*plštym*) were the people of Falsah (*ṕlsh*), a village of the Asir highlands flanking Wadi Bishah from the west. By going out from the land of Mizraim through this Falsah, the Israelites would have proceeded northwards to reach the southern Hijaz, which is where Pharaoh actually wanted them to go. Moses, however, wanted to take them to Central Arabia instead, so he diverted from that road and headed eastwards for Khamāsīn. The Egyptians must have blocked the way and forced the Israelites to move southwards from Khamāsīn in the direction of Wadi Habuna, where an Egyptian force was also lying in wait, as we shall ultimately see.

5. In Exodus 14:8, we are told that the people of Israel were pursued by Pharaoh as they went *b-yd rmh*, traditionally take to mean 'with a high hand' (AV), i.e. 'defiantly'. Actually, Moses had first led the Israelites out of the land of Goshen to Succoth (12:37). In analysing the story of Joseph (chapter 6), we have already noted that Goshen is the present Ghithān, in the Balqarn hill country of northern Asir, flanking the lower course of Wadi Bishah from the west. As for Succoth (*śkt*) it is today the village of Āl Skūt (exactly *skt*), a short distance to the south of Ghithān, or 'Goshen'. From this 'Succoth' the Israelites proceeded to nearby Rīmah (*rmh*). Having arrived there, they turned eastwards, heading towards Khamāsīn in Wadi al-Dawasir, by way of the 'valley of Rīmah' (*b-yd rmh*). There is actual geography rather than a 'high hand' or 'defiance' in question.

The Egyptians, clearly, did not wish to see Moses establish a strong Hebrew community in the Yamamah and the adjacent parts of Central Arabia, where these Hebrews would have controlled the immediate hinterland of Mizraim. They preferred the Hebrews to go elsewhere to the north, far from Mizraim, where they would be kept at a safe distance. The bargaining between Pharaoh and Moses was over this issue. It was finally agreed that the Hebrews would go northwards, but they remained determined to attempt the forbidden exit into Central Arabia. Thus, having gathered themselves in Āl Skūt, the Biblical 'Succoth', in the hill country west of Wadi Bishah, they moved down Wadi Rīmah (Biblical *yd rmh*) to the point of its confluence with Wadi Bishah, and from there headed eastwards to the village of Khamāsīn, which overlooks Wadi al-Dawasir, hoping to make a direct exit into the Yamamah region from there. Stopped by the Egyptians at that strategic point, they moved south to attempt another exit from Wadi Habuna, where they encamped 'above Zephon' (*b-'l ṣpn*, not *b'l ṣpn*, or 'Baal-zephon', as the expression is usually rendered, 14:2). The place indicated is today still called Ṣafan (exactly *ṣṕn*) — a village adjacent to Wadi Habuna from the south. As the awaiting Egyptian forces moved down into the valley to block the Hebrew access into the Yamamah, they were reportedly destroyed and washed away into the wastes of *Yam Sūf* — not the 'Red Sea', but the desert of Baḥr Ṣāfī — by the waters of what could only have been an unexpected flash flood (14:20-30). To appreciate the effect of flood in the area, here is a report about the one which occurred in 1918 in Wadi Tathlith, not far from Wadi Habuna (Fuad Hamza, *Fī Bilād 'Asīr*, Riyadh, 1951, p. 146):

> In 1918, there was a great flood in Wadi Tathlith. It broke through the sand dunes which separate it from Wadi al-Dawasir at Makhtamiyyah, and overwhelmed Wadi al-Dawasir, washing away many of its villages... The flood continued for days, irresistible. The place where it broke through the sand dunes came to be called the Burst of Makhtamiyyah.

A much smaller flood in Wadi Habuna would have sufficed to wash away Pharaoh and his forces to the wastes of Baḥr Ṣāfī, leaving the bodies of the Egyptians lying dead on the edges of the desert after the flood waters had receded (14:30).

It is, in fact, the perfect geographical accuracy of the trek of the Hebrew exodus from Mizraim, when followed on the map of Arabia, that establishes the historicity of the exodus, and of its leader Moses, beyond the shadow of a doubt. Between Egypt and Palestine, this trek cannot be followed at all; for this reason, there are a number of theories about it, some of which doubt that a Hebrew exodus on the scale described in the Bible ever took place. In Arabia, however, this exodus — starting not from 'Egypt', but from the Egyptian colony of Mizraim in Wadi Bishah — can be followed stage by stage (see map p. 140). However I shall spare the reader its reconstruction in this chapter (for the full details, see the Appendix). What remains important is this: there was a historical Moses; there is much accurate information about him in the Bible with its authenticity beyond question; and this information can be salvaged from the maze of legendary and mythical lore with which it is fused. Perhaps, one day, we may have a proper biography of Moses, which his towering stature in world history more than deserves.

9
The Man Who Saw It Happen

In the preceding chapters, we have re-examined the content of the more important Torah stories — as myth, legend or history — against the geographical background of Arabia, on the assumption that they are actually Arabian lore. In the chapter that follows, we shall turn from the Torah to consider the Biblical story of Jonah in the same light. Before doing so, it would be useful to stop and make a summary inventory of what we have learned so far, and assess the degree to which our experiment has been successful.

The pagan origins of Judaism

It has long been accepted that Yahweh, the One God of the Hebrew Bible, was originally a tribal god among many. From our experiment with the Torah stories which speak of him, we have gathered a rich harvest of information about the pantheon to which he originally belonged, and the colourful mythology with which he was connected in ancient Arabia. Here, at one time, every conceivable notion, no matter how abstract, appears to have been represented by a god or goddess, to whom different powers and functions were assigned. To begin with there was a wide array of nature deities: Āl Sādī (Biblical El Shaddai), a mountain god; Āl ʻAlyān (Biblical El Elyon), a god of elevations or mountain country; Āl Sarah (Biblical Sarah), a goddess of the Asir highlands, at first barren, until she is made fertile by Abū Ruhm (Biblical Abraham), the god of drizzling rain and dry-farming. The product of the marriage between Āl Sarah and Abū Ruhm is Isaac (Arabic *Ḍaḥḥāk*, the 'overflowing one') as a god of wells, and hence of irrigation. In the mythology of ancient Arabia, this potent god of wells, by whose 'thigh' (or phallus) people swore, marries Rebekkah, a goddess of fecundity and feminine guile, who bears him twin sons, both of them gods of male fertility: Āl 'Īsā (Biblical Esau), a rugged god of unbridled male promiscuity; and Āl 'Uqbah (Jacob), a smooth god of domesticated masculinity, and hence of regular progeny and family life. Āl 'Īsā is the firstborn of the twins, but Āl 'Uqbah, acting under his mother's guidance, tricks him out of his birthright, thereby establishing the triumph of domestic sex over the 'firstborn', or more archaic, urge of sexual licence.

With Āl 'Īsā and Āl 'Uqbah, we are already moving from the realm of nature gods to that of gods of concepts. Here the ancient Arabian pantheon had countless deities. Āl Ḥayāt, for example, was a god of the abstract concept of life, represented in the Garden of Eden (Junaynah, in Wadi Bishah) by the Tree of Life. Āl Ḥayyah (Biblical Eve), on the other hand, was a goddess of motherhood, and hence of 'all living creatures' or actual life. At the same time, we have Āl Bashar, the god of live flesh, whose vegetarian cult forbade the eating of meat. There was the god of ethical knowledge, Āl Da'yā, represented in the garden of Eden by the Tree of Knowledge. His associate and link with the human world was the serpent god Āl Ḥanīshah, standing for the related but more practical concepts of wisdom, cleverness and wiliness.

Gods were also recognized as representing diverse aspects of human society and social institutions. Āl Nayīḥ (Biblical Noah) was a god of human settlements. His chief ally was Āl Thābit, the god of stability, who guaranteed the continuity and regularity of settled community life. Āl Nayīḥ, however, had another ally: the rainbow god Āl Qays, who guaranteed the regularity of the seasons, his main functions being to tame the ferocity of the cloud god Āl 'Inān, who could devastate human settlements with torrential floods. Āl Shāfī, also called Āl Lisān, was a god of unified speech who promoted understanding and co-operation among people. His natural adversary was Āl Balāl, the polyglot god of misunderstanding and confusion. While Āl Lisān strove hard to bring people together and keep them unified, Āl Balāl strove equally hard to disperse them, destroy their unity, and divide them into different nations, speaking different tongues.

Yet other gods were Āl Rūyah (Biblical El Roi), the god of seeing; Āl Sham'ah (Biblical Ishmael), the god of hearing; Āl Yūsif (Biblical Joseph), also called Āl Yazīd, a god of increase and worldly success, conceived of as being a son of the fertility god Āl 'Uqbah (Jacob). Āl Baram (the Abram of Genesis 15) was a god of male continence and virgin sterility, whose sexual potency could only be unleashed by circumcision. Āl Maylah obligingly served as a god of circumcision for this purpose, making young men ready for marriage, while his associate Āl Dammām, as a god of marriage, stood for the fusion of the 'two bloods': those of the circumcision of the bridegroom and the hymen of the bride.

All these gods and goddesses and many others functioned in their different capacities, undisturbed in the vast pan-Arabian pantheon, until the strangest of all appeared in the local mythology: Yahweh, who hailed from the volcano of Jabal Alhān, the 'mountain of the gods' in northern Yemen. At one time, the original home territory of Yahweh was devastated by an enormous flood, forcing many people to migrate northwards into the Hijaz. One consequence of this migration, it seems, was the introduction of the Yahweh cult to the Hijaz, where the volcanic Medina region could have provided a second home base for this fiery god. In the books of Genesis and Exodus, we have, preserved between the lines, a record of the mythological career of Yahweh as he set out to establish his dominance over the pan-Arabian pantheon.

In a tribal society, such as that of ancient Arabia, it was only natural to conceive of the gods as a tribe of divine beings (the *Benēy hā-Elōhīm*), not unlike human tribes. From the outset, however, Yahweh stood apart from this 'tribe of the gods'. While others consorted freely with mankind to produce races of demigods and giants, Yahweh maintained a splendid aloofness, refusing to contaminate himself with the innate weakness of humanity. According to myth, he would not permit ordinary people even to approach him or see his face. Even those to whom he chose to be especially 'gracious' and 'merciful' were only allowed a fleeting glance of his 'back parts' (Hebrew *'ḥr*, cf. root and derivatives of Arabic *'ḫr*, 'end, bottom, behind', Exodus 33:23).

Among his devotees, Yahweh, with his eccentric habits and unpredictable moods, was conceived as the creator of the universe and everything in it, which to his followers gave him an original pre-eminence over all other divine beings. As a mountain god whose original ḥome was on the volcanic ridge of Jabal Alhān, Yahweh could readily be identified with other mountain gods, such as El Shaddai and El Elyon. It was a different matter, however, with other deities of the Arabian pantheon. A special mythology was elaborated to explain how Yahweh, in his determination to establish himself as the supreme god, and ultimately as the One God, robbed these other deities of their special powers and prerogatives by invading their territories, trespassing over their preserves, pitting them against one another, or playing on their individual weaknesses. Thus, for example, he reduced the gods of life and knowledge to trees in a sacred grove guarded by the cherubim, who were his own priests. The god of prudence and subtlety was turned into a crawling serpent; the goddess of motherhood into a real woman, subject to man, condemned to bear his offspring in pain; the god of human settlements into an actual human settlement; the god of stability into the hulk of an ark; the god of torrential floods into a cloud; the god of the seasons into a rainbow in that cloud. In time he came to be identified as El Roi, the god of seeing, while assuming at the same time the functions of the god of hearing. He also trespassed on the realm of fertility, claiming it as his own — on one occasion, by hitting the god Āl 'Uqbah (Biblical Jacob) on the sinew of his hip, the repository of his generative powers, which left him forever limping. The whole clan of fertility gods and goddesses, represented by Abū Ruhm (Biblical Abraham) and his extended family, were ultimately depotentized and transformed into ordinary human beings — the eponymous ancestors of different Arabian tribes carrying their names.

Once his triumph over the pan-Arabian pantheon was complete, this one-time volcano god, who formerly announced his terrible but invisible presence with fire, blinding smoke and earthquakes, underwent a complete transformation. He now emerged, unrivalled, as the *Elōhīm* or supreme God of Absolute Being, who reportedly chose for himself the name *Ehyeh*, literally 'I am' (Exodus 3:14). As the supreme God of Being, he remained invisible, elusive and unapproachable. His existence, however, permeated all creation. It was this transformed Yahweh, intolerant of the worship of any other deity, who became the One God of Moses and the prophets — the God of the Bible, whose commandments and pronouncements were to be the recognized law and ethics of the universe for all time.

The prehistory of Israel

Our experiment with the Torah has not only yielded a rich fund of information on the pagan origins of the cult of Yahweh, from which Judaism and Christianity, in turn, ultimately developed as world religions. From our restudy of the Torah stories in the light of Arabian geography, we have also learned a great deal about the origins of the ancient Israelites of Arabia — the historical people to whose genius we owe the Bible. Israel was originally the name of a Canaanite-speaking 'Hebrew' tribe of shepherd folk inhabiting the coastal hill country of Asir in the Qunfudhah hinterland, whose special god was apparently El Elyon. These original Israelites, and other related tribes of the region, considered themselves to be descended from a common ancestor, or 'exalted father' (*'b rm*, or 'Abram'). Other West Arabian folk also claimed their 'exalted fathers', or 'Abrams', including the native inhabitants of the Wadi Bishah basin in inland Asir, who worshipped El Shaddai; also the originally Aramean Jacob cattle folk of the Zahran highlands in southern Hijaz, whose god was Yahweh.

Some time in the nineteenth century BC, if we accept the testimony of the book of Exodus,[1] coastal Asir was hit by a severe famine, forcing the Hebrew Israelite inhabitants to migrate inland and settle in the vicinity of Ghithān (Biblical Goshen), on the western side of the Wadi Bishah basin. The local shepherd folk worshipped El Shaddai, and the Israelite immigrants apparently merged with them. In any case, the god of the Hebrew Israelites, El Elyon, came to be identified with the Wadi Bishah god El Shaddai. Wadi Bishah then, including the Ghithān vicinity, formed part of the Egyptian colony of Mizraim, whose capital, in the upper reaches of the valley, survives by name as the village of Miṣrāmah, near the modern city of Khamis Mushait. An Egyptianized Hebrew, originally called Joseph (or so it is said), had risen to high office in Mizraim under the Egyptian name Zaphenath-paneah. While this Zaphenath-paneah lived, the Israelite settlers in the land of Ghithān could thrive under his protection.

1. Exodus 12:40-41 states that the Israelites lived in the land of Mizraim for 430 years. Granting that the Israelites left Mizraim in 1440 BC (chapter 8), they would have originally arrived to settle in Mizraim in 1870 BC. In the absence of evidence to the contrary, there is no reason to doubt the date.

In time, however, the situation changed. As the Israelites in Wadi Bishah grew in number, the Egyptian colonists began to regard them as a threat. Beginning with the middle decades of the fifteenth century BC, the colonists took measures to curb the growing power of the Israelites, placing them under strict supervision and setting them to forced labour, building cities and tending fields — the sort of menial work which pastoral folk have always considered particularly repugnant, much as bedouins do to this day. At that time, an Israelite who is only remembered by his honorific title 'Moses', meaning the 'redeemer', entered the scene. This Moses had been raised as an Egyptian, was deeply involved in the contentious internal politics of Mizraim, and naturally sought a power base among his own Hebrew people. When his political ambitions in Mizraim were somehow frustrated, he decided to lead his people out of the Egyptian-held Wadi Bishah, to establish them as an independent political community under his leadership in Central Arabia, between the Yamamah region and the oasis of Ḍabaṭayn, in Najd. The Egyptians had established the colony of Mizraim with the express purpose of securing the trade of Egypt with South and East Arabia, and were determined not to permit the Israelites access to Central Arabia. They did not want the Israelites to become a thorn in their side, by controlling the vital trade routes with the East Arabian coastlands. At first, they refused to allow the Israelites even to leave Wadi Bishah, as their labour was badly needed. When finally persuaded to let the Israelites go, the Egyptians insisted that they had to migrate not eastwards to the strategic Yamamah region, but northwards to the Hijaz, a safe distance away, with little possibility of causing trouble or harm.

Having secured Egyptian permission to leave, the Israelites, still determined to move into the Yamamah region, made a final bid to reach there by way of the oasis of Khamāsīn in Wadi al-Dawasir. When the Egyptians barred their exit, they turned southwards to attempt another crossing to the Yamamah from Wadi Habuna. The Egyptians tried to bar their exit by that route too, but a flash flood in that valley destroyed their forces. The Israelites hailed the event as divine intervention in their favour, and set out now from Wadi Habuna to the wasteland of Baḥr Ṣāfī (the Biblical *Yam Sūf*, which is not the 'Red Sea'). From this point, they decided to proceed no further in the direction of Central Arabia, realizing that the Egyptians were still determined to prevent them from reaching that area. They had successfully defied the Egyptians by making an exit in that direction; this was a sufficient triumph. Now wisdom dictated that they should move elsewhere.

In the Appendix, the course of the Israelites in their forty-year migration is followed in West Arabia step by step. After their exit to Baḥr Ṣafī from Wadi Habuna, they turned southwards, then back in the direction of the west, crossing the Yemen mountains to attempt a settlement in the coastal Jizan region. The northern Yemen, as already noted, was the homeland of the volcanic god Yahweh. As they passed, the Israelites apparently witnessed a spectacular eruption of the volcano of Jabal Alhān, where Yahweh was thought to dwell. Highly impressed by the experience, they readily adopted Yahweh as their god, identifying him with their own El Elyon, whom they had earlier identified with El Shaddai during their long stay in Wadi Bishah. Thus, while we find Yahweh identified by name as Elyon in Deuteronomy 32:8-9, we read the following in Exodus 6:2-3, where for the first time the secret is given away:

> And God said to Moses:
> 'I am Yahweh.
> I appeared to Abraham, to Isaac and to Jacob as El Shaddai;
> by my name Yahweh I did not make myself known to them.'

Having descended into the Jizan lowlands from the Yemen mountains, the Israelites were forced to flee onwards due to the stiff resistance to their settlement by the people of Amalek (the Biblical *'mlqy*, or 'Amalekites', from *'mlq* — today the village of the Jizan region called Ma'ālīq (*m'lq*)). So the Israelites turned northwards. Passing through the hill country of coastal Asir to the Zahran lowlands, then moving uphill, they crossed the escarpment into the Zahran highlands. Here, for the first time, they came into direct contact with the Aramean Jacob folk of the tribe of Judah (chapter 7), who were old Yahweh worshippers, as the Hebrew Israelites had recently become. With the devotion to Yahweh as a common bond, the Jacob and Israel folk lost little time before agreeing to enter into a confederation under the leadership of Moses, thus forming the people of 'All Israel' (*kl ysr'l*, first mentioned in Deuteronomy 1:1).

One day a careful restudy of the relevant passages of the book of

Numbers may reveal exactly how this confederation of 'All Israel' was negotiated and actualized between the Jacob and Israel folk. For the moment, all that can be asserted is that the Biblical term 'All Israel' has a special historical significance. It does not simply denote all the people of Israel. It refers specifically to the confederation established under Moses in the fortieth year after the exodus, between two different ethnic groups, the Jacob folk and the Israelites, whose initial bond was the common worship of Yahweh.

Balaam: the man who saw it happen

One witness to the historical act of union between the Jacob and Israel folk in the Zahran region was Balaam, whose story is told in the book of Numbers, chapters 22-24. In his time this Balaam, apparently a devotee of Yahweh, was a renowned practitioner of divination and charged substantial fees for his services. He came from the Qasim area, which borders the Taif and Medina regions from the east, where the village of Bil'ām (*bl'm*) still carries his name (Biblical *bl'm*, standard contraction of the Arabic *ab al-'amm*, 'father of the people') — probably not his personal name, but a designation by which members of a local dynasty or cult of divines used to be known.

Balaam, in his own words (Numbers 23:7), said that he came from Aram (*'rm*), from the hill country of Qedem (*qdm*). In chapters 4 and 7, Aram, as the land of the Biblical Arameans, has been identified as the inland territory of the Hijaz, between Taif and Medina, including the region of Qasim. This territory actually comprises the basin of the upper course of Wadi al-Rimmah (*rm*, cf. *'rm*, or 'Aram') and its branching tributaries. The 'hill country of Qedem' (Biblical *hrry qdm*, traditionally taken to mean 'eastern mountains', or 'mountains of the east') is none other than the Qasim region itself, where the Jadhmā (*ğḏm*) folk are still to be found (see p. 131). The king of Moab, a certain Balak, sent after Balaam, we are told, 'to Pethor, which is near the river, the land of his kinsfolk' (*ptwrh 'šr 'l nhr 'rṣ bny 'mw*, 22:5, the expression *'rṣ bny 'mw* here meaning clearly 'the land of his kinsfolk', not 'the land of Amaw', as in some modern translations). The Pethor (*ptwrh*, essentially *ptr*) in question would be the present oasis of Ṭarafiyyah (*trṕ*), on the 'river' or 'water-course' (*nhr*) of Wadi al-Rimmah, whose different tributaries meet in the Qasim region. The village of Bil'ām, which still carries Balaam's name, is found in the same vicinity.

The story of how this Balaam, originally commissioned to pronounce curses against the people of Israel (22:6), was forced by Yahweh to announce favourable oracles instead, can be read as related in the book of Numbers. It bears no relevance to the argument of this chapter. What is important, however, are his four preserved oracles, which distinguish no less than six times between 'Jacob' and 'Israel' (Numbers 23:7, 10, 21, 23; 24:5, 17), in one particularly revealing case also speaking jointly of 'Jacob and Israel' (23:23), thus clearly indicating that two different groups of people were involved in the Israelite union. Two of these oracles, as we read them in the Bible today, bear the clear marks of later redaction. There are references in both to a 'king' or 'sceptre' rising from Israel (obviously King Saul of the Israelite tribe of Benjamin); and one predicts the ultimate political dominance of Jacob in the confederation (an equally obvious reference to King David of the Jacob tribe of Judah, who rose against Saul and replaced him, thus becoming the founder of the dynasty of Judah in Jerusalem). Those are *ex post facto* predictions, interpolated into the original text of the oracles of Balaam at a much later time. Nevertheless, they are equally relevant for the present argument.

At the time when Balaam is introduced on the Biblical scene, the career of Moses was already nearing its end, and the Israelites had reached the final stages of their wanderings, having arrived in the Zahran highlands and 'settled in the plains of Moab, from Eber to the ridge of Jericho' (my translation of 22:1, *w-yḥnw b-'rbwt mw'b m-'br l-yrdn yrḥw*, which readers knowledgeable in Biblical Hebrew may compare with the standing translations). In *The Bible Came from Arabia*, I identified the Biblical land of Moab as the stretch of the Hijaz highlands lying south of Taif, including parts of the Zahran region. Jericho (*yrḥw*), in that area, is the present Warākh (*wrḫ*), at the north-eastern end of the Zahran highlands, while Eber (my reading of *'br*) is Ghabar (*ġbr*), a village of the Ghamid highlands which are adjacent to the Zahran region from the south. Almost midway between Warākh and Ghabar lies the village of al-Mūsā (see Appendix) where, on the first day of the eleventh month in the fortieth year after the exodus, Moses rose for the first time to address 'All Israel' and communicate to them, in a long discourse, 'all that Yahweh had given him in commandment to them' (Deuteronomy 1:1-3f.).

Regardless of the explanations cited in the book of Numbers as to why Balaam, who was originally commissioned by Balak king of Moab to curse Jacob and Israel, decided to bless them instead, it appears to me that he was actually one of the bards who were invited (and in his case handsomely paid) to attend the festivities marking the formation of the Jacob-Israel union and pronounce favourable oracles. In tribal societies, the establishment of a confederation such as that of 'All Israel' is a momentous occasion which calls for extended celebrations. Here is what Balaam said on the occasion, in four separate oracles (Numbers 23:7-10, 20-24; 24:3-9, 15-19, translations reconsidered throughout):

a. From Aram Balak, the king of Moab, has brought me;
   from the hill country of Qedem:
   'Come, curse Jacob for me;
   come, denounce Israel!'
How can I curse those whom God has not cursed?
   How can I denounce those
   whom Yahweh has not denounced?
From the tops of the mountains I see him,
   from the hills I behold him...
Who can count the crowd of Jacob,
   and number the clan of Israel?[1]

b. Behold, I have received a command to bless:
   [Yahweh] has blessed, and I cannot revoke it.
He has not observed wickedness in Jacob;
   nor has he seen evil in Israel:
Yahweh, his God, is with him,
   and the signal of a king is in him...
For there is no sorcery against Jacob;
   no divination against Israel.

1. Traditionally, the Hebrew *'pr y'qb* and *rb' ysr'l* have been taken to mean the 'dust' (Arabic *'ṕr*) of Jacob, and the 'fourth part' (one sense of the Arabic *rb'*) of Israel. Here, however, the actual equivalent of the Hebrew *'pr* is the Arabic *ġṕr*, meaning 'crowd, multitude'. The Hebrew *rb'*, on the other hand, is equivalent to the Arabic *rb'* not in the sense of 'fourth part', but in that equally attested sense of 'extended household, family', i.e. 'kin group, clan', as distinct from the nuclear family or household.

Now it shall be said of Jacob and Israel:
'What a work of God![1]
Here is a people! As a lioness it rises up,
and as a lion it lifts itself;
it does not lie down until it devours its prey,
and drinks the blood of the slain!'

c. How fair are your tents, O Jacob;
your encampments, O Israel!
Like valleys that stretch afar;
like gardens beside a river...
Blessed be every one who blesses you;
cursed be every one who curses you!

d. The oracle of Balaam son of Beor...
The oracle of him who hears the words of God,
and knows the knowledge of Elyon,
seeing the visions of Shaddai...
I see him, but not now;
I behold him, but not nigh:
a star shall come forth from Jacob,
and a sceptre shall rise out of Israel...
By Jacob shall dominion be exercised,
and the survivors of cities be destroyed!

In these four oracles, Balaam not only speaks separately of 'Jacob' and 'Israel', but refers to the Israelite confederation as 'Jacob and Israel'. He also makes reference to God (in the archaic Semitic form *'l* rather than the evolved Hebrew *'lhym*) by three names: Yahweh, Elyon and Shaddai (in the case of Shaddai, twice, the other instance, unquoted above, being in the second oracle, in 23:4). What his oracles actually celebrate is not only the union of 'Jacob' and 'Israel' in the confederation of 'All Israel', but also the formal recognition of their three original tribal gods — El Elyon, El Shaddai and Yahweh —

1. This is my translation of the Hebrew *mh p'l 'l*; literally 'what God has made'. What is in question here is an idiomatic expression of approbation, as I believe it should be translated. An Arabic equivalent, still in regular use, is *mā shā' Allāh*, which literally means 'what God has willed', but is actually used to mean 'how wonderful!'

as being the One God Yahweh for all. The oracles of Balaam are an invaluable historical document, the contents of which can only be appreciated in the light of the sort of analysis of the Torah stories presented by this book. Initally we have a bard, invited to participate in the celebration of a wedding between two different peoples who decide, at a particular moment in history, to become one folk. As in any traditional Near Eastern wedding, he sings the praises of the two parties to the union, invoking blessings, and prophesying every future success. As the bridegroom pays the bard, he therefore normally sings his praises before the praises of the bride. In the wedding of the Aramean 'Jacob' and the Hebrew 'Israel', the bard was an Aramean not a Hebrew, and probably 'Jacob' paid him. Thus, Baalam recognized 'Jacob' as the bridegroom, and 'Israel' as the bride who had been brought to him from afar by divine providence. In all four of his oracles, while lavishing praise on both, he made a point of singing the praises of 'Jacob' before those of 'Israel'. Balaam knew which party, in the end, was going to pay his fee.

★ ★ ★ ★

As this book is not a history of ancient Israel, it will not trace the story of 'All Israel' further. What we have established are the broad lines of Israelite prehistory, as preserved in the books of the Torah. Nevertheless, a general remark on the subject of 'All Israel' may be in order.

In any tribal confederacy, relations between the component tribes — particularly the major ones — are bound to be tenuous. In the confederacy of 'All Israel', the Israelite tribes and the Jacob folk (the latter as the tribe or people of Judah) remained two separate entities. Now and then, they would come together to face a common enemy or make a territorial conquest; otherwise, they were rarely, if ever, of one heart and mind. More than three centuries after Moses addressed 'All Israel' for the first time in the Zahran highlands, Saul, from the Israelite tribe of Benjamin, established an Israelite kingdom which included Judah. His authority, however, appears to have been only reluctantly accepted by the Jacob folk of Judah. Before long David, who came from the tribe of Judah, rose to challenge him and, ultimately, to replace him, first as king of Judah, then as king of 'All Israel' (2 Samuel 5:5). David's kingdom of 'All Israel' was bequeathed to his son Solomon. After Solomon's death, however, the endemic tensions between the Jacob and Israelite folk within the confederacy quickly reasserted themselves. The unity of the kingdom of 'All Israel' broke down, to be replaced by the rival kingdoms of 'Judah' and 'Israel'.

While Hebrew was the official language of both kingdoms, Aramaic continued to be understood and spoken at least by the ruling classes of the kingdom of Judah, in their capital, the West Arabian Jerusalem of the Asir highlands. The officials of Judah, it seems, spoke Aramaic among themselves when they wished to keep their deliberations secret. Thus, when Jerusalem was besieged by the Assyrians at one time, officers of the kingdom of Judah went out to parley and asked that negotiations between the two sides be conducted in Aramaic, indicating to the Assyrians that they understood that language. They made a point of requesting that the 'Jewish' (i.e. Hebrew) language should not be used in the talks, which were held in public, lest the common people standing nearby should understand what was being said (2 Kings 18:26).

Serious religious differences also remained between Judah and Israel, although both sides accepted Yahweh as their God, and the law of Moses as their canon. In post-Biblical times, and even to this day, the religion of 'All Israel' continued, and to some extent continues, in two branches. On the one side are the 'Jews' (*yhwdym*, or *yhwdyym*), whose name actually means the 'Judah people'. On the other, we have communities such as the Samaritans who make a point of calling themselves *Benēy Yīsrā'ēl* (*bny ysr'l*), or 'people of Israel'. Perhaps such communities are remnants of the original Israel branch of the confederacy of 'All Israel'. One thing remains certain: the Samaritans accept the books of the Torah, which include the commandments of Yahweh as articulated by Moses for 'All Israel'. However, they do not accept the other books of the Hebrew Bible, which belong to the tradition of Judah alone, and are not considered part of the shared tradition of 'All Israel'.

10
A Prophet from Oman

Among the stories of the Hebrew Bible, the tale of Jonah is unique in two respects. First, its hero is a prophet to whom no oracles are attributed; second, it is the only Bible story which has a distinctly marine setting. Who was Jonah? What was his real story? Where did he come from?

As already noted in the Introduction, the book of Jonah, as it is found in the Hebrew Bible, is a text probably composed in Mespotamia as late as 350 or even 250 BC. As in the case of other Bible texts, it was no doubt based on earlier sources or traditions. The book, as we shall see, cites a number of place names, all of which are preserved unchanged from the original version of the Jonah story. The author of the book, it seems, had no idea where these places were; he simply gave their names as he had heard or read them. To make his story meaningful to the Mesopotamian Jewish readers, he made a point of changing only one name of the original story, which he rendered as 'Nineveh', the name of the capital of the old Assyrian empire, in northern Iraq. From the other place names, which he failed to alter, and which in some cases he did not even recognize as being place names, the original geography of the story can be fully reconstructed.

The fact that Jonah really existed as a person is beyond question. Apart from featuring in the book of Jonah as the hero of the story of the reluctant prophet who is swallowed by a big fish, then vomited alive, the same man (in both cases called 'Jonah son of Amittai') is also spoken of as 'a servant of Yahweh, God of Israel' in 2 Kings 14:25. In

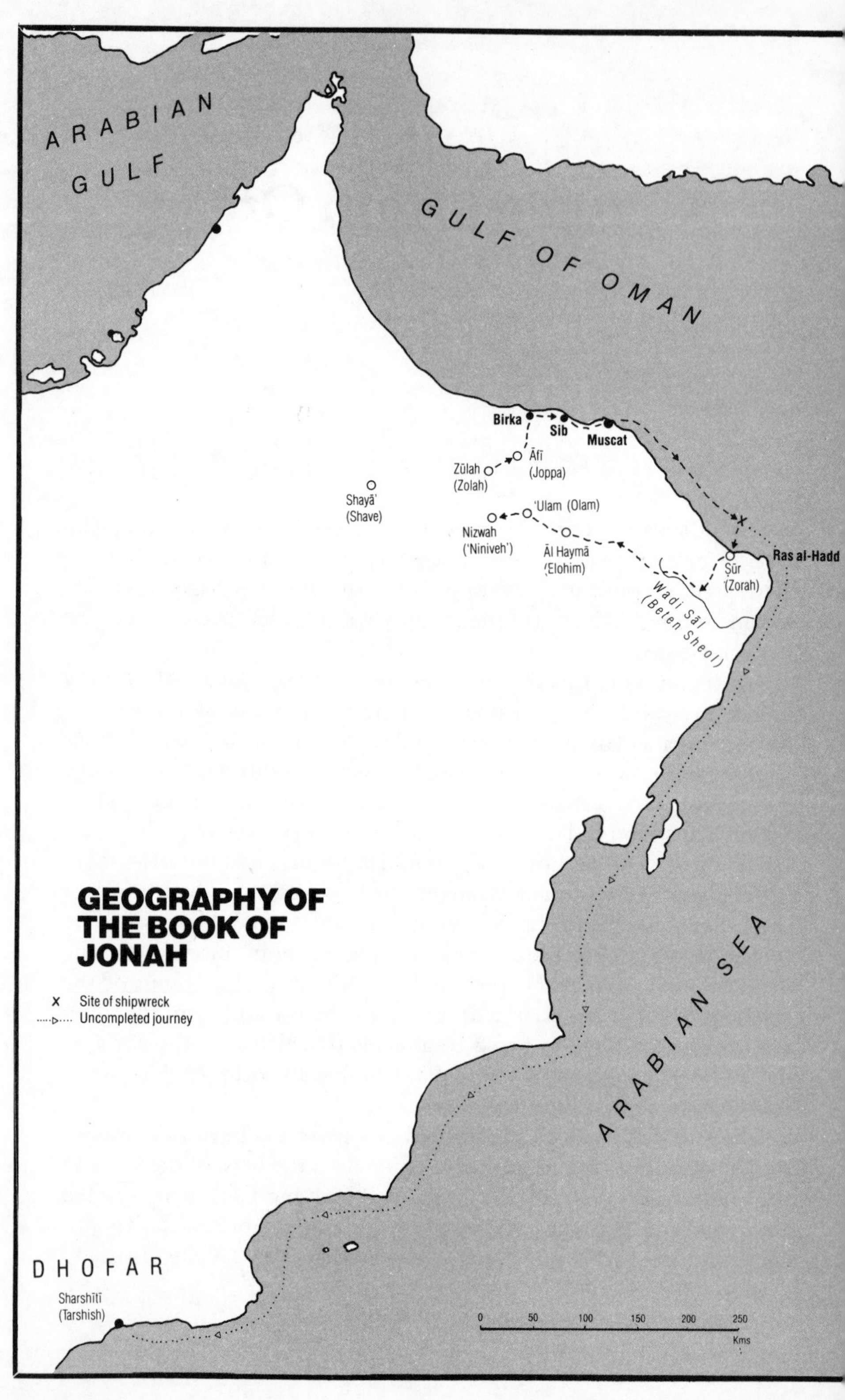
ARABIAN GULF
GULF OF OMAN
Birka
Sib
Muscat
Āfī (Joppa)
Zūlah (Zolah)
Shayā' (Shave)
'Ulam (Olam)
Nizwah ('Niniveh')
Āl Haymā (Elohim)
Ṣūr (Zorah)
Ras al-Hadd
Wadi Sāl (Beten Sheol)
ARABIAN SEA
DHOFAR
Sharshītī (Tarshish)
0 50 100 150 200 250
Kms
GEOGRAPHY OF THE BOOK OF JONAH
x Site of shipwreck
Uncompleted journey

this text it is simply stated that he was a person from a place called Gath-hepher, who prophesied a territorial extension of the kingdom of Israel — an extension which actually took place, exactly as he had prophesied, during the reign of Jeroboam II (c. 786 – c. 746 BC). Here we not only have the necessary evidence about the historicity of Jonah; we also have an indication about his place of origin and the period of his prophetic activity — the middle decades of the eighth century BC at the latest.

Jonah's prayer

The book of Jonah preserves the text of a prayer taken to have been uttered by Jonah from the 'belly of Sheol' (*bṭn š'wl*), understood to mean the belly of the whale that swallowed him. The text of this prayer, I believe, is authentic. It cites a number of unsuspected place names which help establish the geography of the Jonah story, and I would translate it as follows (Jonah 2:2-9):

> I called from Zorah (*ṣrh*) to Yahweh,
> and he answered me;
> From the valley (*bṭn*) of Sheol (*š'wl*) I cried for help,
> and you heard my voice.
> You cast me from Zolah (*ṣwlh*) into the heart of the seas,
> and vastness[1] surrounded me;
> all your breakers and waves passed over me.
> I said: 'I am cast from before your eyes;
> how can I look again upon your holy temple?'
> The waters threw me out onto the same coastland;[2]
> weeds were round about me,
> wrapped to my head.

1. Hebrew *nhr* (*nahar*), translated 'river', is meaningless in this context. In Arabic, however, the same word, which with one vocalization (*nahr*) means 'river', is attested with another vocalization (*nahār*) to mean 'vastness'.

2. Hebrew *'ppwny 'd npš thwm*. For my interpretation of the Biblical term *thwm*, or *tehōm*, see *The Bible Came from Arabia*, pp 76-78. The Arabic *thm*, vocalized as *taham*, also carries the sense of 'land descending to the sea'; E.W. Lane, *Arabic-English Lexicon* (London, 1863-74), I, p. 320. The Hebrew *'ppwny*, from *'pp*, is attested in Arabic in the sense of impatient rejection; hence the Arabic expression *uff* (*'ṕṕ*), to mean 'begone!'

I went down to the extreme parts of the mountains:
  the land of Riheyah (*rḥyh*);
  afterwards to Olam (*b-'dy l-'wlm*);[1]
  and you brought my kinsfolk up from Shahat (*šḥt*)[2]
  O Yahweh, my God!
In my despair,[3] I remembered Yahweh:
  my prayer came to you,
  to your holy temple.
Those who serve the idols of Shave
  abandon their fidelity.
I, with the voice of gratitude,
  sacrifice to you what I have vowed;
  I complete it:
  may its goodness be for Yahweh!

From this prayer, as I have retranslated it from the original Hebrew, we learn the following:

1. Jonah experienced a disaster at sea.
2. In his despair, he made a vow to offer a special sacrifice to Yahweh.
3. The survivors of the disaster were washed ashore onto the same coastlands from which they had set out on their journey.
4. Jonah himself had set out on his journey from a place called Zolah.
5. Either before or after the disaster, he had twice successfully

1. Hebrew *w-t'l m-šḥt ḥyy*, usually rendered 'Yet thou didst bring up my *life* from the *pit*' (RSV). Here, the Hebrew *ḥyy* (contruct of *ḥy* with the first person pronoun) is better interpreted to mean 'my tribe, kinsfolk' (Arabic *ḥy*, vocalized *ḥayy*), rather than 'my life'. For *šḥt* as a place name, see below.

2. Here, the problematic Hebrew *b-'dy*, in my opinion, must be interpreted in the sense of the Arabic *ba'd* (contraction of *b-'d*, literally, 'in the going beyond'), meaning 'afterwards', 'beyond'.

3. Hebrew *b-ht'tp 'ly npšy*, literally 'In the languishing of my soul over me'. The usual translation, 'When my soul fainted within me' (RSV) is untenable, because the Hebrew *'ly* means 'over me', not 'within me'.

invoked the assistance of Yahweh in prayer: once at Zorah, and another time in the valley of Sheol.

6. From the place where he was washed ashore, Jonah made his way to a region of mountains, first to Riheyah, then to a place called Olam.

7. His kinsfolk came up from a place called Shahat to meet him.

8. Jonah completed his vowed sacrifice to Yahweh, apparently upon his arrival at Olam, and his prayer was composed to celebrate the occasion.

9. While he sacrificed to Yahweh, others broke faith and served 'the idols of Shave' — the implication being that those were fellow Yahweh-worshippers who had experienced the same disaster and made the same vow of sacrifice to Yahweh, but broke their faith by offering their sacrifices to the 'idols of Shave' instead.

There is no mention of a 'big fish' in the words of Jonah's prayer. Had he been swallowed upon falling into the sea by such a 'fish', perhaps a sperm whale, he would not have lived to compose his prayer. There actually exists a record of a man who fell into the sea and was swallowed by a whale, which his companions pursued and killed. When they recovered his body from the whale's belly, his chest was crushed, and the creature's gastric juices were already working upon the corpse. An investigation of the possibility of a man entering the belly of a dead sperm whale convinced the investigators that any person would be dead before reaching the stomach, let alone surviving there for any length of time.[1]

Still, one cannot rule out the possibility that Jonah could have had an accident with a large fish at sea, which left him virtually unharmed. In the Koranic version of the story (Koran 37:142-144), the fish certainly takes him in by the mouth (Arabic *iltaqama*, 'make a mouthful of', not necessarily implying actual swallowing). The Koran simply adds that had he not been a true believer, he would have stayed in the belly of the fish forever. In the chapter of the Koran that actually carries the name of Jonah (10:21-23), no fish are mentioned. The story indicates that some people were sailing with a fair wind at sea when a tempest broke out. As the waves rolled

1. Jacques-Yves Cousteau and Philippe Diole, *The Whale: Mighty Monarch of the Sea* (London, 1972), pp. 134-135, with reference to the study of whales by Egerton Y. Davis.

over them, they beseeched God to save them. God thereupon intervened, and they were rescued, but failed to show their gratitude. In fact, they proceeded to behave abominably. This is exactly what Jonah himself points out about his travelling companions in his prayer: after being saved, they showed infidelity by serving the idols of Shave, instead of participating in the sacrifice to Yahweh. Clearly, what we have in the Koran is a correct account of the historical event.

One can easily perceive how it came to be assumed that Jonah uttered his prayer 'from the bowels of the fish' (*m-m'y h-dgh*, Jonah 2:2). In the text of the prayer, Jonah says that he cried for help from the 'valley of Sheol' (*m-bṭn š'wl*). Because the Hebrew *bṭn*, as a common noun, means 'belly' (in Arabic it also means 'valley'), the phrase *m-bṭn š'wl* was understood to mean 'from the belly of Sheol', and the enigmatic Sheol was taken to be a reference to the fish, or perhaps its name.[1] It is possible that the whole story of Jonah's three-day stay in the belly of the fish was originally woven out of the misinterpretation of this one phrase from the preserved text of his prayer — a text rendered verbatim in the book of Jonah, which was a work of much later composition.

The evidence from the book of Jonah

In the book of Jonah, we have additional information about the man and his career. Here is a synopsis of the story, with the additional information included:

1. Jonah son of Amittai (*ywnh bn 'mty*) was asked by Yahweh to go to the 'great city' (*h-'yr h-gdwlh*) of 'Nineveh' (*nynwh*) and denounce her wicked ways (1:1-2).
2. Unwilling to undertake this mission, Jonah 'went down' (*yrd*)

1. Sheol features in other Biblical passages as the name of the place where the dead go — a sort of underworld. For the Sheol of Jonah, see below. The other Sheol could have been an ancient West Arabian necropolis. The name survives in different parts of West Arabia as Shawlā', Shawalah (both *šwl*), Sāyil or Sāyilah (both *syl*). One, Āl Sāyilah (*'l syl*, the 'god of the underworld'?) is a village of the Najran valley. If the Biblical *š'wl* is equivalent to the Arabic *syl*, meaning 'flow', said of a torrent or flash flood (hence Arabic *sayl*, meaning 'valley of the torrent, flood'), the biblical concept of the world of the dead would be that of the gorge of a torrent, which would make sense.

to Joppa (*ypw*) and found a ship going to Tarshish (*tršyš*); so he paid his fare and went aboard (*w-yrd bh*) to go 'with them' (*'m-hm*), away from the presence of Yahweh (*m-l-pny yhwh*, 1:3). Two things are implied here: first, Tarshish was a distant place reached from Jonah's home country by sea; second, Tarshish lay (or was imagined by Jonah to lie) outside the realm or reach of Yahweh.

3. At sea a mighty tempest broke out which threatened to wreck the ship. To lighten the craft, the mariners threw its cargo overboard; then they cast lots to determine which person was responsible for the calamity befalling them. The lot fell on Jonah, who identified himself as a *'bry* — normally taken to mean 'Hebrew', but possibly, in this case, meaning the native of a place called *'br*. He confessed his guilt through his disobedience to Yahweh, and suggested that he be thrown overboard so that the tempest would subside. After all attempts to row the ship back to shore had failed, Jonah was finally thrown into the sea, as he himself had suggested, and the tempest was stilled. Thereupon a 'great fish', specially appointed by Yahweh, swallowed Jonah; he remained 'in the bowels of the fish' (*b-m'y h-dg*) three days and three nights (1:4 - 2:1). Here again, two things are implied. First, the ship going to Tarshish was a trading vessel carrying cargo, with no passengers other than Jonah (at least, no other passengers are mentioned, only 'mariners', Hebrew *mlḥym*). In the Koranic version of the story, it is actually specified that the ship was a 'vessel laden with cargo' (Arabic *fulk mashḥūn*). Second, the sea where the ship sailed was one in which 'great fish' capable of swallowing people (i.e. whales) were found.

4. After three days when the fish finally vomited Jonah on dry land, Yahweh came to him a second time and asked him to go to 'Nineveh' to proclaim to its people that their city was going to be destroyed in forty days. This time Jonah was prompt in obeying (3:1-3a). Here the Hebrew text adds, as I read it: 'Nineveh was a great city, to Elohim, a journey of three days' (*w-nynwh hyth 'yr gdwlh l-'lhym mhlk šlšt ymym*, hitherto taken to mean 'Nineveh was a great city to God (*l-'lhym*), a journey of three days', which makes awkward sense). Jonah 'turned round' (*w-yḥl*) to enter the city, which made his journey from Elohim take four days (3:3b-4a) instead of three.[1] What is implied is that Jonah went to 'Nineveh' from a

1. In usual translations, 'Jonah *began* (*w-yḥl*) to go into the city, going a day's journey' (!) (RSV). This translation takes so many liberties with the

place called Elohim (*'lhym*, not to be translated here as 'God'), and that the journey took him four days (a marching distance of about 120 kilometres).

5. When Jonah prophesied in 'Nineveh' that the city was going to be destroyed in forty days, its inhabitants, who 'believed in God' (*w-y'mynw b-'lhym*), proclaimed a fast and put on sackcloth. The 'king' of the city 'arose from his throne, removed his robe, covered himself in sackcloth, and sat in ashes', ordering his people to 'cry mightily to God' to spare their city. The city was actually spared, to the disappointment of Jonah who had left it and was waiting nearby to 'see what would become' of it. It is clearly implied in the story that the king and people of 'Nineveh' believed in the same God as Jonah. Like him, they worshipped Yahweh (3:4b - 4:5).

6. Jonah was disappointed because his prophecy concerning the destruction of 'Nineveh', at Yahweh's urgent request, did not happen, thus discrediting him as a prophet. To console Jonah, Yahweh pointed out the terrible consequences of destroying a city 'in which there are more than a hundred and twenty thousand persons... and also much livestock (*bhmh rbh*)' (4:11). From this, it is clear that the 'Nineveh' of Jonah was a city much of whose wealth was in livestock. In fact, the king of the city, when he asked his people to 'cry mightily to God' to spare its destruction, enjoined them to go on a fast, so that 'neither man nor livestock (*bhmh*), cattle (*bqr*) or sheep (*ṣ'n*) taste anything' (3:7). The 'Nineveh' of the story must have been the principal market city of a rich pastoral region.

Surely, Jonah's 'Nineveh' as a city of 'livestock', 'cattle' and 'sheep' was not the Assyrian Nineveh of northern Iraq, which in the eighth century BC was the capital of a military empire of much more varied wealth. The people of the Assyrian Nineveh were certainly not Yahweh-worshippers. So far, it has been assumed that Jonah went to this Nineveh from Palestine, where his Joppa (*ypw*) was Jaffa (Yāfā, or *yṕ'*). Had this been the case, he would not have been able to reach the Assyrian capital in four days using a roundabout route. The distance between Palestine and northern Iraq is about

Hebrew original that I find it grossly misleading. Actually, the Hebrew *yḥl* means 'turns round'. For the identification of Elohim as a place name, see below.

1,400 kilometres by the shortest route, which would take the better part of three months to cover on foot, or by mule or camel, without making any stops. Before we can hope to discover the actual location of Jonah's 'Nineveh', we must first determine where he came from.

The geography of the Jonah story

Jonah's country was located by a sea with a known whale population. This sea could hardly have been the Mediterranean, into whose waters whales rarely stray. On the other hand, it could easily have been the Arabian Sea, where whales abound. After all, the ambergris which was first gathered off the shores of South Arabia, and which is indispensable in the manufacture of expensive perfumes, is a secretion of the sperm whales swimming in the waters of the Indian Ocean, of which the Arabian Sea forms a part.

In the Indian Ocean, the sperm whale is only found in the winter season, when the waters of its summer home in the Antarctic are frozen. For Jonah to have had an accident involving a whale in the Arabian Sea, he would probably have been travelling in winter. In the Indian Ocean, this is the season of the north-east monsoons, when traditional seafaring along the coast of South Arabia moved from Oman in the north-east, by way of Dhofar, to the Yemen in the south-west. The summer season, which is that of the south-west monsoons, would have been the time of the return journey from the Yemen to Dhofar, and from there to Oman. On this basis, we may assume for a start that Jonah's home base, and the port from which he set out on his sea journey, was in Oman. This is no more than a guess, the evidence so far being in no way conclusive.

Jonah, however, was reportedly travelling towards Tarshish when his ship was hit by the tempest. To Biblical scholars Tarshish has long posed a problem. Guesses about its location have varied widely between Tartessus in Spain, Debaia el-Shrirah in southern Tunisia and different suggested locations in the Red Sea basin and elsewhere. I am personally convinced that the Biblical 'Tarshish' (*ršyš*) was actually an ancient name for coastal Dhofar, where a village called Sharshītī (*šršyt*) is still to be found. Throughout history, the harbours of Dhofar have been important stations for South Arabian maritime commerce, the country itself being, in a special way, the land of the famed South Arabian frankincense. In the Middle Ages, the harbour city of Dhofar, whose ruins can still be seen outside the present city of Salalah, enjoyed world fame as a leading market for the 'spices' coming from the different countries of the Indian Ocean basin.

To determine whether or not Jonah had set out for 'Tarshish' from Oman rather than the Yemen, or perhaps coastal Asir or the Hijaz, we have to identify all the place names in his story — among them, possibly, Amittai. As the 'son of Amittai', Jonah need not have had a father called Amittai; he could have come from a place by that name. In Biblical Hebrew, as in Arabic, one can be the 'son' of a place as well as of a parent. I have examined all parts of Arabia, and other parts of the Near East, for the place names cited in the book of Jonah. With the exception of 'Nineveh' they are only found collectively in Oman. According to 2 Kings 14:25, as already noted, Jonah son of Amittai came from a place called Gath-hepher (*g̲t ḥpr*) — I would say the 'hill country' (Arabic *ġṭ*, from the root *ġṭṭ;*) of Hepher (*ḥpr*). From Joshua 19:13, we learn that this Hepher, and another place called Kazin (*qzyn*), were located 'to the east (*qdmh*), towards the sunrise (*mzrḥh*)'. In Arabia, no region lies further 'to the east, towards the sunrise' than Oman, where the place names cited in the Bible in connection with the career of Jonah can still be found to this day (for the locations, see map p. 178):

1. Amittai (*'mty*): Imṭī (*'mṭy*), two villages by the same name.
2. Hepher (*ḥpr*): Ḥafrā (*ḥṕr*).
3. Kazin (*qzyn*): G̲hīzayn (*g̲zyn*).
4. Joppa (*ypw*): Āfī (*'ṕy*).
5. Zolah (*ṣwlh*): Zūlah (*zwlh*).
6. Zorah (*ṣrh*): Ṣūr (*ṣr*).
7. The 'valley' (*bṭn*) of Sheol (*š'wl*): the valley of Wadi Sal (*s'l*), where there is actually a village called Bāṭin (*bṭn*, meaning 'valley'), and another nearby called Abū Yūnah (*ywnh*) — none other than the name of Jonah (Biblical *ywnh*).
8. The 'land' of Riheyah (*rḥyh*): Ḥārah al-Riḥī, literally the 'settlement' of Riḥī (*rḥy*).
9. Olam (*'wlm*): 'Ulam (*'lm*).
10. Shahat (*šḥt*): Shaḥḥah (*šḥh*, or *šḥt*).
11. Shave (*šw'*): Shayā' (*šy'*).
12. Elohim (*'lhym*): Āl Haymā (exactly *'l hym*), the name of a village and a mountain ridge in the same location.

On the ship, Jonah reportedly identified himself as being a *'bry* — here not a 'Hebrew', but the native of a place called *'br*. This, on a purely linguistic basis, could have been the present town of 'Ibri (*'bry*), in inland Oman. The coordinates of the Jonah story, however, point to the two villages called today Ghabarah (*ġbr*, linguistically the exact equivalent of the Biblical *'br*), each of them near one of the two villages called Imṭī, or 'Amittai'. Usually, in regions where the economy is largely pastoral, as is the case of Oman and other parts of Arabia, the presence of sets of villages of the same name in areas not too far apart reflects the common practice of transhumance, already referred to in chapter 7.

That Yahweh-worshipping communities, such as the one to which Jonah belonged, should have existed — even flourished — in Oman in Biblical times, at a considerable distance from the West Arabian land of Israel in Asir, is not at all surprising. The worship of Yahweh could have reached Oman from Asir at an early time, either as a result of Israelite migrations there, or by missionary preaching. Throughout known history, migrations between West and East Arabia, as well as regular commercial relations by land and also by sea, are regularly attested. It must be observed that in 2 Kings, Jonah is not spoken of as a 'prophet of Israel', which would have made him a native West Arabian Israelite. Rather, he is spoken of as a 'servant of Yahweh, the God of Israel' who came from Gath-hepher — the land described in the book of Joshua as being in the extreme east, towards the rising of the sun (see above). The indication is clearly that he did not belong to the native folk of the West Arabian Israel, but to a community from elsewhere which happened to worship the God of Israel.

The real story

Having established the obviously Omani setting of the Jonah story, we can easily reconstruct the events of the tale. Jonah came from the village of Imṭī (Amittai), near Ghabarah (*'br*), in the hill country of Ḥafrā (Hepher), on the coastal slopes of the Oman mountains west of the seaport and modern capital city of Muscat. He and his kinsfolk led a life of transhumance, moving their residence seasonally between coastal and inland Oman, where another Imṭī stands near another Ghabarah, and where two villages called 'Ulam (Olam) and Shaḥḥah (Shahat) are also located. Jonah was at Zūlah (Zolah), near the Imṭī and Ghabarah on the maritime side of Oman, when he decided to go by sea to 'Tarshish'. So he 'went down' by way of the valley of Wadi al-Mu'awil to Āfī (Joppa), to book passage on a cargo ship with a sea captain whom he knew there. He then proceeded down the same valley to reach present-day Birka, where he turned eastwards, passing through Sib (today the Muscat airport), and boarded his ship in one of the Muscat creeks — the only good harbours in that part of the country. From Muscat, his ship began to coast its way eastwards, to make a right angle turn at Ras al-Hadd and proceed along the South Arabian coast to 'Tarshish' or Dhofar.

Jonah's ship, however, was destroyed by a violent tempest before reaching Ras al-Hadd. The survivors of the shipwreck managed to reach land (the 'same coastland', or *npš thwm*) at the harbour of Ṣūr (Zorah), where Jonah invoked Yahweh to guide him and his party safely home. From Ṣūr, the travellers crossed the mountains inland to Wadi Sāl (the Beten of Sheol), where Jonah invoked the help of Yahweh again — probably in the village of Abū Yūnah (the 'father', or 'god' of Jonah), which still carries the prophet's name in its exact Biblical spelling.

Leaving Wadi Sāl, the travellers headed north-west in the direction of the Izki region of inland Oman, where Jonah had relatives living in the village of Shaḥḥah (Shahat), close by the local Imṭī and Ghabarah which also belonged to his folk. There Jonah stopped at the village of 'Ulam (Olam), and his relatives arrived to meet him. At 'Ulam (Hebrew *'wlm*, the 'everlasting', one of the epithets given to Yahweh in the Bible), there appears to have been a sanctuary dedicated to Yahweh which was considered particularly sacred — the 'holy temple' of Jonah's prayer. The prophet, now reunited with his relatives, proceeded to make a burnt offering to Yahweh, in completion of the vows he had made at Ṣūr and in Wadi Sāl, and perhaps also earlier at sea. His fellow travellers, however, did not stop at Olam with him to complete their vows to Yahweh. Instead, they moved further on to the 'Ibri region, to offer their sacrifices there to the 'idols' of what is today the village of Shayā' (Shave).

Why did Jonah undertake his journey to Dhofar, which ended in disaster and was never completed? Perhaps Jonah was not fleeing the face of his god, but as a 'servant of Yahweh', he had intended to undertake a preaching mission there — a mission which was never fulfilled. Upon his safe return home, the prophet settled for a time in Āl Haymā (Elohim), about 60 kilometres east of 'Ulam. He then resumed his missionary work nearer home, in 'Nineveh', which was only a march of three days away — about 90 kilometres by the shortest route. Jonah took a roundabout route, reached the city in four days, and proceeded to announce its imminent destruction because of the wickedness of its people. What was this 'Nineveh', which was so clearly in Oman?

From Āl Haymā, a three-day journey could have brought Jonah to Nizwah, the largest and historically the most important town of inland Oman. By a detour into the Izki region, where the prophet had relatives, the journey would have taken him four days. In the town of Nizwah, the livestock of a rich pastoral area has traditionally been traded, including sheep (*ṣ'n*), cattle (*bqr*) and pack animals (*bhmh*), such as the special breed of asses of the neighbouring Jabal al-Akhdar. I am convinced that the 'Nineveh' of the Jonah story was none other than this Nizwah. The author of the book of Jonah, I would say, took the name 'Nizwah' (*nzwh*) and changed it to 'Nineveh' (*nynwh*, essentially *nnwh*) by the alteration of one consonant — the change of the *z* in 'Nizwah' to the *n* in 'Nineveh'. He was writing his story for Mesopotamian Jews familiar with 'Nineveh', which was still a thriving city between the fifth and third centuries BC, as it was to be for centuries to follow, when the book of Jonah was written. On the other hand, few Mesopotamian Jews at the time would have been able to tell where Nizwah was.

As it turned out, Jonah's prophecy of the destruction of 'Nineveh', which I shall take to be Nizwah, failed to happen. This was probably the turning point in his career. Discredited as a prophet in his home country, Jonah had good reason to decide to leave Oman. Next we find him in the land of Israel, in West Arabia, where he made the prophecy concerning the extension of the territory of the kingdom of Israel. His words eventually proved true, and in consequence he gained some renown — enough to secure for him a passing mention in the annals of Israel. Among the Israelites, however, who had known a number of great prophets, Jonah was not fully accepted. To them, he was no more than an outlandish 'servant of Yahweh, God of Israel' who came from the distant hill country of Hepher, in the extreme east.

One question remains to be asked: was it only the misreading of the expression *bṭn š'wl* (the 'valley of Sheol') in the text of Jonah's prayer — his only surviving words — that gave rise to the legend of his three-day sojourn in the belly of the whale? In the world of the Indian Ocean, many such stories must have been told, first because whales are found in abundance in that ocean; and second, because these monstrous creatures have always been the object of fascination. If the story of Jonah belongs to the world of the Indian Ocean basin on its Arabian side, there is a similar story that comes from the Indian side, and the two stories are no doubt more than geographically related. In the Indian story, the ancient hero Śaktideva goes searching for the Golden City, is swallowed at sea by a fish, then disgorged intact. Is it possible that the story of this Śaktideva was picked up one time in Oman and woven into the story of the local prophet called Jonah? Or was it the story of some hero of Omani legend, perhaps called Jonah, that was picked up in India and woven into the legend of Śaktideva and his search for the Golden City? The story is certainly the same one. What is not possible to determine is who borrowed it from whom. However, one thing remains certain: there was a historical prophet from Oman called Jonah who lived in Biblical times and experienced a sea disaster at some point in his career. He could even have had an encounter with a whale on that occasion. On the other hand, Jonah the prophet was surely not the original hero of the ancient legend about the man who stayed alive in the belly of a fish.

Appendix
Geography of the Exodus

The territory of the Egyptian colony of Mizraim (present day Miṣrāmah, near Khamis Mushait) must have comprised the whole Wadi Bishah basin. The Hebrew shepherd folk of Israel were settled in the land of Goshen (*gšn*) — today the village of Ghithān (*ġṯn*), in the Balqarn hill country, west of the lower course of Wadi Bishah (chapter 6). In the same Balqarn region, these Hebrews (Exodus 1:11) were put to forced labour to build two store cities for the Egyptian colonists, called Pithom (*ptm*) and Raamses (*r'mśś*), the name of the second city being a construct referring to a shrine for the Egyptian god Ra (*r'*) in a place called Mesēs (*mśś*). The two store cities in question are today the local villages of Āl Fuṭaymah (*ṕṭym*) and Maṣāṣ (*mṣṣ*).

When the Hebrew Israelites, under the leadership of Moses, decided to leave the territory of Mizraim (chapter 8), the Egyptians forbade them to move inland into Central Arabia, towards Zebotham (*'l ṣb'tm*, 6:26; 12:51), hitherto taken to mean 'by their hosts' (RSV), but actually the village of Ḍabaṭayn (*ḍbṭyn*). They were willing, on the other hand, to let them go north towards the Hijaz, by way of the land of the Philistines (*plštym*, 13:17, from *plšh*) — today Falsah (*ṕlsh*), in the Khath'am hill country, directly north of the Balqarn region. The Hebrew Israelites, however, were determined to attempt an exodus to Central Arabia. This is what they did:

From a gathering point in the Balqarn region at Maṣāṣ (Raamses), they first moved south, and uphill, to Succoth (*śkt*), today Āl Skūt (*skt*) in the adjacent hill country of Bani 'Amr. From there, they descended to Wadi Bishah by way of one of its tributaries, Wadi Rīmah (*b-yd rmh*, 14:8, hitherto taken to mean 'with a high hand'). Their plan was to head first for Ḥamūshīm (*ḥmšym*, 13:18), hitherto translated 'equipped for battle' (RSV), which is today the oasis town of Khamāsīn (*ḫmsyn*) in Wadi al-Dawasir. From there, they could have directly reached Ḍabaṭayn (Zebotham), in Central Arabia. The Egyptians, however, were already pursuing them in that direction (14:8). So the Hebrew Israelites turned southwards from Khamāsīn to Wadi Habuna (the Biblical *Yād Ḥazāqāh*, or valley of Ḥazqah, which is the name of one of the local villages), encamping in the heights south of that valley in a location described as *b-'l ṣpn* (14:2) — not 'Baal-zephon' (*b'l ṣpn*), as traditionally rendered, but 'above' (*b-'l*) a place called Zephon (*ṣpn*), today the village of Ṣafan (*ṣpn*). This Zephon faced Pi-ha-hiroth (*py h-ḥyrt*, the 'mouth' of Hiroth), today probably the village of Āl Ḥarah (*ḥrh*, or *ḥrt*), in the same vicinity. Both Zephon and Hiroth are Biblically described as located between Migdol and the Yam (*h-ym*, usually rendered as 'the sea') (14:2). Migdol (*mgdl*) appears to refer to the present village of Maqlad (*mqld*) in Jabal Faifa, at the headwaters of Wadi Habuna. As for the Yam, it is none other than the pastoral desert of Bilād Yām, fringing Wadi Habuna from the east.

When the Egyptian forces reached the valley of Wadi Habuna, they were overtaken by a flash flood which took a heavy toll of them (chapter 8). The Israelites waited for the flood to subside, then made a swift descent from their encampment at Ṣafan (Zephon) to Ḥazqah, in Wadi Habuna (*b-yd ḥzqh*, 'by Wadi Ḥazqah', not 'by strength of hand', as in the standard translations, 13:3, 14). From there, they made their exit to Yam Sūf (*ym śwp*, 15:22) — not the 'Red Sea', nor the 'Sea of Reeds', as usually rendered, but the desert of Baḥr Ṣāfī (in Arabic, literally, the 'sea' of Ṣāfī, or *ṣṕ*, see chapter 8). From there they proceeded in the direction of Shur (*šwr*, 15:22), today Sharī (*šr*), in the desert valley of Wadi Khubb, about 120 kilometres south of Wadi Habuna. For three days they went without water. When they reached Marah (*mrh*, 15:23), today Murrah (*mrh*) in Wadi Khubb, they found its waters too bitter to drink. The name of this place, in its Biblical as in its present Arabic form, actually means 'bitter'.

Before their exodus from Wadi Bishah, the Egyptians had made it clear to the Israelites that they could not proceed to or settle in

Central Arabia, 'not even by way of Wadi Ḥazqah' (*w-l' b-yd ḥzqh*, 3:19). The Israelites had made a point of moving out of the land of Mizraim by that route, in defiance of the Egyptians; but now they decided to press their luck no further. Hence they moved south to Wadi Khubb, to take the road from there which crosses the Yemen highlands to the Jizan region. In that region, their first stop was Elim (*'ylm*, 15:27) — today al-Yāmiyah (*'l-ym*), in the valley of Wadi Dhabhan. Next they proceeded to the 'wilderness' of Sin (*śyn*), today Ṣin (*ṣyn*), downhill from al-Yāmiyah in a southerly direction. This 'Sin' lay 'between Elim and Sinai' (16:1), the coordinates being correct. The Sinai (*śyny*) in question is today Wadi Sayān (*syn*) in the northern Yemen. The Israelites, reportedly, reached this 'Sinai' in the third month of their wanderings (19:1). It was there that they apparently witnessed an eruption of the volcano of Jabal Alhān (19:16), which made them adopt the local volcano god Yahweh as their god (chapter 8).

The Hebrew Israelites might have settled in the Jizan region and the adjacent parts of northern Yemen, had their reception been more friendly. They had hardly reached Rephidim (*rpydym*, 17:1), today Radfayn (*rdṕyn*), at the edge of the Jizan coastal plain, when the people of neighbouring Ma'ālīq (*m'lq*) — the Biblical Amalek (*'mlq*) — came out to fight them (17:8f.). Upon first arriving to encamp outside Radfayn, the Israelites had found no water to drink (17:1f.); thereupon Moses reportedly took his rod and struck water for them out of the rock of Horeb (*ḥrb*, 17:6). The Horeb in question is today the village of Ḥabarah (*ḥbr*) in the same vicinity. Moses, it is said, called the place Massah (*mśh*) and Meribah (*mrybh*) (17:7). There is no 'Massah' to be found in that location now, but there is certainly a 'Meribah' — today the local village of Marābī (*mrb*).

At this point, the report of the trek of the Israelite wanderings becomes confused, mainly because of similarities in place names. The very fact that the place where Moses struck water out of the rock is given three different names in the same context points to this confusion. Moreover, while 'Horeb' can be the Ḥabarah of the Jizan region, it can also be either of the two Ḥāribs of the Yemen (see chapter 8), one south-east, the other south-west of a 'Meribah' which is the historical and present Maarib (Ma'rib, or *m'rb*). On the other hand it can be the Ḥārib (*ḥrb*) of coastal Asir in the hinterland of Qunfudhah. There one finds not only a 'Meribah' (this one Marībī, also *mrb*), but also a 'Massah', which is Ḥillat Maṣwā (the 'settlement' of *mṣw*).

Faced with stiff resistance in the Jizan hinterland, the Israelites, it appears, lost no time in turning northwards to establish a temporary settlement for themselves around this second 'Horeb' of coastal Asir and the 'Massah' and 'Meribah' of its neighbourhood. How long they remained there is not clear. At this point, the book of Exodus ceases to relate their wanderings and turns instead to speak of the laws given to them by Moses. In Numbers 10:11-12, there is a hint that the Israelites had already moved to the wilderness of Paran (see below) 'on the twentieth of the second month of the second year' of the exodus from Mizraim, which would mean that their stay in the Qunfudhah hinterland was no more than a matter of months. Next (Numbers 11:3), we find them at Taberah (*tb'rh*, archaic noun derivative of the verbal root *b'r*) — today Ba'arah (*b'rh*, also noun derivative of *b'r*), a village which controls one of the main passes across the Asir escarpment into the Zahran highlands of the southern Hijaz. From this point on, the narrative of the wanderings is resumed.

Having crossed the Ba'arah (Taberah) pass into the Zahran highlands, the Israelites proceeded first to Kibroth-hattavah (*qbrwt h-t'wh*, Numbers 11:34), then to Hazeroth (*hṣrwt*, 11:35). As a place name, Kibroth-hattavah means the 'graves' (Hebrew plural of *qbr*) of *h-t'wh* (*t'wh* preceded by the definite article). The place in question, in the Zahran highlands, is today Qubūr (Arabic plural of *qbr*, also meaning 'graves'), near the village of Ṭawī (*ṭwy*, cf. *t'wh*). As for Hazeroth, it could refer to a number of places there — most probably the densely-forested ridge of Jabal Khuḍayrah (*ḫḍyrh*, or *ḫḍyrt*). From this 'Hazeroth', the Israelites proceeded to the wilderness of Paran (*p'rn*, 12:16): today the nearby ridge of Jabal Farān (*ṕrn*), where an oasis by the same name is to be found.

From the Zahran highlands, Moses led the Israelites further north into the Taif region. His trek in this direction is described in detail in *The Bible Came from Arabia* (p. 207, n. 5), and the account need not be repeated here. Once the Hebrew Israelites had arrived in the Zahran highlands, however, they were already in the territory of the Ya'āqīb (chapter 7) — the Aramean Jacob people of the southern Hijaz, among whom the tribe of Judah was the most prominent. Here, for the first time, the two peoples became fused into one folk — that of 'All Israel' (chapter 9). The place where the terms of the confederation were concluded was most probably the village called today al-Mūsā, which actually carries the name of Moses in its Arabic form. It was here, apparently, that Moses rose to make a formal address to 'All Israel' for the first time. For the identification of the coordinates of the place, as given in Deuteronomy 1:1, see *The Bible Came from Arabia*, p. 204, n. 8.

Thus, in West Arabia, the full trek of the exodus and wanderings of the Israelites under the leadersip of Moses can be retraced, down to the last given detail (see map p. 140). This is sufficient to establish their historicity. So far, the same Israelite wanderings have not been successfully retraced between Egypt and Palestine, and this for a perfectly understandable reason: historically, the wanderings occurred elsewhere.

Index